AnnMarie Wolpe was educated [...] an honours degree by the age [...] Wolpe in 1955, after a two-ye[...] three children. Her first job [...] Industry Medical Aid Society, and a[...] daughter she worked part time running a bursary fund for African students. The events of 1963, as described in this book, resulted in AnnMarie and her family fleeing to England.

Her first job as an academic was in a Unit of Yugoslav Studies at Bradford University, where her husband was also working. They then moved to London and AnnMarie became a researcher, then a Sociology lecturer at what is now Middlesex University. She developed the Women's Studies programme there in the 1980s and worked at this until her return to South Africa after she and her husband were given indemnities in 1991.

AnnMarie Wolpe has published three academic books: *Feminism and Materialism*, edited with Annette Kuhn; *Is There Anyone Here from Education?* edited with James Donald; and an ethnographic study of a London School, *Within School Walls*. She is also a founder member of the leading feminist journal *Feminist Review*.

AnnMarie and Harold now live and work in Cape Town, where they are both involved in research on educational issues. Their eldest daughter lives in rural France with her two children, the younger daughter lives and works in London. Their son returned to South Africa with them as he feels that is where he belongs.

The Long Way Home

ANNMARIE WOLPE

Published by VIRAGO PRESS Limited, June 1994
42–43 Gloucester Crescent, Camden Town, London NW1 7PD

A CIP catalogue record for this title is available
from the British Library

Printed in Great Britain by
Cox & Wyman Ltd, Reading, Berkshire

This book is dedicated in the first instance to my family who are wonderful, and to all those people who contributed in some way to the success of that daring escape. This book was written not only to chronicle some historical events but also as an attempt to draw attention to all those countless women whose stories are hidden and yet without whom liberation politics could never occur.

Acknowledgements

My editor, Lennie Goodings, has nurtured me through the final stages of writing and given me all the encouragement needed. Without constructive ideas and criticisms this book would still have been a draft sitting in my files. It has not been possible to mention individuals who helped in a variety of ways in the course of writing. The absence of their names is no reflection of my feelings.

Contents

Going Home

February 1990–June 1991

Going Home

FEBRUARY 1990

T ODAY IS an unusually sharp, bright, sunny day for
February, cold but dry. The geese of Trent Park seem to
recognise that spring is not far off. They waddle proprie-
torially along the grass banks at the side of the mansion house
that once belonged to Sir Phillip Sassoon, a man whose life
seems to have been devoted to the pursuit of pleasure and
aesthetics. Sassoon would have been horrified at the desecration
of his home by the educational administrators who have allo-
cated the building to teacher training and other further education work since 1947. Fortunately, they could not destroy the
wonderful views to the river two hundred yards away from the
house, but they managed to deface the interior.

The tranquil landscape belies the tensions and pressures of
working with mature students at Middlesex Polytechnic. I'm in
early to meet my new group of students, and I pass Norman
Levy – a South African friend and colleague. He is beaming.
His usually solemn, owlish look is completely transformed.
'Have you heard the news?' he asks. No. 'The ANC has been
unbanned, and the Communist Party.' I am stunned.

I walk into our general office. 'I can go home again, I can
go home again,' I say, and am astounded by unexpected tears
which course down my face. Where do they come from? Fiona,
our administrator, looks bemused. She thrusts a glass of sherry
into my hands, even though it is only 9.30 in the morning.
Clearly she thinks this will help me pull myself together. 'I
thought this was home,' she says.

So had I, until that moment. Harold and I have been
twenty-seven years in England, and I've been at the Poly for the

past twenty-two of them. Our daughters Peta and Tessa were six and five when they arrived in London; Nicholas was only a baby in arms when he followed some months later, and we have all been here ever since. Suddenly I find myself proclaiming my connection to South Africa, a country I have hated passionately for years for what it has done to me and my family. I am confused.

I thought I would never live to see the day when I could visit my country again. I thought I would be long dead before it would be possible for the likes of me to return. Now all this has changed. The chance of 'going home' fills my consciousness.

My students look totally bemused when I stand in front of them shortly afterwards. A middle-aged, middle-class white woman, walking with the aid of a stick, speaking English with only the slightest trace of a South African accent, greets them with 'It's a momentous day for us all. My country is undergoing a change, and I am totally overwhelmed by the news. Now, for the first time in twenty-seven years, it is possible for me to return and visit my own country.' The new batch of students are there to learn about the condition of women in the Women's Studies programme I run at the Polytechnic. This is our first meeting, and they don't want to hear about politics in far-off South Africa, or the reasons for my exile.

Harold is at Essex University today. He has heard the news by the time I get him on the phone; we're excited, but there's no time to talk about it. We'll wait until we're at home.

Our eldest child, Peta, comes home with her two-year-old son Jonathan in tow. Tessa rushes in from work, anxious to know what the implications are of the unbanning of the ANC. Nick is there with his girlfriend Remedios, whom we call Meme. We are glued to the box for the six o'clock news. 'What's going to happen?' Peta asks the inevitable. Nick looks interested in Peta's question. Tessa hovers in the background.

As a family well versed in the problems of exile, we (surprisingly) don't talk politics at home. Home is where we chatter about what has happened today, and there's a wonderful film on TV tonight, and work was absolute hell, and so and so phoned to invite us to dinner on Saturday night . . . Politics enters the conversation only when something extraordinary happens, and tonight is just such an occasion.

We're all flabbergasted by the news. The kids have grown up accepting that the ANC – the African National Congress, the black oppositional force in South Africa – and Harold's life are inextricably linked. They don't really know anything of its history, except that Harold was a lawyer associated with it, and had it not been for his jail break he would have spent most of his life in jail, as the now famous Rivonia trialists – Nelson Mandela, Walter Sisulu, Ahmed Kathrada and the others – have done. They have known that Joe Slovo, Harold's oldest and closest friend, works full-time for the ANC in exile in Lusaka, Zambia, and arrives in London from time to time on missions that no one asks him about. They have known that the ANC has operated in exile as long as they can remember. They have watched with us the news (even though it has been censored by the South Africans) that cannot mask the living symbol of resistance – the black, green and gold ANC flag, which only recently has been defiantly draped over the coffins of the martyrs and victims of state violence. The unbanning has allowed the ANC to emerge from the shadows of its clandestine existence.

Peta's question about the implications of the unbanning is an interesting one. It is not only about the political import, but about what effect this could have on our lives. 'Does that mean you'll be able to go and have a look at the country?' asks Nicholas. He's the only one who has any idea of what South Africa is like, having worked there for six months as a trainee manager for Woolworths in Cape Town before going to university. Harold smiles and says that he supposes so. Tessa immediately looks anxious. 'You can't go there, it's just not safe.'

Of course there is no way that we will go there. I couldn't even get a guarantee of a safe passage when my mother was so ill in 1975, and never did see her before she died.

Nelson Mandela is freed from jail. We and the world watch his walk to freedom. It is like nothing I have ever seen before. We strain as though peering closer to the TV screen will give us a better view of this outstanding man who has captured the imagination of the world.

A few days after this I get his phone number and phone him direct at home. He is amazing. He recalls Peta's and Tessa's names. When I express astonishment, he tells me how important memories were during his prison sentence. 'Without them I would never have survived. I can remember well the dinners we had with you.' He is curious to know what has happened to us all. As I'm talking Nick walks in the door in his big black winter overcoat. His mouth drops open when I mouth that I'm talking to Nelson. I say to Nelson that the baby who was born after his arrest has just come home from work, and would love to greet him. Nick splutters, and then collects himself and exchanges a few words with Nelson. The call is over. Nicholas is beside himself with joy. 'Wait till I tell them at work tomorrow,' he says. 'The only trouble is that they won't believe me.' Everyone thinks that Nicholas's stories are fabricated, and he does have some amazing stories to tell. Maybe our personal circumstances have something to do with why we are such a close family, still very much living together. Meme says that she finds us dauntingly close. She has settled into a warm relationship with Nick. This wonderful friendly Spanish woman, who came into our lives as an *au pair* when I was still badly crippled after my second hip replacement operation, has now become an integral part of our family.

But Nick and Harold have quite a turbulent relationship. It's not just that Harold supports Arsenal and Nick supports Manchester United. Nick craves Harold's approval, which is seldom forthcoming. We have endless rows over domestic labour. Nick is a past master at avoiding it. Forever my baby, I suppose, even though he is twenty-eight now. Harold rants and raves about it, and I try to intervene. Nick should have moved out of the house by now, but the cost of renting in London is exorbitant, we have room, and it doesn't make sense for him to live elsewhere. This doesn't help in the development of independence and severance from the family. Anyway, Nick looks as though he will make a good living working for the large insurance company Allied Dunbar. He appears to be a whizz kid at selling insurance policies.

It is strange that after virtually their whole life here in England, none of our children identifies with the British. At the same time they feel no affinity to South Africa – far from it. Nicholas has always said he feels more comfortable in America than anywhere else. Peta and Tessa feel alienated, belonging nowhere. Is this peculiar to our family, or is it a twentieth-century phenomenon?

We are caught up in an euphoria about what is happening in South Africa. First Walter Sisulu and Ahmed Kathrada and other Rivonia trialists freed. And now Nelson Mandela, who retained the Presidency of the ANC even though he was serving such an inhuman sentence. Mandela handles the international press as though he has always been in the spotlight. It is awe-inspiring to watch and listen to this regal man, particularly recalling how he spent more than twenty years on Robben Island, for fifteen of which he was forced to break stones at the quarry. I recall seeing Robben Island, a little blob in the distance off the coast of Cape Town – a place that was a refuge, a source of food for passing seamen, and finally a prison for the insane, the criminals, and now political prisoners.

Part of the excitement gripping South African exiles is attached to the plethora of rumours of a major breakthrough in negotiations with the South African state. People like Joe Slovo are even more optimistic than usual. I could never understand how Joe maintained his sense of confidence that the South African apartheid regime would be defeated. He thought that even when the South African government was killing off its opponents. They blew Joe's first wife, Ruth First, into little pieces with a letter bomb when she was working in Mozambique. They locked up opponents to apartheid in jail without trial, they tortured them to death, they even tortured children. That is hard to countenance. When you have seen the scars on young bodies and heard the stories of the state's brutality, it is difficult to maintain any feeling of faith and hope. Joe, on one of his many trips, reported on the historic meeting on strategies for negotiations with the South African government agreed by the African Front Line States. And Harold, too, was optimistic. After all, he had been one of the delegates at another historic meeting in Dakar in 1987, when Afrikaners and other moderates met ANC officials for the first time.

Events speeded up when F.W. de Klerk succeeded the former President of the country, P.W. Botha. Funny how South African leaders are always referred to by either their initials or their nicknames. F.W. seems hell-bent on beginning to effect these 'winds of change'. Nicholas's eyes shine when he says, 'He's getting to be just like Gorbachev.' Nicholas is like Joe: he is optimistic, and expects great things will now happen.

Every time there is a meeting at the house of one of the ANC groups Harold discusses the possibility of political exiles being allowed to return to South Africa. Six months ago this was the thought farthest from anyone's mind. 'What guarantee is there that the state won't arrest people on their return?' asks Harold. Obviously this is a crucial question. 'The office is buzzing,' says another exile, referring to the ANC headquarters near the Angel, Islington. 'Whenever I go there everyone is talking about going home!'

The ANC is now my organisation – I joined it only a few years ago, and I find myself talking about our chief rep in London, and our leaders on Robben Island. I have become part of this movement. I have moved away from what I had felt was an almost moribund feminist movement in the UK, and found a new home in the ANC.

I head the Welfare Committee. I've enjoyed the involvement, and found the struggle to get our members to be receptive to the provision of psychotherapeutic services quite a challenge. Alcoholism is just one of the problems London ANC members have. It doesn't take a lot to understand the extraordinarily damaging effects of torture or the sudden and irreparable separation from families on young adults who had to flee South Africa rather than face torture, imprisonment or death. If my children have problems because their parents were in exile, then how much worse must it be for the people with no family support?

All sorts of other reasons why it is unnecessary to get any

psychological help are given by the ANC members: it's not a good idea; talking to a therapist presents a security risk. We all know about the network of informers, yet it is stretching the imagination to think that psychotherapists fit this bill. I think people fear that admission of the need for help can be read as a sign of personal weakness. In the end we win, and together with the support of Percy Cohen, a dentist who was with Harold in Pretoria jail during the Sharpeville Emergency thirty years ago, we co-operate with various groups, including the Medical Foundation, who have provided an amazing support system for people seeking asylum.

Phone calls have begun to be exchanged with alarming frequency between Harold and people at the University of the Western Cape about relocating RESA, the research project he founded on education in South Africa. 'We've got a mass of research documents and material, and a number of ideas about what needs to be researched,' says Harold. 'It now makes sense if we can relocate the offices there down south.' The Rector of the university, Jakes Gerwel, is reputed to be an outstanding man who has systematically fought against apartheid and struggled to open up the gates of the university to all people and create a first-class black university: to transform it into a centre of excellence. I know that there are others who are working to reconstruct education provision in opposition to the state, and that always takes a lot of courage.

I look at my husband, this man who still has a twinkle in his eye, although his beard is now quite grey, matching his hair. In winter, when his face has the English pallor, beard, hair and pale face merge into one. In the height of summer, when he is tanned a deep bronze, the contrast is striking.

I have no idea where the University of the Western Cape is.

I listen to these conversations, and a sense of apprehension overwhelms me. I'm not part of the research outfit. What place could there be for me?

MARCH 1990

Harold is getting decidedly excited about the thought of returning to South Africa. He is not one to be overtly enthusiastic: his hallmark is restraint and level-headedness. There are not many things that get him really worked up. One is bad driving in London; another is a really good intellectual argument. He is like a terrier, worrying at the problem and never giving up. The cross-examination skills he acquired as a barrister stand him in good stead. The children get furious with him if they have an argument. 'We can't win. He's impossible,' Nicholas complains, and I tend to agree. Sometimes I have to pacify wounded feelings when people take his arguments as personal attacks. They never are; Harold just loves a good discussion. We are so very different. I get excited; he remains composed. Unlike me, he seldom gets worked up over situations or events or people, and is irritated by what he calls my extreme responses. Just as well. It would be impossible if we were similar.

'I'm bored at Essex,' he says. This is only part of the story. He is disenchanted with the department, which fails to give him any tangible recognition for things he has written which have had a major impact in South Africa and among Africanists in general. 'Essex Sociology Department appears singularly unimpressed. The trouble is that what I write is not regarded as sociology,' he adds, somewhat wistfully. This was evident in his belated promotion to Senior Lecturer and then never getting a chair. 'And I have to retire in a few years' time, in any event. I might as well go to South Africa, where it seems I can go on and on working.' Of course there are other, even stronger reasons pulling him back, chiefly a sense of obligation. 'They're going to need people like us, with our expertise. There's so much work to be done when the apartheid system goes. While the problems are going to be enormous, it will be tremendously exciting helping to build a new South Africa. It isn't going to be easy,' he adds, anticipating my doubts about people in our age group having enough stamina to cope with the difficulties, even assuming that the political harassment by the state ceases. 'I have been free all these years. I owe it to the others. I can't say now: Tough shit, you get on with the work while I enjoy life in London and Europe. I can't do it. It would deny all that I believe in. It would make a mockery of my political beliefs, and everything I have stood for and done in the past.'

I understand that and believe, as our children do, that his politics have always been his driving force. The children are proud of Harold, and respect him. I, even more than them, am aware of the extraordinary integrity, selflessness and honesty by which he has lived his life. Acknowledging that does not make it easier for me. The payoff is zero financially. It certainly doesn't help with the bank balance. Worse than that, the struggle against apartheid has been a particularly bloody one and left a trail of broken lives, and the impact on us has not been inconsiderable.

It is quite simple: I don't want to go back. 'I wouldn't mind seeing the place, but live there – never. Anyway, it won't be safe. There's bound to be someone who wants to get you.' I say all this unconvincingly, because I know now without any doubt that he wants to return. Any move by us will have massive repercussions for Peta, Jonny, Tessa and Nicholas, and I am torn by misgivings.

APRIL 1990

In March I thought spring was here, but the weather is always deceptive. A blossom comes out, the sun shines falteringly for a day, and the birds cavort around. Then we're plunged cruelly back into cold, dreary, gloomy days. 'It's at times like this,' my eccentric neighbour Phoebe once said, 'that people commit suicide. They think everything is getting better. They are fooled – it doesn't.' Now it really is spring, and I understand well the old saying I used to hear as a child, and which never made sense: 'Ne'er cast a clout till May is out', because the temperature doesn't equal the burgeoning new growth. The darkness has lifted, the days are getting longer, blossom is everywhere, although the horse chestnuts are late this year. I always feel better when summer is round the corner.

There is little doubt now that sooner or later Harold will go to South Africa although, of course, the question of his indemnity has yet to be resolved. 'It's impossible to get any clarity,' he complains. 'No one knows whether the co-conspirator charge has been proscribed. Even if it has, there's always the possibility that they will find some other reason to detain me.' I worry less about formal imprisonment than about his being on a hit list. I have yet to be convinced that the change of heart extends to those people who have been responsible for the murders of so many apartheid opponents in the past.

After more than thirty-five years' of marriage, being with someone becomes something of a habit. That isn't what our relationship is all about. I can't say simply: I love him, and will follow him to the ends of the earth. It isn't like that after all these years. Our lives are inextricably tied up with our children, although Nicholas and Tessa in particular complain that Harold's involvement in politics takes precedence over everything else. And there are times when I have felt the same. From time to time I have craved his undivided attention, but have had to share it with all his other responsibilities, including his political ones. I would down everything for him in a crisis. I had never been absolutely sure that he would do the same for me, until I had the hip operations. He was incredibly supportive over the long recovery period. It must have come as a huge shock to see me so vulnerable and dependent. Normally I have been strong and able to bear all sorts of adversities. He is not demonstrative, yet I know that he depends on me every bit as much as I depend on him, although for very different reasons. We share many interests, and are excellent companions. He has been my mentor, and now he is my sharpest and most reliable critic, even if I always throw my hands up in horror and threaten to give up academic life after he has dissected what I have written. He is used to my histrionics, and I am used to his low-key responses.

Could I possibly allow him to go to South Africa without me? Could I really not go with him? Every now and again I entertain the idea. Contrary to my expectations, I unexpectedly loved living on my own in Berkeley when I taught at University of California, Davis in 1985. I wallowed in the freedom of being answerable to no one, coming and going when I liked, buying my own car, having my own bank account, eating when I felt like it – although it was a bit lonely, and I would set out my tray in front of the TV. I did not have to think about anyone except myself. That was for a limited period. Could I do it now, calculatingly, going on sixty? Somebody I know separated from her husband recently, and she says she is deliriously happy doing her own thing. Harold and I enjoy being with each other, we have fun, and we have our serious moments. Being with Harold is a consolidation of years of trials, tribulations and love. I can't leave him.

The trouble is that I do not feel duty bound to return to South Africa. I have always had doubts about the role of white people, particularly in my age group. I doubt whether black people would welcome the likes of me back. If I was black, I think I would feel hostility towards all white people.

Then, of course, there are Peta and Jonathan, Tessa, and Nicholas. Our departure would disrupt their lives as much as it would mine and Harold's. Tessa is the most blunt: 'I hate South Africa for what it has done to our family and to all our friends. And I am angry with you for being involved.' She directs her remarks to Harold. Her unhappiness is transparent. Late at night Harold and I talk about this, and wonder whether it wouldn't be a good thing for her to be separated from us. She seems to have been the one most affected by our exile. Perhaps she would finally come to terms with it and live her own life. Her ties to us appear to be even stronger, particularly since my operations, when she was supportive to the point of decimating her own social life. Tessa's ambition is handicapped by her low self-esteem. She has extraordinary bright blue eyes, and exudes a sexual appeal which she always tries to hide. In order to cope with a hard time at school she joined the local gangs and opted out, in spite of being so bright. She left school without any qualifications, which has disturbed her ever since. She is enormously talented, a highly imaginative textile designer who gave it up because she did not have the necessary business acumen. After a series of dead-end jobs and bouts of catering, she moved into the film world, starting as the dogsbody, and she has been there ever since. She is an amazing organiser and fixer. Yet we both worry a great deal about her, even though she is clearly intelligent and has a driving ambition to do well in the film business. It's a tough world.

And I don't dare to think about what will happen to Peta

if we go. How will she manage? She can't afford to live in her flat, and have a nanny for Jonny, so she has let it furnished and is camping with us. At least Jonny has his own room, although Peta has a bed in the front sitting-room. She feels the loss of her independence, privacy and own home. I don't know how she copes after a tough day in Walthamstow, dealing with all the myriad problems a psychiatric social worker has to face. She picks Jonny up from his nanny, and then devotes herself entirely to him. He's at the terrible twos stage. He has a ridiculously deep voice for someone so young, is never still, and has a raucous sense of humour. Jonny eats with us at night and joins in the conversation as much as he can, babbling away, mimicking the adults even before he could formulate words, and clinking his bottle, teat and all, with our wine glasses.

Peta is an exceptional mother, devoted, caring, consistent – all this, and without a partner. I can't help wondering what went wrong. Somewhere along the line she has been let down in her relationships. Her affair with Yves had all the trappings of a storybook holiday romance, but real life is very different. The massive cultural differences between them are a stumbling block. He retains all the chauvinism of a French countryman, with hunting and daily bar rituals, and no acceptance of a sharing of childminding. Apart from her wonderful sense of humour and calm wisdom, she is able to lift people out of a sense of gloom. She has always played the difficult role of mediator in our family. Tall, thin, with a wistful expression, she reminds me of one of Michelangelo's Sibyls in the Vatican. Peta is reserved until she is comfortable with a person. She is a born therapist: quiet, dependable, and with great inner reserves.

Nicholas, I am always confident, will be all right, although he too suffers from low self-esteem. He has had to battle enormously to get where he is. His early illness appears to have caused massive dyslexia, which the school ignored, treating him as though he was just thick. It was only at the age of fifteen that he began to be able to read. By then it was too late at school, and he went to several colleges to get some A levels, and then on to university. By dint of his own sheer determination he got a degree, and has learned all about the financial world. He has great charm, and is well informed about world events. I am always surprised by his depth of knowledge, which comes out in social situations. People tell me that he looks like Harold. I see shades of my brother Jimmy in him.

I wonder why our children relate to us in a way which is so different to our own relationships with our parents. My father, Hooks Kantor, was always somewhat distant; and Polly, my mother – well, she was Polly, someone who never did like to talk about problems. She avoided them altogether.

MAY 1990

Went to see *Sunday in the Park with George*, the first time either of us has seen a production of Sondheim's work. It is a treat, and the sets are breathtaking, Seurat come to life. 'Why don't we do this more often?' says Harold, as we come out beaming. 'It requires my organisation, and I just don't get around to doing it,' is my response. I'm by no means as busy as Harold. I certainly don't work as hard as he does. I suppose I'm not yet attuned to being well and able to walk and out of pain. My resilience is less than it has ever been. The hip operations and the continuous pain last year have all taken their toll.

The phone calls between Harold and South Africa don't abate. Harold is now being coerced to agree to take up a post either as Professor of Sociology or as a director of a research unit at UWC. It seems a *fait accompli* that he is returning to South Africa. Somehow we don't sit down and talk about my desires or hopes or wishes. It seems to be taken for granted that I too will return. Harold is vague, but says there should be no problem in my getting a job as well. I certainly won't entertain the idea of going out to South Africa if I don't have a job waiting for me.

Jakes Gerwel is stopping off in London *en route* to New York, where he is being awarded an honorary doctorate, and the message is that he wants to meet people who would like to come to UWC. Harold organises a get-together at our house. At least I'm not expected to cater. I can't do that and teach all day.

I collect the food from Majio's, our local Indian takeaway: some dahl, my favourite gram flour dumplings in a yoghurt sauce, lamb and peas, chicken tikka, a potato curry. The food is splendid, though nobody seems to appreciate it fully. Everyone is concerned with what Gerwel has to say. Nicholas hovers in the background, intrigued to meet this man about whom he has heard so much. Jakes Gerwel, a small, dapper man with a pointed goatee beard, and bright eyes, who speaks with that distinctive accent of the coloured people of Cape Town, appears shy. Obviously, beneath this gentle, almost hesitant, exterior is a man with an iron will.

'What work do you want to do?' Jakes asks me. I can't give an adequate answer, nor is there time to explain why I am so hesitant. A Women's Studies course such as I have been running at the Poly is not really transferable to South Africa. My brand of feminism is really Eurocentric. Questions relating to the construction of gender identity somehow do not seem entirely appropriate in a country where the ravages of apartheid have overriden any gender issues. Anyway, do I want to develop new courses at this time of my life? On the other hand, I do have a range of skills, knowledge and experience. I know a great deal about why girls, overall, do badly at school; I am a good teacher, and I get good results from my students; I have more than twenty-five years' experience in higher education, a M.Sc. and Ph.D. under my belt. Yet on reflection, it seems almost impossible to insert myself into a black academic institution. I don't begin to know what the problems are: how universal are the ideas I have been playing around with, and how applicable are they to a possible post-apartheid society? People are talking as though massive events are about to happen in South Africa – as though apartheid is in the process of crumbling away, and change is around the corner. I am sceptical. And yet at supper, listening to Gerwel talk about the changes he would like to see, and the benefits that people sitting round the table could bring to a country cut off from the rest of the world, reeling under the effects of the cultural boycott, removed from the world of ideas, is seductive. I am momentarily excited: the spirit of hope and optimism is infectious, and I begin to think that maybe there is a place there for me, maybe I could do something constructive.

I have difficulty sleeping, and it's not because of the spicy food – it's the prospect of returning home after twenty-seven years. I had left at twenty-four hours' notice with a small suitcase and £100. I abandoned my three children and fled in a state of anxiety, terrified for my own safety, vowing then that I would never return to the country that had inflicted so much hardship on me, and on others I knew and loved. How do I reconcile myself to these contradictions? Once again I seem to have no control over the pathway my life is taking. There are forces out of my control. In the background I feel that my life is being dictated by Harold's wishes, Harold's options. Shades of the past.

My tired academic colleagues all see my 'going home' as a tremendous challenge, an opportunity they would love to have. 'I envy you the chance to start again,' the head of our department says. 'You're really very lucky, you know. Just think. You can leave this place' – and he glances round his shabby office cluttered with files and papers, with a few books on the shelves. Polytechnics haven't been happy places for some years.

I set up an appointment and see my Dean. His initial reaction is horrendous. Leave of absence? Never. Replacement for me? Never. What about my students? What about the courses I've developed? What about the future of Women's Studies at Middlesex Polytechnic? He's smiling, then irascible – the quintessential bureaucrat. When I am close to tears, he grudgingly says he will see to it that I get a year's leave of absence. No more.

South Africa will be a foreign country. I will be a stranger in my home country. I find myself trying to catalogue in concrete terms what I will actively miss, and I have games with myself as I drive along the streets of London trying to work out exactly what it will be. It is difficult, because there is so much one takes for granted, like the specialist shops. I know where to buy the best Turkish sweetmeats, I know who the best fishmonger is. It is having oysters for starters and goose for Christmas. It is knowing which bargains to go for at the January sales. It is walking in the back streets of Mayfair and marvelling at a gem of a house that you suddenly come upon. It is the annual summer Channel crossing and drive through sleepy French villages, remembering the siestas that go on from midday through to 2.30. It is our friends and the interesting and stimulating intellectuals; exotic meals cooked by Sami, one of my closest friends; browsing in Camden Lock, and always returning to my favourite stalls, where I know I will find the right present for someone; instant access to books hot off the press; my teaching and my studens. It is the delight of the flower market in the East End on Sunday mornings; the best TV in the world; our best friend Roy, who visits us regularly when he has a gig on in or near London.

Perhaps most importantly, it is far from the violence and the red dust and the heat and the noise and the children who run barefoot through the veld.

Going home. Those words, once spoken spontaneously, are no longer in the same league as 'I want to visit the Far East', 'I want to go to Mexico', 'I would love to see what Johannesburg looks like now', or 'Wouldn't it be lovely to go and stay with my sister, Betty, and walk on the squeaky white sands of Clifton Beach'. Going home is no longer fantasy.

The academic year is drawing to a close. I always mourn the departure of my final-year students, whom I have got to know well, even to love.

Before the final marking starts, Tessa and I go to Paris for a long weekend. It is years since I have been there, and I can't leave Europe without visiting Paris again. I don't feel guilty about leaving Harold – he has travelled extensively without me. We have a wonderful time. Tessa and I walk, we look, we meet a relative of ours. Our weekend is over too soon, and we return to London rejuvenated and happy.

Tonight Joe Slovo phoned from Cape Town. History is

being made. Joe is enemy Number 1 in South Africa. With true white South African chauvinism, he is depicted as the brains behind the ANC, as though a black person is incapable of running a resistance organisation. Joe, and other members of the ANC executive in Lusaka, have joined Nelson Mandela's delegation, which is having an historic meeting with de Klerk, the President, Pik Botha, the Foreign Minister, and other dignitaries of the apartheid state. This is unprecedented. We wait with bated breath to hear the outcome. Joe, as always, is amusing. He describes his ride in a big black Mercedes surrounded by security officers. He laughs and says, 'I had a vision of them pulling my nails out. It was jokes all round. When the formal introductions were being made I referred to myself as Colonel Slovo of the KGB and there were loud guffaws.' The South African press, in their personal attacks on Joe, have said, quite ridiculously, that he has a summer retreat outside Moscow, a gift from the Soviet Union.

The ANC delegation is paving the way for negotiations to begin, and these include the possibility of the return of the likes of us. The BBC and ITV news capture the broad smiles of the former bitter enemies. I cannot understand how someone like Mandela can reconcile himself to talking to the people who were responsible for his more than twenty-five years in jail.

We are all together when Joe phones. This opens up the way yet again to Tessa's anguish. She doesn't talk about it. Instead she becomes withdrawn, a clear sign of how unhappy she is. Peta, too, keeps her own counsel.

A few days later, Harold says casually, 'I've been invited to attend a conference in Johannesburg.' He is obviously excited, but apprehensive at the same time. We're all at the table having dinner when he drops this bombshell. 'Will you be allowed in?' Tessa asks anxiously. 'Look, some people have already gone in and not had any bother,' Harold replies. 'The ANC is organising visas, and temporary indemnity is being given.' I don't voice my ever-present fears about what will happen if the press get to know of his presence. He is bound to be newsworthy, if only because of his involvement in the Rivonia Trial which sentenced all those fine men to imprisonment for life.

That night my usual nightmare disturbs my sleep. It is always a variation on the same theme: Harold invariably insists on returning to South Africa, for some reason or other. My response never varies: I argue categorically that whatever the reason, it is sheer madness. In spite of this, Harold returns, and the variations relate to the manner in which he falls into the hands of the police once again, and how I seem to follow him, also landing in trouble.

We're sitting having a drink at Fred and Maxine's next door. Nicholas rushes in, face flushed, eyes wide, clearly excited. 'The most extraordinary thing has happened.' He pauses dramatically. 'I've had the most amazing phone call. Some guy says to me, "You won't believe what I'm going to tell you, but I know all about you, your father" . . . and he goes through all our names. He knows everything about us. He knows about my work for Allied Dunbar, and tells me things about all of us. He tells me not to try and trace his call. He puts the phone down and then phones again.' Apparently, soon after moving into a new home, this stranger found tapes of our telephone conversations. It confirms what I have always suspected: that our phone is bugged. Funny things have happened in the past, like hearing a recording of a meeting which has been picked up on our answering machine and recognising the voices of members of the ANC or the banned South African Communist Party.

There's nothing we can do until such time as this man sends the tapes, which he promises to do. It is creepy.

The indemnity certificate which will be issued by the state office in Pretoria allowing Harold to enter the country for a restricted period seems at last to have arrived at the Johannesburg ANC offices. Harold has gone quite frantic over the last few weeks, talking to a range of people, to ensure that it comes through. He won't risk going back without his clearance.

Harold leaves tomorrow evening. I am tense. My nightmare returns.

I have arranged to see some students at the Poly. No

possibility of rescheduling this. I will be with them when Harold is due to arrive. I've told him to phone me the minute he is through Customs and immigration. I have to know that he is safe and sound. I have to know that he has not been arrested or molested in any way. Returning to a country from which he escaped twenty-seven years ago is unlikely to go without a hitch. I can't help the tears. This time I curse and swear at the government. I explain to my switchboard about the call that may come from South Africa, and urge them to put it through to me immediately. I tell them at which number I will be. I have a sense of high drama.

In the midst of the tutorial, the phone rings. Harold's voice is at the other end. Quite normal. No tension. 'I'm sitting in Jack's garden and the sun is shining, although it's winter. The sky is bright blue. It's amazing and it's also quite strange.' 'What happened when you arrived?' I am desperate to know all the details. 'There was no real trouble at the airport. I was waved into the South African citizen line, which had emptied, and we gave in our British passports, and the woman said, 'Do you mind if I stamp it?' I laughed and said no, not at all. I sailed through and went to the carousel. I felt really peeved – a let down after all this time. The least I expected was some recognition that I was coming home, but no. While I was waiting for my baggage, the woman who had stamped my passport came up to me and said the computer was down when we had gone through and would I return with her. I went back to the immigration cubicle, and what seemed like the senior guy asked me whether I had a visa. I told him there was one waiting for me at the airport somewhere. I sweated for a moment, thinking the bloody ANC had muffed it. There was a flurry and a phone call. Whatever it was was traced. I was waved on. The immigration officer then wished me a happy stay. It is bizarre.' He goes on to describe the weather and the magnificence of Jack Unterhalters' house and the garden, where he will stay in the guest cottage. 'Are you sure it's safe,' I question Harold urgently. He laughs and says of course it is. I suppose there must be some form of security – from what one reads, everyone in the white Johannesburg suburbs is security-conscious.

Harold keeps using the word 'strange'. Everything he describes is strange. 'I feel like a stranger here. Somehow it is all familiar, yet at the same time totally unfamiliar. You can't imagine just how much Johannesburg has changed.'

We don't talk for long, and I arrange to phone him first thing every morning.

While he is away a small parcel arrives addressed to Nicholas, his name written in big block capitals, as though to disguise the handwriting. There is no doubt in our minds that it contains the telephone tapes. Nick and I drive to the ANC offices. We want to have the parcel checked for a letter bomb. It is cleared. There are two tapes, with the dates marked on them.

We listen to them in the car on the way home. They are unbelievably boring. The first few conversations are mine with Peta while she is in France, giving her good Jewish mama advice about the advantages of breastfeeding and telling her to ignore her French friends' advice about weaning Jonny. When I listen to myself, I am appalled – I do go on and on. Nicholas roars with laughter. 'Imagine some poor bastard Special Branch agent sitting down and listening to all this crap. There's nothing subversive at all.' He sees the funny side of it all. Does the listener get involved in the lives of the people on whom he is eavesdropping? I think momentarily, then I get angry at the sheer chutzpah of the whole business.

I am not sure what to do, and so I call in the local police to tell them I have evidence that our phone is being bugged. They are perplexed, and keep asking me whether I am part of the diplomatic corps. I keep assuring them that I am not. Someone comes round to see me, then refers the matter to Scotland Yard. Nothing happens, and I decide to shelve the matter until Harold's return.

Harold and I talk every morning, and every day he tells me how strange it is. 'What happened to the shooting in the trains?' I ask. The press had described in full how masked men had attacked commuters on the train from Soweto and randomly killed people on their way to work. There was speculation that this was the work of a third force. 'I've been so busy with meetings I haven't watched any news or even seen the newspaper. Mind you,' he adds, 'it probably wouldn't have made the news. It is unbelievably parochial and boring.'

When he returns we're fascinated, and listen avidly to his accounts. Even though he is tired, he tells us all about it.

'It really was an extraordinary experience, you know. In the context of these changes, the fact that I was there, and I was attending a meeting together wth Tozie' (Tozamile Botha is a black activist who had to flee the country twelve years ago and was given a hero's welcome when he went back to his home town of Port Elizabeth) 'was enough to blow one's mind. There were such direct contrasts. On the one hand I intellectually marvelled at what was happening, that we were attending a meeting called by the NECC, that petty apartheid had disappeared. On the other hand, emotionally, I was left with a weird feeling of anticlimax almost. No – not anticlimax, so much as I had an unreal feeling that everything around me was familiar. At the same time I wasn't really there. I kept thinking to myself: It's going to be wonderful meeting with old friends. That too was disappointing. I didn't have much spare time, and met only a few people. Like the time I got together with an old lawyer friend of mine. He asked me what I had been doing these past twenty-seven years, and never stopped to listen. It was as though he had to justify his remaining on in South Africa and making a really good living. He wasn't interested in me at all, and told me all about his famous cases. There were also some memorable moments. I went to a meeting that Jack was chairing for the National Association of Democratic Lawyers, who were listening to a report by Arthur Chaskelson, an old friend, a member of the team which had drafted the Namibian constitution. I walked in a bit late, and Jack stopped the proceedings and said: "That grey-haired gentleman who just walked into the hall is none other than Harold Wolpe returned from exile." There was a huge round of applause. And I went to a meeting with some sociologists at Witwatersrand University' (the children knew that was our alma mater) 'and I was told that the postgraduate students had strung up a poster or a banner saying "Wolpe Live 12 Noon Today".'

Of course he had seen Joe, and even managed to get to see Helen Joseph, my erstwhile boss, activist in the movement, and a legend in her lifetime. I was particularly keen to hear about his visit to UWC. 'I couldn't get over the fact that Tozie was staying with us at this rather posh hotel, the Winchester Mansions in Sea Point, and there was no trouble.' When we had left the country it was impossible to meet Africans in a public place, and hotels would never have admitted or served a black man or woman. Harold was enthusiastic about the people he had met in Cape Town, and about how warm and friendly everybody had been, and how they had expressed their delight at our impending arrival.

We discuss the matter of the tapes with Maxine and Fred. Fred Halliday is a political scientist who has reported extensively on the Arab world and the Soviet Union. He is familiar with dirty tricks campaigns. He suggests that we contact Duncan Campbell, an investigative journalist. Campbell is unashamedly intrigued, and together he and Nicholas pull up carpets and follow wires. *Voilà!* The bugging devices – there are two of them – are neatly attached to the outside of the wall of the house, connected to some plastic container that Harold had carefully picked up and put down for years when he cleaned out gutters. It was there for all to see. Had we even noticed it, we would have assumed it was something to do with the phones.

Campbell is like a little schoolboy who has had his secret wish granted. He all but jumps for joy at his discovery. It is the first actual bugging contraption he has found, although he has investigated a number of other cases, including the bugging of his own phone. And through further investigations he is able to establish that it has transmitted to a recording device, which runs on batteries, within a hundred yards of the house. Even this information does not get the police moving, and we try to investigate further, but to no avail – although we all think that one of the dilapidated garages higher up the road must have stored the equipment.

I find the whole incident menacing – all the more so when, the day after the removal of the device, there is clear evidence that someone has been round to the house to check it out. A TV set that had stood in the alleyway outside has been moved next to the wall. Someone needed this to stand on to check what had happened! I write to our Member of Parliament, but get no joy from him. Campbell writes an interesting article for the *New Statesman*, and the Special Branch police take the tapes and the envelope they arrived in. Nothing further is heard.

JULY 1990

Summer again in our house in Provence. The magic of the area shrouds all my lurking anxieties about the return. We are all together, including Nicholas, who is there with Meme. Peta wonders whether she can live with Jonathan's father, Yves. Tessa, who had not planned to come this year because of a trip to Los Angeles, changed her arrangements because she is convinced that this will be the last time we are all together.

We all pretend this is a summer like all the others we have spent in this wonderful village. Tessa, though, doesn't allow us to forget that she feels we are abandoning her. 'Look at what happens to so many people,' I try to reason. 'Children move away from their parents when they grow up. Everyone I know in America lives thousands of miles away from their parents. And all those masses of South Africans who have left their parents and gone to Australia, or England, or Canada, or America . . . Look at the Bermans. Not one of their four daughters lives in England.' Myrtle and Monty are very dear old friends of ours. I used to look after their daughters while the two of them were in jail during the Emergency in 1960. They migrated soon after. 'That's not the same,' Tessa remonstrates. Tessa is the most up-front about her anguish. She says that politics are intervening and upsetting – if not destroying – her life yet again. 'Look what we've been through. If it wasn't for Harold, we would probably have grown up in a normal way in South Africa. Peta and I have often thought our lives would have been very different if you hadn't had to leave the country. We would have grown up in a conventional way, and been confident and happy.' How can I tell her that there was no guarantee of normality in South Africa? Anything could have happened to her, or to us. The slightest involvement in oppositional politics could have signed our death warrant, and I am grateful that my children did not have to make any decisions about joining the resistance movement, being subjected to the constant harassment that has affected so many people. She rejects any logical argument. 'It's what I feel that's important. I don't care about other people. I am so angry with Harold for his unswerving commitment to the struggle in South Africa. Why did he have to do all those things?' How can you answer this question adequately when someone is so badly hurt?

The anger is dissipated by the dry heat of the sky-blue days. She and Harold ride together on their bikes. She manages to keep up with Harold, riding her heavy little bike with no gears. They go to Carpentras. I warn them that it is much too hot, particularly in the midday sun, to ride home. They are both obstinate, and in the end I have to fetch them because they lose the key to unlock the chains protecting their bikes. I drive back to Carpentras to rescue them; my blue *fripé* silk top changes colour with the salt from my perspiration.

It is a summer full of nostalgia: visits to markets checking that the aubergines are garden-fresh, buying little Mediterranean fish for soup, sipping cold beer in the street cafés and chatting to friends, swimming at the local baths in Tulette, sitting out on the patio until midnight, talking, and eating and drinking. The mistral seems to blow even fiercer on the west side of the Rhône, where the Romans planted the first vines; and the landscape is rugged to the point of savagery. The sense of history is present everywhere. The history of South Africa is in the present, and there is no 'smell of antiquity'.

I look at the hills and the valleys. I etch on to my mind's eye the countryside I have grown to love, so that I shall be able to recall these delights in the future. I want to be able to evoke the memory of the tall cypress tree on the hill near Villedieu, the fields of sunflowers miraculously turning their heads before finally drooping, the purple lavender fields which perfume the air, the farmers filling the water tanks with the spray for their vines, the view of Cairanne perched on the hill as the road winds down from the mountain to our village. Harold keeps reminding me how beautiful Cape Town is. I acknowledge this, but I love Provence. I know what to expect. I know what the life is like. I can walk at night without fear. I can drive without fear. The local fascists confine their attacks to the desecration of Jewish graves in Carpentras, and put up posters supporting Le Pen.

The summer speeds by. Tessa returns to London, Nick as well, and Remedios goes back to Spain. We remain on with Peta and Jonathan for a few more days.

The market at Tulette is small and unpretentious – unlike nearby Vaison la Romaine, which is chic, filled with tourists and kitsch arts and crafts stalls. The local farmers treat Monday market day as a major social event. There is an excellent stall with Ardèche sausages and salami. On my last morning I find I have only forty francs left, and I want to buy some salami to take back to London. Forty francs is not enough. The woman on the stall, who knows me as Jonathan's grandmother, smiles and says: Pay me next year. I explain that I might be in South Africa next July. She expresses her concern, and then takes whatever money I have and brushes away the question of how I can pay the balance.

It is hard to imagine a summer without being in Provence. It is hard to imagine a July that is wet and cold and windy, as I am told it is in Cape Town.

SEPTEMBER 1990

More phone calls to South Africa. Harold is anxious. UWC haven't come up with contracts for our employment, though apparently there is no doubt this will happen. It adds to the feeling of suspended animation. We are going back – the question is when, and to what?

As I write, the low-slung grey clouds move slowly but purposefully across the skies. The last roses of the late summer still magically open up their new buds. The oak tree, sad with its scar from the amputated trunk following the devastation of last year's hurricane, shows the telltale signs of autumnal onslaught. The squirrels are frantic in their search for food to

stock up for the hazards of the winter months. And suddenly I
see a dramatically marked nuthatch, with its sharp nervous
movements, eagerly snatching at the pieces of fat on the bird
table. And there is Mingi, the neighbours' predatory Burmese
cat, voraciously gnawing the lamb knuckle that Nick has thrown
for the fox whose visits are becoming more and more frequent.
I even saw it, quite at home, curled up on the middle of the
lawn for an afternoon nap. I love our house. It has warmth and
a welcoming glow.

I know the birds of our woods – Queens Wood part of
Highgate Woods, small, compact and mysterious, filled with a
variety of trees, a paddling pool for dogs and a more serviceable
one for young children. The barn owls nest there, and even a
kestrel in flight has been seen. I anticipate the change of season
with a sense of awe. I hate the damp and the greyness in
January and February, except that the trees in winter, with
their spidery thin branches caught up in the half-light of a dark
winter's day, lend an aura of mystery. And spring is only a few
months away.

What is Cape Town like? I really don't know it. What are
its seasons like? I am a Johannesburg person, after all. Even as
I say this I realise that I am no longer from Johannesburg. I am
from London.

Things seem to go from bad to worse. Tessa has just been made
redundant. She is devastated. And Nick wants to quit his job
with Allied Dunbar. I tire of the bright voices who continually
congratulate me on my luck at being able to return 'home'. I
have taken to waking at dawn. I wrestle with sleep, which
doesn't return because I go over and over all the problems, and
fret about how everything will resolve itself.

Harold expresses his worries so differently. It's largely
cerebral, and it shows in his irritability with me. There are
definite signs of increasing irascibility on both our parts. We
bicker in an unpleasant way. Tessa says we don't express our
feelings or anger openly. Everything is suppressed.

Mostly I feel quite cheerless. It's like all those days long ago, when I used to fret about Harold's involvement in the underground movement. 'Well, if you want to leave the country you can, you know,' he would remonstrate with me. How could I leave the country on my own, with small children, no capital and no income? I felt then that I had no choice, and the same feeling has returned. I don't want to separate from Harold. This is the only option if I want to remain in London. For Harold it is quite simple.

I am diverted from these concerns by the beginning of the new term. Study skills classes with a new batch of students, helping to organise the students' timetables and choices. In the midst of all this I have a series of medical checks which seem to indicate that everything is working perfectly.

OCTOBER 1990

The weeks seem to fly by. My list of what I will miss in London gets longer and longer. My children don't feature there. They aren't things I will miss. The separation will simply leave a gaping wound. I love having three generations living under one roof. I feel really privileged in living with and close to our children all the while. Albertina Sisulu, Walter's wife, last saw her son Max in 1963, and didn't recognise him when he stepped off the aircraft in 1990. So many women have had to endure separation from children as exiles.

Harold doesn't seem at all upset at the prospect of leaving London, except for the loss of the children. He begins to work out who among our friends we will miss. The trouble with London is that you manage to see some people only once or twice a year at the most. 'We'd probably see more of our friends if we visited occasionally.'

We have no friends in Cape Town. Betty, my sister, lives in the Wilderness and has a business in George, a long way away. Joe Slovo and his second wife Helena will be living in Johannesburg. So many of our old Johannesburg friends shunned us when they visited London. They were probably scared of the long arm of the Secret Police. I am not sure that I want to renew those friendships, and anyway, they all live in Johannesburg.

In the 1960s it was chic to have a black journalist at dinner parties. Will it be chic to entertain ex-terrorists, as Harold has been described? I express my fears to him. 'Oh, we'll easily make new friends,' he reassures me. 'Don't forget that UWC is filled with academics who share our views. I've already met some of the people, and they are incredibly warm and friendly. I feel so different with South Africans.' He pauses then adds: 'You remember when I was in Dakar' (referring to that historic meeting in 1987 between ANC people and South Africans keen to meet with the ANC, a meeting sponsored by Madame Mitterrand of France). 'I told you that within a very short while people who previously would never have talked to each other were behaving as though there were no barriers to friendship. It was extraordinary that even with the Afrikaners I had a fellow feeling. It is a shared history. There is an ease that you find with South Africans which is missing from relationships with the English. The longer I live here, the more alien I feel. I feel really relaxed when I am with South Africans.' I don't want to point out that there are a whole mass of South Africans with whom I never want to be friendly.

I wonder about my type of feminism, even though Harold tells me that some women in South Africa are looking forward to my arrival because my work is known and respected. I have enormous doubts about this. The feminism I know and work with is rooted in a Western European tradition. Although the core problems may be the same, the lives of the women in South Africa are so different. Do the white women still talk about the servant problem? Do they sit on one side of the room while their husbands talk man talk on the other? Middle-class white women have flocked into the world of work. Their level of education is still surprisingly low. The world of the African women is so different. Those who have been politically active have suffered so greatly. I met a woman named Joyce recently. She came to London for a brief spell to learn about research methods in education. She told me how she had been arrested when her youngest child was one, and imprisoned for seven years. He was eight when she was released. Her troubles didn't stop there. She was re-arrested and separated from her children once again. Her goal is to return to the Northern Transvaal, where she hopes to live and work in some peace together with the family she hardly knows. 'Even then I can never get back all those years I have lost. They are gone for ever.'

It is difficult to know in advance what being a feminist, particularly a feminist in my age group, will be like in South Africa. There seem to be younger women addressing questions of feminism. The movement is underdeveloped, and reports of the mass democratic movement indicate that feminism may be on the agenda, but in practice it has had little impact. It is men who dominate the committees, the power bases – women do the work on the sidelines.

OCTOBER 1990

Although I'm disenchanted with British feminism, it has been an integral part of my life for the past twenty years. Looking back, I can't help feeling proud of what I did in the midst of raising the children, running a home, and becoming an academic at a mature age without any support system. And initially Harold behaved like most men, not lifting a finger to help in the house. It has been tough, particularly as the younger feminists were initially intolerant of me as a wife with children. It was only when they had established their careers and begun to have their own children that their attitudes changed.

I could land up fighting the same feminist battles all over again. That is daunting.

Irrespective of whether we rent or sell our house, twenty-seven years of accumulated jumble has to be sorted and dealt with. It was much more straightforward leaving South Africa: I just packed a suitcase and left. Moving like a refugee, without any thought or any baggage or any planning, is simpler. Sometimes returning feels like death.

NOVEMBER 1990

Suddenly there are contracts for both of us, and they will be sent to us for signature. I am still not sure what I shall be doing, except that I will be attached to a centre for adult education. It isn't an area I know very much about. Harold's work is clear-cut: he will be starting up an education policy unit. Apparently there are several in different universities. The children's reaction is predictable. Nick says, 'I think it's a wonderful idea. The two of you are going to love it there. It will be the best thing you can do.' He doesn't express any of the anger and trauma that constantly haunts Tessa. Peta says she will give up her job, go and live in France for a while, then come out to South Africa as well. 'I've thought about it quite carefully. Jonny's childhood is going so quickly, and I only really spend time with him over the weekends. This isn't what I wanted. I don't want to work and miss all this.' I know Peta well. It is not a decision she has reached lightly. Once she has made up her mind, nothing will deter her, however difficult that decision may be. However wonderful it would be to have her live with us in South Africa, I am none too happy at the prospect of her bringing up her child in that sort of environment.

Things are looking up for Tessa and Nicholas. She has landed an amazing job in the Dick Williams animation studio. He is doing a film that he has planned for the past twenty years, and Tessa is to be the studio manager. She works an amazing seventy-hour week, and will be earning a fortune while the job lasts. Although she is exhausted, I hope it will take her mind off our impending departure.

Nick, too, seems to have found himself a good job. Against all advice, he gave notice, gave up his company car, and sat for a month reading about financial issues. Finally, he sent a letter to fifteen firms and got very positive responses. Within a week he had been offered a job with a small firm – run, ironically, by expatriate South Africans who are out to make money and don't see a lot wrong with the ruling party in South Africa!

Living in London is more than the culture, the climate, the trees and the beauty of the seasons, friends and family, intellectual stimulation, the markets and the people and the irritation of congested roads and aggressive drivers. It is safe. Nobody runs through the commuter trains hacking to death and shooting innocent workers. No rival gangs vie with each other in ghetto areas to wreak havoc among their own people; there are no white men with bull necks, short bristling hair, arms folded over huge chests, muscles threatening and straining at their tight shirtsleeves, listening enraptured to their leader, Eugene Terre'Blanche, inciting them on to murder and mayhem because of their fear of the ANC, and in the name of the preservation of the white *volk* (people) and its exalted civilisation. Those white people who support fascism in England are, luckily, not immediately visible as the South Africans are.

It is comforting to know that my fears and apprehension are being experienced by so many of the exiles I talk to. It is, perhaps, even stronger among the black people who, over the years, have built up lives for themselves in which they enjoy a sense of dignity, and whose children have jobs and are treated like people. However much is written about institutionalised racism in England it is simply not comparable with apartheid in South Africa. We as white people will enjoy a privileged existence by virtue of being white in South Africa, but the returning black people have no such assurance. It could be almost impossible for someone who is used to living in Islington to go back to life in Soweto.

1 DECEMBER 1990

Today is my sixtieth birthday, and we decide to celebrate it. We will have a small party of about thirty people. It is a wonderful evening, the first birthday party I have had since . . . I can't remember when I last had one. I don't mind leaving my fifties. There is too much else to traumatise me. We are due to leave for my first visit to South Africa in a few days.

12 DECEMBER 1990

I am sitting in my sister Betty's beautiful garden under a circular thatched gazebo, looking out at the lagoon. She lives opposite ex-President P.W. Botha in this idyllic retirement village, Wilderness, on what is known as the Garden Route. Beyond the lagoon the thundering Indian Ocean is visible. There is an extraordinary variety of plants – dianthuses and dahlias mixed together with lettuces; herbs rubbing shoulders with zinnias. The riot of colour is reflected in the honey birds feasting on the nectar of the great hibiscus bush which stands three metres high, and as much again broad. How different is the real hibiscus in comparison with the small indoor plants that are given as Christmas presents in England. Honey birds are exquisite: sharp curved beaks, luminous backs, and a streak of bright red on the breast. They pierce the base of the flower to suck out the nectar. I cannot accustom myself to the Technicolor of the countryside and the bird life after the greys and muted colours that I have come to associate with England.

The air is heavy. In place of a blue sky is the white mist cloud. The whir of the electric polisher that Sarah, Betty's coloured maid, is using indoors intrudes on the sounds of nature. Sarah is busy clearing up after Sunday's luncheon party.

That was my first introduction to new white South Africa. Betty's friends are a most heterogeneous group. There is her hairdresser, Errol, shirt open to the waist, in his brief – and I do mean brief – denim shorts, which reveal long tanned legs, and not an ounce of fat anywhere, camping it up and getting pissed out of his mind. Errol is no admirer of Nelson Mandela, and makes no bones about his racism. And Tom Sprong and his wife, owners of the local restaurant. Tom came to help Betty cook in the morning and the drinking of delicious white wine began at eleven o'clock. There's the farmer from over the hill too – he produces artichokes but says the Capetonians don't appreciate them and he'll change his crop; and Betty's gynaecologist – he looks after her in general. He supports the ruling Nationalist Party. His beautiful, thoroughly bilingual wife supports the Democratic Party – obviously room for conflict and struggle there. And another six people, none of whom, except for Betty, can quite get around to supporting the ANC.

I felt apprehensive at first. This was the first time I had sat down to a meal with anyone who supports the government, and I was distinctly uncomfortable. Betty handled it with her usual devil-may-care attitude. She believes that everyone has the right to believe what they want to believe. Politics should not interfere with whom you like and whom you don't, and life is there to be enjoyed. Good wine, good food and pleasant company – what more could one want? Betty wanted to launch me on her friends, who are a little curious about me. I cannot be quite so sanguine, knowing that there are people around who would like to see the likes of me safely locked up behind bars, and our children eradicated. I am asked what it is like being back. It is not clear whether they really do want to hear anything that borders on controversy, although it still arouses some curiosity.

The luncheon was a great success, and we moved into the dining room for dessert. By this time most of the guests, Betty included – were quite drunk. I was conscious of the need to keep an eye on the gate that opens on to the main road below. Betty's precious dachshunds were always threatening to run into the road, where they would be run over. Betty had disappeared by the time one of them had been rescued. 'I'm glad she didn't see that,' I said. 'Oh, don't worry,' retorted Errol, 'she's gone to bed. She always goes to bed.' I guffawed and said, 'Impossible. She has all you people here' – gesticulating to the gathering. 'Oh, but she always does that,' Errol assured me. 'You'll find her on her bed, fast asleep. When we want to go, we tidy up and leave the house.' He was right.

Betty's parties, I discover, are notorious: the food, the wine and the laughter. Wherever Betty is, there is always bound to be a party. Maybe it's just as well that Harold was in Durban. I don't know how well he would have coped with the heterogeneous company.

Today everything is quiet. Betty is at work, and four coloured men are supposedly finishing the paving round the small swimming pool that has just been built. I had thought British workmen were bad. By comparison they are paragons of virtue; they are Stakhanovites; they deserve the Order of Lenin. Only one of the four men seems to be doing anything. The others keep on disappearing in the vicinity of the garage. And what is worse, the paving is decidedly crooked. It is quite obvious that it will have to be redone.

Betty works really hard in her café/restaurant in the Pick 'n Pay store complex in George. When she comes home at night she is exhausted, and sinks into her armchair with a vodka and soda in her hand. Her maid, Sarah, always sets out a tray with a bucket of ice, glasses and drinks for her. It is at this time that we indulge in our early memories.

We talk about our mother, Polly, and recall how difficult her youth had been: she had been impoverished. Her mother never seems to have had the means to look after her, so she was farmed out to relatives in the countryside. She told us how she had gone to a dentist for the first time when she was eighteen, and that was because he was a new arrival in Parys, where she was living, and an eligible bachelor. Anyone new in that little dorp was worthy of pursuit. Lucky thing: she had a perfect set of teeth, and had lost only one by the time she died at the age of seventy-six.

She became a secretary in a legal firm in Johannesburg. She was fond of telling us how she spent all her spare cash on glamorous clothes she could wear at the afternoon tea dances in the heart of the city. She had two dresses for work, which she alternated each day. The photographs of her then showed no signs of the wrinkles that caused her so much concern when she was older. She made me so self-conscious of my own. She wore her hair short and bobbed in the latest fashion, and struggled to get it to lie flat. It was normally curly and unruly.

We both agreed that she was a snob through and through. She would reject her many suitors, knowing their antecedents, on the grounds that they were uncultured, or had no breeding. It was what their parents had done, not how much money they had, that was her criterion. 'Oh, his family were little short of horse thieves,' she would say dismissively, irrespective of the son's success. Annie, her eldest sister, was well ahead of her time. No doubt she had all the elements of a hippie. She eschewed make-up and brassières, and left her husband. She interfered or supported – depending on what side you were on – in other people's lives. She was quick to condemn, and had felt largely responsible for Polly, who lived with her when she came to the big city. Annie watched over Polly as though she was her own daighter, and she was horrified when Polly eloped with our father, Hooks.

Our mother was contemptuous of the nouveaux riches, yet at the same time she enjoyed all the trappings of money. She had impeccable good taste, and bought some beautiful furniture and various *objets d'art* on her one and only trip to Europe as a young woman. Betty has the magnificent oak dining-room table.

Polly's early married life seems to have been carefree. She had servants and nannies. Betty remembers Miss Torman, our small, gaunt, austere German nanny, far better than I do. All I recall is her insistence on all three of us chewing our food to the count of a hundred before swallowing. I know why I never insisted that Nicholas chews like that, although he almost swallows his food whole. I don't seem to have had the authority with my children that Miss Torman had with us. Chewing slowly is a habit I have never quite kicked. Miss Torman was succeeded by Miss Clark, an attractive Englishwoman with a conventional peaches-and-cream complexion. She did not last long, because she started to go out with one of Polly's admirers. From then on we had black nannies.

We don't talk about our brother Jimmy. We both still find it painful that he died in his late forties after a massive heart attack. I always attribute a large part of his stress to his traumatic divorce from Barbara, and his subsequent difficulties bringing up his children on his own. His succession of house-keepers never solved the problem. I also know that Harold and I contributed in no small way to the stress and strain he endured. I have never come to terms with the fact that Jimmy was charged with treason, together with all the other Rivonia trialists. Even his acquittal months later could not eliminate my abiding guilt. Betty and I both acknowledge that Jimmy was Polly's favourite, but neither of us seems to bear any rancour.

George Mbumbi became the mainstay in the house of our later childhood. He was a short, stocky Zulu who ran the house and seemed to be most caring of the three of us. George had what seemed like masses of younger brothers, one of whom would relieve him when he wanted to return to his home in Zululand. I still shudder at the memory of writing out a pass for George which would allow him to leave our home on his 'days off'. Without that scrap of paper he could have been arrested – never mind that it was obviously written by a childish hand.

It is good to be able to recall these times together.

Harold, who has been in Durban at some conference since our arrival in South Africa, is due here tomorrow. We will stay a further two days, then we fly off to Cape Town.

9 DECEMBER 1990

We manage one visit to UWC, where I go to the centre where I shall be working and meet the Director, Shirley Walters, who gives me all the recent publications and extends a warm welcome. We have tea with Jakes Gerwel in his office together with some other returnees; and I feel that I talk too much about feminism, and try too hard to sound interesting.

The campus is miles from Cape Town, past the airport. It is a huge sprawling place, with buildings scattered everywhere. Harold points out all the new buildings enthusiastically. I do not find the architecture engaging, and I get the feeling that it is a rather bleak campus. I didn't know what to expect.

12 DECEMBER 1990

We are flying to Johannesburg to spend two days there before leaving for London and Christmas with our children. We hope to see someone in the ANC offices to finalise details about the necessary documents if we are to be given amnesty.

Harold suddenly thumps me and gestures towards the man sitting in front and to his right across the aisle. I look, but I can see nothing. The man is reading a newspaper. I need my long-distance glasses. I put them on, and see headlines in Afrikaans:

Harold Wolpe mag ook terugkom na SA vrywaring: name van 730 bekend.

Harold Wolpe may also return to South Africa indemni-fied: names of 750 well known.

The man reading the paper is deeply suntanned. He must have been on holiday in the Cape. He has a short moustache and a beard. The gold signet ring on the little finger of his left hand, an expensive-looking wristwatch with a natty dark tan leather strap, a gold ring on the right hand, and a gold identity chain spell out money. His wife and two children looked casually yet expensively dressed.

We wait for him to finish reading the newspaper so that we can borrow it. His son keeps interfering with his reading. Harold leans across and taps him lightly on the shoulder. 'May I borrow your newspaper?' he asks. 'I've an English-language one if you want that,' the man replies. Harold shakes his head. 'No, I should like that one' – pointing to the Afrikaans paper. The man shrugs and hands it over. We both scan the article. My Afrikaans is too poor to allow me to understand anything more than the headlines. I wonder what the man's reaction would have been had he known Harold was the object of that news report!

I can't wait to see Johannesburg again.

We rent a car at the airport and drive straight into the centre of town to the ANC offices. I look around me in utter amazement. Near the central library – where I used to work as a student and skip through the streets with a fellow student, a thoroughly extrovert young man who wore his hair long twenty years ahead of his time – I stare in amazement. Numbers of black women are squatting on boxes selling various foodstuffs. I can't believe this. The streets are filled with black people, and the street vendors seem to be doing a roaring trade. Not many white people around. Harold tells me that not only is this, the informal economy, a feature of the Third World, it also represents a significant breakthrough. Previously street vendors were prosecuted, and only recently have they been allowed to ply their trade. One of the rationales for their exclusion was to prevent the South African economy from approximating a Third World one!

I've been warned about the crime in the centre of Johannesburg, and I clutch my bag tightly.

The ANC offices have strict security. Another unbelievable

phenomenon. Official offices, above board and operating in the open! Very different from the small building housing the ANC in London. These offices are spacious, and occupy several floors. The man we are due to see isn't there, even though we made an appointment and came to Johannesburg a day early for this express purpose. Charitably, we say that it is too close to Christmas, and everyone seems to be in a party mood. This does not prevent us from feeling intense irritation at what appears to be another example of the ANC's administrative incapacity.

We both feel strange. I understand now why Harold used this word when he described his first visit here. And I recognise the inadequacy of my expressions to convey my immediate impressions. I, too, repeat: 'It's strange, it's really strange.' Petty apartheid has disappeared. The banks have black tellers who share the same office space as white workers. There are black people in places where before only white people were allowed. There were even black people on the plane – and not only business or professional men. When I flew to George, a sleepy strung-out town with single-storey buildings that reminded me of small-town America, there was a black woman on the plane who had clearly never flown before. The air hostess was considerate and polite, and showed her how the table unclipped. White serving black is a strange sight in South Africa.

I cannot recognise any buildings in Johannesburg. Everything seems to have changed. The city has undergone a metamorphosis – except the street names, which are familiar.

We decide to drive around a bit, with Harold acting as guide. This is a role reversal: normally he has no sense of direction. Our next stop is Maxie Street, where we lived. As we drive through the suburbs, I realise that everything looks vaguely familiar. It is a little like a dream where you struggle to identify exactly where you are. We come to the long drive leading down towards Killarney, and I ask Harold to go on a detour there before we get to Louis Botha Avenue and the turnoff to our old house. I am even more amazed at what I see.

I now feel like a patient suffering from amnesia who has flashes of recall that point to an elusive history.

We pass where I think the tennis courts stood where we played on Saturday afternoons. They aren't there. Have they moved, or are we in the wrong street? Landmarks have disappeared. 'The rondavels where Polly and Hooks lived are no longer there,' Harold tells me. I can't make out where they stood in relation to what I see now.

We get to Maxie Street. Everything looks different, our old house in particular. The tin roof has gone, the cannas in the pavement outside are no longer there. Instead there is the obligatory high wall, and the security gate with the number 11A in big gilt figures. You can't see into the house or the garden, as you could before, because there is another closed, solid, white-painted high gate. The farmhouse atmosphere has been replaced. A new house stands where the servants' rooms used to be.

Houses tell stories, and when we lived there it felt that 11 Maxie Street had always been a happy house. I had known immediately I saw it that I wanted to live there. It was an untypical suburban house, small by professional white standards and idiosyncratic of design. The pathway between the garage and the side of the house led to the sitting-room. There was no front door. Trumpet vine, with its long red summer flowers, was everywhere. The garden was large – the house obviously occupied two plots – and dominated by a large old oak tree, unusual for Johannesburg. The acorns would ping on the corrugated-iron roof, and a thunderstorm would bring them clattering down in a cacophony of sound, just like hailstones. Once I had been told that an oak tree in your own garden was good luck – an old Russian superstition – and I believed that.

We never seemed to have enough money to furnish the house in a way most people did. We had splashed out on a good hi-fi set in anticipation of Harold being placed under house arrest. The fire was effective, although it was small. On winter nights I would sit there reading in peace, broken only by the occasional night-time sickness of one or other of the girls: teething, or some other childish problem. Harold was out so often at some clandestine meeting. It took up so much of his spare time. Polly would phone me and say, 'Are you doing anything tonight, and how is Harold?' I would tell her he was playing bridge somewhere.

Harold turns to me and says, 'I told you it was very different from the time when we lived here.' We are both silent, deep in thought.

South Africa has not stood still. Nor, for that matter, have I. My face, like the fountain in St Roman, shows the signs of physical change. The jaw line is no longer firm. There is more than a trace of a double chin. The lines of my face now crisscross each other like a detailed Ordnance Survey map. I realise that the lines will go on and on, new ones appearing with quite unrelenting regularity. But the changes in me go far beyond those telltale lines on my face and the liver spots on my hands. They go beyond my friends, my children. They are an accumulation of all these elements which have constituted my life in a British climate and environment over the past twenty-seven years. I am very different from the frightened woman who fled the country in 1963.

'I must see Bryanston,' I say. Harold agrees. We drive there in search of the house I lived in as an adolescent, and throughout my student days.

My father made a killing on the stock market and we moved to Bryanston, ten miles from the centre of Johannesburg. With its huge plots, it promised to become an exclusive area.

Wartime building restrictions placed limits on the square footage that could be erected. Stefan Ahrends, the leading domestic architect at the time, came up with a wonderful plan which provided five bedrooms and an extraordinary living-room with a large open copper-hooded fireplace. The room was double height, open thatch, which gave off a sweet smell when the rains came. The cabriole-legged cabinet was filled with fine porcelain and china. The Meissen ballet dancer, with extended points in a tulle china dress, and the Wedgwood lord and lady, in their golden-coloured clothes, which stood elegantly next to a pair of Dresden candlesticks, were my favourites. The paintings included work by some fine South African artists. The large sitting-room was invitingly comfortable. The dining-room table stood at one end. My Siamese cats thought that mealtimes were their times as well. Poetsie would sit on the arm of the carving chair, and quite nonchalantly take a dainty morsel from my father's fork. Not that he did not encourage her to do so. The cats were in the habit of walking across the table from one side to another. None of us thought that at all odd. The dogs were better behaved. Flush, my cocker spaniel, was really old and sleepy most of the time.

The dining-room looked out over the veld, which stretched away endlessly. Our three-acre garden had no boundaries. There was no need, because we had no neighbours. We built a swimming pool, but no filter plant. The money must have run out.

There were miraculous afternoons of solitude. I would walk for miles and miles through the endless stretches of dried yellowing grass, swaying in the summer winds, reflecting a golden light as the shafts of sun played on the seeded heads. As usual in the Transvaal, there were few trees around. The sky was wide and open, with large cumulus clouds in the far distance. My sole companion was Jimmy's beautiful red bull terrier – sleek of build, with a body taut like wire. Suddenly she would see or smell something. Her body stiffened, poised for the leap into the air before she pounced on her prey. Although she never did catch anything, that moment when she appeared suspended in air was beautiful to watch. The sun would beat down, even on winter days, and in the solitude I would experience an overwhelming sense of freedom and harmony.

It was a lonely time. My mother never seemed to be interested in my school work, and never looked at my books. She was quite satisfied that I did well, and was not the problem that Betty seemed to be. Betty, the middle child, seems always to have been in trouble. Jimmy had it easy: he was the eldest, and the favoured one.

Being clever was not necessarily a prized quality, and when I suggested that I wanted to become a doctor, she was horrified. 'You don't want to be like Dr Getz!' she remonstrated when the topic was broached. Dr Getz, who was sometimes called in, was businesslike, wore sensible dowdy suits and sensible shoes. Her hair was short, back and sides – unfashionable. She walked in a brusque, determined way, carrying her medical bag with authority. She did not look at all feminine. My mother did not regard her as a suitable role model for me.

'Anyway, it takes six years to study, and then you have to work in a hospital. Much too long a period for a girl.' She dismissed the subject.

A career for me was not something my mother took seriously, although exactly what she wanted for me was never clear. Perhaps a good marriage to a wealthy, attractive, personable, interesting man. Yet at the same time she was critical of conventional Jewish society, and mocked the nice Jewish girls who married their nice Jewish boys and lived happily ever after. She did not realise that she was giving me contradictory messages. She had planted the seed of discontent, but did not know how to make it bear fruit. She herself had potential that was never realised. She led a life of ease, even when money was so obviously tight. Although she was no longer able to buy good clothes, she always managed to look extremely well dressed. She had flair. She had style. She had beauty. And she was witty, with a delightful sense of humour and a great gift for telling jokes. In short, she was the sort of person everybody loved having around them. She had the ability to lift the mood of everyone around her, and inject a feeling of gaiety and laughter.

All sorts of events were occurring which passed me by. The black mine workers had begun to be more militant. These were men who came from all over Southern Africa to dig the rich gold out of the bowels of the earth. They began objecting to their meagre food rations. They wanted more money, they wanted better working conditions, they were tired of being treated like workhorses. Wildcat stoppages occurred and then dramatically, in August 1946, between sixty and seventy thousand men downed tools and refused to go on shifts bringing out the gold that made their bosses rich but kept them in poverty. The week-long strike was broken. The caged strength of the black worker had become fleetingly visible.

I knew nothing of the meeting in Market Square, in the centre of Johannesburg, which called the strike. I did not know that within days there were 150,000 men on strike. I did not know that white people, including members of the Communist Party, had been engaged in helping with the organisational tasks of duplicating newsheets which were distributed to mine compounds at two or three in the morning. I did not know that students from the university, including Harold, were helping, and barely sleeping at all. He was to recount these events in the years to come.

I knew nothing of the problems generated by the shortage of staple foods, like rice. In Ferreirastown and Fordsburg, areas close to the centre of Johannesburg inhabited largely by Indians and other non-white people, the Indian shopkeepers were refusing to sell rice to customers unless they bought other goods. The people could not afford to do this, so they gave up buying rice altogether.

The Communist Party organised a series of food raids. Their members, including some young activists from the university, would simply walk into shops, go behind the counters, serve people with rice, charge the non-inflated price, and hand it over to the shopkeepers. The poor were quick to learn of this. Within days huge queues formed behind these activists, who would lead the people into shops. Nor was this confined to areas like Fordsburg and Ferreirastown. In Alexandra Township – a sprawling mess of corrugated dwellings, rough, unpaved, pitted sand roads, isolated taps providing water for complete households and smoke rising skywards at dawn from myriad fires lit by women preparing some meagre meal before their husbands' and their own departure for work in white areas ten miles away – similar activities took place. One day Harold and an older man, Louis Joffe, wandered the disorderly roads like Pied

Pipers. As they walked, more and more people joined in, until finally there was a gathering of some five thousand anxious for action, wanting to raid more and more shops. These two men were quite unprepared for this reaction. They were amateurs in the business of mass action, mass reaction, and support. A hurried little speech from a makeshift orange-box podium, then flight from the crowd demanding action.

The end of the day's activities would be marked by eating and drinking in the home of Indian friends. There would be celebrations on the successes of the day, and the genesis of a feeling of comradeship which transcended all racial barriers. Not all of them were Communists.

None of this impinged on my life. I was concerned with getting through matriculation. It was at this time that Jimmy was demobbed. He had spent a while in North Africa. Luckily for him, he had never been engaged in active service. A tailgunner's chance of survival was not, apparently, good. He looked far older than his twenty years. He became articled to my father, and duly qualified as a lawyer after the statutory period, joining my father's firm. His name was linked with glamorous women, and in spite of his youth he became very much a man about town, cultivating the playboy image. Meanwhile Betty, who had left school, became a clerical worker and fell out continuously with my mother, who discovered a Dutch cap in her bedroom. Betty and I never did discuss with whom, and when, she had lost her virginity. My own sex education had consisted of my mother telling me, laughingly, that it was all right down to the waist, but not below. She gave me no guidance on the thrust and fumble that I was to experience in the future.

So I knew nothing of current events. I did not read the daily paper. We never talked about such things at home, and I was wrapped up in my own little world. The prospect of going to university was my immediate goal, and entry into a social life.

University opened up a whole new world for me. To begin with I was totally bemused by the sudden immersion into an intellectual life, combined with an intense social whirl of differing hues. Suddenly I was on the way to becoming an adult: sixteen going on thirty. I looked far older, and covered my insecurity with an air of confidence. Walk straight, don't look left or right, and no one will know just how shy you feel. New impressions scattered around me like blowing autumn leaves. It was bewildering. A lyric from a Cole Porter song suddenly became something that could be read and analysed. I learned for the first time that Afrikaans need not always sound harsh and guttural. Our lecturer, who had piercing blue eyes, read from *Uit Oerwoud en Vlakte*, which described the veld and the life of a pack of lions, so that you could smell the dry grasses, hear the sound of the wind, and feel the heat of the sun on your back. I still retained a dislike of the language and a distrust of its people. I began to learn about the social sciences and started to realise just how much I did not know, how circumscribed my life had been, how boring my school days and school friends were.

As we drive towards Bryanston, these glorious carefree days flash fleetingly through my mind. Harold points to the place where he thinks his old Peugeot car broke down one night. He had not been part of the wild parties we had held there. He was far too serious, and not an integral part of the arty set in which I moved, although he knew them all.

Nothing is familiar. No more veld – houses everywhere, with well-established gardens. Along the roadside are black vendors with Ndebele dolls, soapstone sculptures, large crocheted tablecloths, traditional clay pots. We get to the corner where I think the turnoff to our house was. The dirt roads have been replaced by wider tarred highways. Gone is the shelter indicating the terminus for the creaky bus that ran a few times a day, whose driver would take pity on us having to walk the mile to the house and would, from time to time, career along the dirt roads and drive us all the way home.

I direct Harold to the road where I think our house is. We stop outside a thatched house that should be ours. Somehow it doesn't look quite right. I think my memory is playing odd tricks, and I ring the bell at the security gate, hoping to speak to the owner and find out if it is really where I lived. A black voice answers on the intercom and says the madam and master are away on holiday. There is no sign of any white people at all, although down the road are some black people. I then realise that everywhere we have driven, the streets are devoid of white people, who all seem to be securely locked behind their high walls; the only pedestrians are black. In the suburbs the black women still wear the obligatory domestic worker's pink or coral or blue overalls, with matching caps and little matching aprons.

I take a picture of the house through the security gate, not quite convinced that I have found the right place.

On the way home we are on a freeway when I see a large board saying 11de Laan. I recognise that: I recall 11th Avenue, a long road. We lived off this road in Lower Houghton for about nine years. 'Turn,' I say urgently to Harold. I am feeling quite excited. 'I know where I am now. We lived here when I was five. We lived in a street called 5th Street, which goes off at right angles to 11th Avenue. I want to see where I lived as a child. Oh, how exciting.'

I am again in memory lane.

In 1935 Lower Houghton was just being developed, and the house was new. It was a house that held all sorts of intriguing places for a child. A bedroom on the first floor opened on to a large terrace which, in turn, led to a hidden nook between the two pitches of the roof. We could smuggle tins of condensed milk and sit there licking the white, thick, sticky, sweet liquid. My mother did not approve of giving us sweets or biscuits; no doubt this led to my adult passion for all things sweet. Underneath this balcony my father had a huge aviary built, and filled it with exotic little birds.

The walls of the house were painted in Art Deco style, with stuccoed swirls. In the darkened, slightly sombre rear of the sitting-room was the big black Bechstein grand piano on which my mother occasionally played some Chopin preludes, sighing how she really could have been a concert pianist if only she had had lessons.

The house was set well back from the road, in large terraced grounds, the tennis court filled the lower terrace, and the succeeding two terraces leading up to the house had long rockeries in which the black gardener toiled hour after hour, although the results were never very rewarding: no cascade of bright flowers, no exotic plants – a rather dull rockery, for all his labours. The construction of the steep driveway was completed by black prisoners, who would arrive early in the morning in shorts and striped tops. These young black men would wield the pickaxes rhythmically, waiting that split second with the handles held high in the air, until the call from the leader would bring them down on the ground in thudding unison. All the while they chanted in harmony. The muscles in their arms and legs glistened in the hot sun with the sweat of their effort. They did not look like desperate criminals, these young men. They just did not have a passbook – after all, if you were black and male you had to have the correct documents to say that you were allowed to be in the urban area and seek work. The armed warder, a white man with a thick neck, looked thoroughly bored, a cigarette in the corner of his mouth, dreaming about the time he could knock off work.

It is a dark night, although stars are out in the sky. We have absolutely no trouble finding 5th Street. We turn right into it, and I immediately recognise where the house stands. Its position is absolutely indelibly etched in my mind. Yet again, security gates block all view. These gates are very different from the ones at 11 Maxie Street: bigger and grander, reflecting the difference in the value of the properties. This time they look fifteen feet high, set back slightly from the driveway. Large curved white gates. No sign whatsoever of the house beyond. No sign of the tennis court. I am disappointed. 'We must come back tomorrow – please.'

I find it difficult to fall asleep, and my mind courses over the past. Funny, how little I have thought about my early childhood. It was carefree. Betty and I rode our bicycles everywhere. Jimmy, as the eldest and the only son, took his position in the family somewhat seriously, and did not often deign to play with us.

I recall the names of the only children who lived near us: Myrtle Stein and Pat Mockford. The Mockfords clearly did not like Jews, so we seldom went to their home, which seemed to be barricaded against all those Jews who had invaded the road. Myrtle's family was Jewish. Myrtle was the youngest, and her mother had ambitions for her daughter, whose name she could pronounce only as Mecghtil. Myrtle wasn't much fun. She had to practise the piano for interminable hours. She struggled endlessly with the Turkish March. The tempo would falter at the crucial passage, and the notes collided with each other. She had water blisters on all her right-hand fingers, which she managed to suck simultaneously.

22 DECEMBER 1990

It's the Saturday before Christmas. A beautiful Transvaal summer day, with bright blue skies and still cumulus clouds in the distance. Just a slight breeze to ease the intense heat. The bird calls are prolific. The only ones I can recognise are the turtledoves and the piet-my-vrou. We breakfast on herbal tea, dry biscuits and sweet marmalade. Mynah birds and Egyptian ibises stroll casually along the banks nearby: fat, luscious yellow weavers and red bishops dart around. Bird life here is incredible.

We have tea at Hyde Park, a shopping mall, with Harold's sister, Margery, and her daughter, Joan, sitting at marble-topped tables with chairs that resemble Bauhaus, eating pancakes coated with cinnamon, sugar and lemon and drinking healthy fruit juice – mine a mixture of carrot and pineapple. Joan talks rapidly about her job and her life, while Margery, with her sweet shyness, engages in earnest conversation with Harold.

There are four Wolpe children. The eldest, Joe, is an internationally recognised psychologist. He is the king of behaviourists, one of the major proponents of this school of thought. Then there is Margery who has read voraciously all her life. Her husband, as a staunch supporter of the state, loathes

Harold. He was even one of the country's emissaries for a while, in Chicago. This has made life very difficult for Margery who is unable to have Harold or myself visit her home. Then comes Mickey, who is patient, kind, exceedingly thoughtful. She devoted years to nursing her sick husband, and has now emigrated to Canada to be near her daughter. At a relatively late age she renewed her studies, and has become a psychotherapist. Quite an amazing family. There is a gentleness and shyness about all of them.

When we lived here I never did see much of any of them, except for Harold's parents. His family is so different to mine. His father was a self-effacing man, interested in the world and discussion. He would sometimes join in the group of men who met on Sunday mornings in Doornfontein, the Jewish ghetto. They would stand on street corners arguing and discussing a range of topics. Was it from his side of the family all the children inherited questioning minds? I know that Joe, twelve years older than Harold, was an important influence in his life, although Joe was never involved in radical politics. When the two brothers get together, they discuss and argue.

Harold's parents would visit us regularly on a Sunday afternoon for tea, bringing barley-sugar sweets for Peta and Tessa. Through dedicated struggle his mother had become financially independent, and owned a number of properties in Johannesburg; while his father had been employed as a book-keeper for a firm of offal suppliers. After working diligently for forty years, he was summarily dismissed without any compensation.

Margery and Harold reminisce about their family, recalling with delight some of Harold's exploits, and how Joe was not only his mentor but also his protector. They are into 'Do you remember . . .', then going off into peals of laughter.

It's hard to believe this is just three days before Christmas. The shopping mall is deserted and dead by London standards. No maddening throngs frantically buying last-minute presents. 'The whites are feeling the pinch,' explains Joan, 'and anyway, people have gone away.' The annual white exodus from Johannesburg to the Cape and Natal has occurred.

Downtown Market Street presents a totally different picture. Significantly, as we drive we close windows and lock car doors from the inside. 'You can't take any chances,' Joan insists. Margery takes her gold chain off her neck and puts it into the glove compartment. The market stalls represent the new South Africa: black and white stallholders next to each other. Apartheid doesn't operate here. We park under the old railway lines; the cars are guarded by young black men who whistle you into your parking space and then ease you out again. The urban poor are streetwise the world over.

After lunch we go to see Helen Joseph. She is a remarkable woman, indefatigable, one of the leaders of the women's movement. In October 1955 she and a woman called Bertha Mashaba mobilised and led two thousand women to Pretoria. They marched to the Union Buildings, the impressive state administrative centre, to hand in their petitions against unjust laws. They told the Prime Minister that he had struck a rock. Helen was named, banned, put under house arrest and continually harassed over the next twenty years and more. This tall, elegant, beautiful Englishwoman withstood all these onslaughts, and survived. She will certainly go down in the annals of South African history. She tells us that Harry Belafonte is planning to make a film based on her life.

She is obviously delighted to see us. She and Harold talk about the period when he tutored her as a student at Witwatersrand University. She and I recall the years when I worked as her secretary. On my return from London in 1954 I had hoped to do an MA. Hooks, my father, had no money, and it was clear that I had to earn my own keep. I landed up working for the Transvaal Clothing Industry Medical Aid Society as Helen's assistant. My God, she exploited me. I did the bulk of her work, which released her for her political activities. We talked about that, and the march to Pretoria, and how she had used the office to house all her files. The office, of course, was raided from time to time by the Security Police. They would invade the premises looking for incriminating documents. Helen was a prime suspect because of her work with the women's groups. It was on one such occasion that Naomi Wallis, one of the office staff, saved the day for Helen. With great foresight she walked into Helen's office and picked up her briefcase, which contained all the relevant files the police were looking for, under their very eyes. Armed with Freda Katz's dog, Naomi left the office and spent the rest of the day walking the streets of Johannesburg until the police had left. Freda, another close friend who worked in the same office, had brought the dog to work every day since her father's death. We laughed over that incident, though it was not amusing at the time.

It was while I was working with Helen that Harold and I finally married, in November 1955. We had been dating since 1948 and lovers since 1950 – I had held out for a long time. In those days virginity was guarded quite jealously.

I learned a lot from Helen. When I resigned, she sent me out to buy myself some clothes and appointed an assistant for me. I finally left when I got the job at the Institute of Race Relations managing a bursary fund for black children. That suited me far better, as it was mostly part-time, leaving me free to spend afternoons with the children.

Late-night dinner with Joe Slovo and Helena Dolny, his wife. Helena looks slightly frazzled; she is desperate to settle down. They have bought a house in Isipingo Street, which is far from secure, surrounded by flats on all sides. A sniper could easily get at Joe. Bulletproof glass is too expensive, he says. Joe's attitude is that it will take them – the enemy – some months to get their act together, by which time he will have set up a security system or they will have moved. Helena feels more vulnerable here than she did in Lusaka. I wonder how much of our conversation is being listened to. Joe and Harold assume all of it.

23 DECEMBER 1990
Our last day in South Africa. We drive to Soweto to visit Walter and Albertina Sisulu. Walter, one of the Rivonia trialists, was

released before Mandela. He had been Secretary-General of the ANC.

We drive down the N1 towards Bloemfontein. We lose our way, of course. Soweto is an endless series of small houses in somewhat desolate streets, with nothing obvious to the outsider to demarcate one area from the other. How strong the contrast is with white suburbs! After the third stop to ask for the street, Harold says, 'We're looking for Comrade Walter Sisulu's house.' Immediately the rather surly response when we had first said a polite 'Good morning, I wonder if you could help us' gives way to broad smiles. We are literally round the corner. It is a small house, with a high wall and a sliding white security gate. Bodyguards are in evidence. Walter looks amazing, smiles and welcomes us into the house. An L-shaped living-room, grey leather-upholstered settee on one side, another settee in the other part facing the TV, which is on. In a cabinet a photograph of Albertina with President Bush, and a plaque by a newspaper commemorating their award as the Family of the Year.

We spend two hours with them. I speak to Albertina about the women. She says that, unfortunately, so many women are ignorant. They will follow their leaders without knowing why. 'We need help. They need to be organised; they need to learn; they need to understand. Whatever help you can give is welcome. We need all the help we can get.' I wonder what sort of help? 'I'm too tired to stand for the executive. I'll work in the office. More than that I can't do. I've been to the Eastern Cape, Transvaal and other places trying to organise women. It's time for somebody else to take over.' Undoubtedly she is a remarkable woman. I remember a time when the wives of the various leaders used to sit quite quietly at the parties at the Fischers' or the Slovos'. It is good to see women coming into their own at last, and being recognised for their courage and political actions.

At the airport I set off all the security systems. I say brightly, 'It's my artificial hips that do that.' No one takes any notice, and I am escorted to a cubicle where a grim-faced young woman feels me up and down the front, the back and the inside leg. As she is feeling me, I say, 'Ooh, that's nice. More please.' No response. Sullen silence.

This sparks off thoughts of how I will cope with living in a country in which white thugs can strut around like puffed-up cobras, with their guns dangling like phalluses. It is not only the threat of fanatical upholders of a particularly nasty European tradition that bothers me. Part of me fears these people. Part of me worries that somewhere one of these men is skulking in the back and beyond, waiting to wreak revenge for what happened so long ago when Harold escaped from jail and evaded the fifty thousand men who were deputed to find him. Part of me cannot sweep aside the traumas of 1963.

There is a man sitting to the right of us. He is tall, large; his hair is cut like the French Foreign Legion, almost a clean shave. He has a dark moustache, and on the side of his head is a fine scar. He looks like a mercenary. He has a well-worn leather holdall slung round his broad shoulders. It looks as though it has seen much wear and tear. I entertain sinister thoughts about what brings a soldier of fortune to South Africa.

Once more I am winging my way back to London and the world I do know.

JUNE 1991

All our attempts to sell 19 Onslow Gardens have failed. I am pleased. I so love this house. Both Tessa and I fantasise that one day she or Nick or Peta or all of them will return to live there. Number 19 is a large Victorian semi-detached house. It has always exuded a welcoming atmosphere, even though when I first saw it it had been sorely neglected. We have no alternative but to rent the house, and have entered into a two-year contract with some tenants.

It is now some months since I last expressed my anxiety about leaving. Peta cured me of it.

One morning she suddenly screamed at me and burst into tears: 'If you don't want to bloody go then fucking don't go. Stop this moaning. I can't stand it any more. I can't. I have to cope with what is happening to me and your moaning is making everything worse.' She screamed and wept and stormed out of the room. She is normally so calm and controlled. She is always the one who receives other people's problems, and does not discuss her own feelings very much. Perhaps this is her way of maintaining her independence with us.

I am stunned by this outburst. Not even as a child did she display any temper tantrums. I have never seen her behave like this before. Unlike Tessa, she does not normally express her own fears and desires. On a number of occasions, though, she has said somewhat ruefully, 'I swore I would never move my children around the way we moved around when we were young. And now look at me. Since Jonny was born he's been in three different homes – first Stoke Newington, then France and now here.' She plans to buy somewhere else together with Nicholas, and Tessa if she wants to join them.

At last, after a great deal of searching, all three have found a house in Crouch End that they can buy jointly. Tessa can have a one-bedroomed flat on the ground floor, and Nick and Peta another on the next two floors. It is a handsome Edwardian house, desperately in need of tender loving care – a euphemism for massive renovation and restoration.

I feel a tremendous relief.

I have begun sorting out the accumulation of the past twenty-seven years. Harold's work is so demanding that he has no spare time for this. He will go through his study, and I will be responsible for the rest of the house. Sifting through possessions, tidying and throwing away, parades the past in front of you. Discarding those parts of your life that you define as redundant. It brings into sharp relief aspects of your life that are taken for granted, and highlights how the minutiae of life create the understandable, the comforting, the everyday fragments that are recognisable.

Twenty-seven years of photographs, all in their envelopes. If only I had put them into albums as I started accumulating them. That, unfortunately, I have never done. In the end I choose some photographs, including those from my mother's trunk that she left with us before her final return to South Africa, and leave the majority for the children to sort through and take what they want.

There are too many cooking utensils, old towels and sheets. There are mementos, postcards from all over the world, documents associated with my work over the past twenty-seven years. There are files I have kept, although some are now obsolete. 'Estate' deals with the many years following Jimmy's death, until his younger daughter reached the age of eighteen. It is not pleasant to be reminded of those events. Nor can they be thrown away like bits of household garbage.

Suddenly, over the past month, all our friends have realised that we are leaving the country, and invitations to dinner pour in. I enjoy the socialising, but the repetitive and inevitable questions about how we feel about returning to South Africa are tiring.

Harold is due to leave in two weeks' time. He has been frantically busy completing a report on human resources development for the Commonwealth Secretariat, and yet he finds time to sort through his study and leave meticulous instructions for all of us about arrangements with the bank. It doesn't make sense to me that he should rush out ahead of me.

'Why don't you postpone going and come out with me later?' I suggest. Harold is stubborn. I recognise that Wolpe trait; Peta has it too. 'I can't see that it will make any difference if you go now or in August.' It does not make sense for him to rush there. Our goods will not arrive in South Africa until September at the earliest.

We have decided on the shippers and agreed together what is to go. But no – he wants to get there and begin his new life as soon as possible. He is restless and seems eager to leave London. How different from me! 'I want to get cracking,' he says. He has made up his mind, and won't budge.

Tessa is absolutely distraught about Harold's departure. I don't have time to think about it – I still have too much to do.

In the background, like my guardian angel, is Roo. Such a ridiculous name, Roo. 'My name is really Robert. I hate it, and I like the character Rooster that John Wayne played. I couldn't really call myself Rooster, so I settled for Roo,' he explained one day.

Roo is tall, and wears bizarre clothes: voluminous Turkish-style cotton trousers, a colourful scarf tied like a bandanna round his head, short cropped hair and a single gold earring. He does not look one slightest bit like a nanny, which is what he is at the moment. In his twenty-three years he seems to have tackled a hundred different jobs, and learned something useful from each of them. He has taken me in hand, and is organising the final sorting of my cupboards. It's an art. I am like a hamster, collecting for the day of need that is sure to arrive, so it is difficult to cast anything aside. Roo doesn't allow me to move one pile to another. Ruthlessly he insists that we go through each item, deciding what to cast aside, which to include for sending to South Africa and what to do with those items which don't belong in either category. Oxfam will benefit.

I have given way to bouts of public sobbing, and Harold's departure has no doubt contributed to this. I go to Enfield, one of the Polytechnic sites, to see my Dean. By now I have decided that leave of absence is nonsensical, and it would be better if I could be granted an enhanced pension related to early retirement. It will make a significant difference both to the lump sum I get and to my annual pension. The Dean is his usual forthright, aggressive self. 'You've blown it this time,' he greets me, thumping down on the desk a photocopy of *North Circular*, the Poly's house paper, which carries a picture of me being given a bunch of flowers by the woman taking over from me at the party the students organised for me. 'Now you'll never get an enhanced pension. I had Personnel phoning me about your leaving the Poly. They were under the impression that you were simply taking unpaid leave.' No comment about the uniqueness of students organising a large public farewell party for a member of staff! I rush from his office sobbing, saying, 'I might as well leave.' Then I return, because I think it is too easy for him, and amidst loud sobs I say, 'Do you think I want to go? I don't. I don't want to go back to South Africa. I don't look forward to the work I shall be doing. I don't want to live in fear. Harold is probably a target for the wretched right bloody wing. I have had to buy security devices. And I need whatever money I can get. We're short. And after all these years, why the hell can't I get an enhanced pension? Others have.'

The Dean tries to soothe me, and says, 'Go Home.' The trouble is that I no longer feel that I have a home to go to. My reserves seem to be seeping away at an alarming speed. The now familiar tension in my head, presaging high blood pressure, does not seem to abate.

There are still a number of loose ends to tie up – particularly at work. Exam board meetings. Farewell parties. Sorting out my office, and deciding which books to take.

And then, suddenly, it all happens. Peta, who has decided to take a period of leave from work and go to France, leaves with Jonny. The overseas shippers are in the house for two full days. In spite of all the careful labelling and marking, they have me running up and down stairs with some query or another. It is an exhausting two days, and tension is increased with the deadline on the exchange of contracts for the children's house in Crouch End being delayed. By Wednesday night the house looks forlorn, with the remainder of the things due to go to Crouch End clumped together in various rooms. I have left a load of things for the children, including some precious objects which I would rather they derive benefit from, as well as useful things.

My last night in the house is unexpectedly simple, delightful and calm. Number 19 is a wonderful house – it even looks great without furniture. Our bedroom, with all the bookshelves that housed my collection, looks delightfully refreshing and cool; the dining-room extension, doors open to the garden on a warm summer evening, is magical. Just Nicholas, Stephanie, a friend of his, Roo and myself. Tessa is still at work. We didn't want to eat in a stuffy restaurant. It is one of those rare days in London, hot and still. Much nicer to picnic on the bare dining-room floor with Chinese takeaway. Stephanie provides the crockery and a bottle of champagne Nicholas had given her some months earlier. Maxine and Fred join us for some wine.

It is a quiet end to our stay in Onslow Gardens. I have a premonition that I will never live in London again.

The Escape

June–August 1963

Nicholas

2 JUNE 1963

A DATE that is imprinted on my mind for ever. We are meeting Joe and Ruth Slovo tonight for a clandestine farewell dinner. Joe is being sent out of the country on a secret mission by the underground movement. As the government steps up its attack on anyone who opposes it, the underground movement – led by the ANC and its fledgling army, UmKhonto we Sizwe – is attempting to meet this opposition with its own stratagems. But I have no idea what these are; presumably Joe's departure from South Africa is connected with this matter. Joe is stateless, and has no passport. The organisation must be quite sophisticated if it can organise his departure as well as his return.

Although Joe claims that Harold kicked him off the football field when he was a nine-year-old, soon after he arrived in South Africa from the Soviet Union, it was only at university that they became friends, and they have remained friends ever since. Harold has known Ruth since childhood, and the two of them went off to Europe representing the Progressive Youth Council in 1946, just after World War Two. All three have been very active in the struggle; all three were members of the Communist Party up to the time of its banning in 1950. And now they are all named and banned, an effective ploy devised by the South African government whereby everyone defined as its enemy is named and then banned from being members of a wide range of organisations. One of the effects is that Harold is not supposed to meet Joe or Ruth publicly, but nobody seems to take much notice of this stricture.

The restaurant, near Zoo Lake, is relatively new, small and

intimate. Gingham tablecloths and curtains hanging from a wooden rail cover only half the window. Candles on the tables and discreet, softly playing piped music add to the atmosphere. These touching attempts do not quite capture the atmosphere of the restaurants I recall from my brief visit to Paris more than ten years ago.

Ruth, dressed impeccably as usual, is in a quietly expensive navy suit. Her lustrous black hair is well styled, controlling an unruly, almost frizzy mop. Behind her glasses her eyes are bright. Joe – heavy-set with broad shoulders, thick glasses, bushy eyebrows and a dense mop of hair – tells jokes with great gusto, and does not conform at all to the image of a revolutionary. He is a successful barrister. Ruth is the Johannesburg editor of the left-wing weekly paper *New Age* (it is hard to keep up with its name: it gets banned and emerges, like a phoenix from the ashes, with a different name). She is an intrepid journalist, manifestly successful and already well known outside South Africa for her exposure of some of the excesses of the regime.

'How long will you be away?' I ask. A shrug and a noncommittal 'Some months' is the answer. We could not know then that it would be more than twenty-five years before Joe would return, and that Ruth would be murdered in Maputo by a letter bomb in 1982.

All our attempts at light-hearted chatter sound false. There is an air of quiet tension, and even foreboding, as we eat our peppered fillet steaks with round blobs of garlicky breadcrumbs on top. Joe and Ruth have a warm but undemonstrative relationship. Tensions arise from their political differences, but they avoid any altercations tonight. I wonder how Ruth is feeling, but she isn't the sort of person you can ask that question.

'Ruth is really a tough person,' I say to Harold on the way home.

'Yes. I've known her such a long time and I have never seen her show any sign of emotion or weakness,' says Harold admiringly.

Joe and Ruth have been married for twelve years and have

three daughters. Although they are Harold's dearest friends, it has taken me some years to feel at ease with them. Initially all Harold's Communist friends went into mourning when we got married, anticipating that I would drag him down. They were convinced that I was a middle-class 'kogel', a spoilt Jewish woman whose sights were set on money, comfort, trivia and self-indulgence. It has taken time for me to be accepted. The 1960 Emergency did it. It was sparked off by the massacre at Sharpeville, a then unknown African township near a small town called Vereeniging, where the police opened fire on unarmed demonstrators against the carrying of the hated pass-books which were obligatory for all African men. They killed sixty-nine people, of whom eight were women and ten were children. After this the townships were like tinderboxes and the government swooped, to curtail the unrest, arresting several thousand people – including every known white activist – and declaring an emergency which lasted three months. Harold was among this group, as were so many of our friends. During this period I kept a watchful eye on the teenage children of our friends, the Bermans and the Bernsteins, because both parents had been arrested. I entertained some of these children for supper every Friday night. They were missing their parents. I found Ruth a hiding place in Johannesburg, and ran errands for Harold and his comrades, who were held in jail without trial. I smuggled messages from them, proving that they were on hunger strike. I provided them with the food they wanted, like Calamata olives. All this upped my credentials. I was finally accepted.

Joe is now flirtatious with me, and Ruth is quite warm. She is an incredible woman – witty, beautiful, intelligent, and able to insert sharp epithets into the conversation. She is intolerant of small talk, and if she gets bored she takes off her glasses, closes her eyes, covers them with her hand, and simply shuts off. If you are in the middle of a sentence, this can be devastating, so I am guarded about what I say. Even if I wanted to enter into the political discussions, they would not listen to me. I would voice common-sense ideas and views. I was not brought up on political theory and knowledge, and I had never been a member of the Communist Party – nor of any other party for that matter. At dinner I play the role of hostess, seeing to the food, making sure that the glasses are filled and the bread basket is replete. My role is fixed and clear: I am the woman of the household, and as such I do what is expected of me. But this does not still my resentment at times.

I still recall with anguish the hours I worked in the kitchen for a dinner party with the Slovos and the Mandelas. Then I followed recipes slavishly, and spent time planning a balanced meal. The dessert was a ginger cake served with apple purée, a Betty Crocker recipe. That ginger cake was perfect. It came out of the rounded tin evenly. It looked just like the picture in the recipe book. Ruth tasted it, and pushed her plate away with a shrug. I vowed to myself never to work as diligently again for an unthinking guest.

'But what about the kids? How on earth are they going to cope with Joe's absence?' Underneath my admiration is a moral anger at what I regard as Ruth's neglect of her due maternal responsibility. My mother would constantly harp at me for coming home from my half-duty job and spending time with the children in the afternoons instead of handing them over to Angelina, their nanny. I would protest: 'I want to bring up my own children. That's why I have them. I don't want to hand them over to someone else.' But Ruth works full-time, and more. Her mother is always at hand at a moment's notice, to take over when necessary. And then there are the servants. Ruth can carry out her journalistic duties without any problem about fetching and carrying the children. They can go to school and do all the out-of-school activities that require a mother or a mother substitute who fetches and carries.

Ruth and I are good friends now but there are limits to what we talk about. I can never enter into a serious conversation with her. We talk about clothes, and food, and babies, and the latest film or book we have seen or read.

It isn't late when we get home. I go to see Nicholas, who is almost seven weeks old. He has proved the easiest of my three children. Perhaps I have been more relaxed with him than with the two girls, though the political tensions are worse than ever before. His birth seems to have coincided with a number of menacing events. The first was Harold's court appearance on behalf of two young Indians, Abdullah Jassat and Mosie Moola, who were finally charged after being held in solitary confinement for ninety days. Harold discovered they had been tortured, and so he kicked up a huge fuss, demanding that they be transferred from the police station to the local jail, where he felt they would have some small measure of protection. This was the first known torture case in the country. I listened to this when Harold visited me in hospital, but its full portent washed over me. I was far more interested in my lovely baby, and what to call him.

Two days after I returned home with Nicholas, Harold went into semi-hiding. There were rumours that people were soon to be placed under house arrest, and Harold's name was reputed to be on that list. A close friend of ours gave him shelter, so Harold continued to work during the day but lived away from home. All raids and bannings took place at night. If people were away from home, they could be warned and avoid contact with the police.

Despite all this, I feel relaxed and happy with my new baby. Each successive child is less frightening, and this time round I am going to enjoy him. I give him his mid-morning feed listening to Mozart, or even dramatic Sibelius. I enjoy playing with him, and don't mind if he doesn't sleep when the book says he should.

'The baby's sick,' says Angelina on our arrival. He seems OK to me, and I don't take much notice. I am thinking about Joe's departure, and wondering what I will do if Harold is instructed to leave the country. Harold goes off to bed. But I can't get Nicholas to settle down. Maybe there is something wrong with him.

He seems to have difficulty in breathing. I pace the floor, I fill a kettle and steam the room. I do not undress, and by 5.30 in the morning I am desperate for both of us. Dr Levy, our GP, responds to my call and visits at seven o'clock. 'Keep an eye on him,' he says, prescribing some medicine. Harold goes off to work, and Nicholas finally seems to go to sleep.

Betty von Ahleveldt, a close friend of the family, visits mid-morning. She takes one look at the baby. 'He is really ill. You'd better get the doctor in,' she says. 'He's not sleeping, I think he's in a coma.' I must have sounded hysterical on the phone. The doctor is there in a short while, and arranges for Nicholas to be placed in an oxygen tent at the Children's Hospital. In my anxiety I rip a button off the shift dress I am wearing as I get into the car. Betty holds Nicholas.

Nicholas is desperately ill. He has pneumonia; a succession of doctors are called in, and confer with each other just out of earshot. Harold joins me. All the doctors have long faces, and warn us that there is little hope.

I am so frightened I do not know what to do. I cannot bear to watch this beautiful little baby so still in an oxygen tent. Betty sits in the room, constantly tapping his tiny little hand under the tent. 'Even though he is in a coma, he must know that someone is with him,' she insists. I cannot do it. I think he will die; I have never seen death before, and the thought of my perfect little baby dying is unbearable.

Betty sits there all day. And all that night. Barbara, my sister-in-law, Jimmy's wife, joins her later on. Betty and Barbara say, 'Go home and get some sleep. We will watch over Nicholas.' Harold and I return home to be with the girls. Peta is just six, Tessa not yet five. They are too young to understand the gravity of Nicholas's illness. There seems little we can do, and I am exhausted from fear and lack of sleep.

He survives the night, although it is obvious that the nurses and the doctors anticipate that it is just a matter of time. A nurse gives me a little hand bell – 'in case you need someone in a hurry', she says. Privately, I think it is for me to summon them when he dies! The nurses seem to be avoiding Nicholas.

The paediatrician arrives, and orders a bronchoscopy to relieve the congestion in the bronchial tubes. A chest surgeon is to perform this, and the only one available at such short notice is Gerson Katz. He is a tall, dark-haired man who tilts his head to one side as he speaks. He is quiet, with a solemn manner. His almost-black, penetrating eyes slope down, and the dark rings under them add to his melancholy air. He is an extraordinary man. Afterwards we learned how he himself had lost a child through a tragic accident, and also how difficult it has been for him to practise as a surgeon. It seems that there is a monopoly, and it is hard to gain entrance to this exclusive group. It has taken Gerson Katz months to penetrate the tight little cabal.

Harold and I watch from afar as a team of people work on this tiny baby. Nicholas resists the intrusion of the tubes into his lungs, and struggles furiously in spite of his illness. Several nurses hold his body down so that the surgeon and the anaesthetist can continue with their work. The bronchial tubes are mechanically cleared of all the muck that is blocking them. The doctors are concerned for the trauma of the procedure on so ill a baby.

It is successful, but the effects are limited. The following day an x-ray reveals an ulcer. This, too, needs to be dealt with mechanically. I understand that Dr Katz has to insert a tube into the spot, and then drain the pus from this ulcer into a bottle which has to be suctioned on the hour, twenty-four hours a day. The tube is almost one centimetre in diameter, and you can hear the rush of air that should have been filling the baby's lungs hiss out, only to be followed by a mass of foul-looking pus. It is inconceivable that that amount of pus can be lodged in such a tiny little thing.

Nicholas is still in a coma. His body is being pumped full of every known antibiotic to combat the infection that is destroying him. The paediatrician warns us that his blood chemistry is likely to be severely disturbed by the drugs, and that this also might prove fatal. There is no aspect of the treatment which does not contain the elements for Nicholas's destruction.

Harold and I move into the hospital during the day. We talk of little else except the daily battle being conducted. I begin to help the nurses with cases that aren't so desperate, but mostly we sit, watch and wait for the latest medical report. Peta and Tessa barely see us. We have a brief meeting late at night when we get back from the hospital. Angelina has taken over the household entirely, including looking after the girls when they come home from nursery school.

I condemn myself for having contemplated an abortion. If I had not been scared of the future, and scared of what is going to happen to Harold, I would not have any doubts about having Nicholas – nor a fourth child, for that matter. I always wanted four children. Betty, as the middle pipper in our family, had a tough time; and Jimmy, as the eldest and the only son, was clearly my mother's favourite. I benefited from being the baby of the family, and a compliant child. Now I say to myself, 'You're being punished for having wanted to end Nicholas's life. This is your retribution.' I am convinced that I am guilty. If only I could pray to a God in whom I believed, I would do so. I vow that I will give up smoking if Nicholas lives. Harold makes the same vow.

Now our life's rhythm is dictated by the timetable of the hospital and Nicholas's struggle to live. We speak of little else, apart from our concern for both our daughters. I know nothing of the outside world, and our only contact with it is through friends who phone solicitously to enquire after Nicholas.

The daily X-rays reveal a second ulcer, and a third. Gerson says solemnly, 'I think we need full-time nursing care for Nicholas, day and night.' Arrangements are made to employ a day and a night nurse through an agency. That is how we get to know Marlene.

Marlene is stunning. She could easily step into a Hollywood film. She has a sexy figure which even the dreary nurse's uniform cannot mask. She is tall, slim, her auburn hair tied in a French knot and a nurse's cap neatly perched on top, not a hair out of place, and satin-smooth skin. Her lips glow, and her lipstick never seems to fade. She smiles easily, displaying a perfect set of teeth.

Unlike other nurses, who scamper down the corridor, Marlene never runs; she simply increases the pace of her walk, and her hips sway casually from side to side. Every doctor preens himself when Marlene comes on the scene. Even Gerson seems susceptible to her charms, and she can raise a smile from his otherwise serious countenance. She is a brilliant nurse, and she shares with Gerson the determination to keep Nicholas alive and overcome the pneumonia.

Gerson joins us on the hard bench in the waiting area. 'We have reached another crisis point,' he says. 'Nicholas must have a tracheotomy. There is no problem in performing it – it's just a simple snip in the hollow below the Adam's apple. The trouble is, we have never performed one on so young an infant before. We have a new respirator on the market. It's the one made famous by Elizabeth Taylor when she had a tracheotomy last year and was connected up to this machine.' Oh yes, I recall the hullabaloo when it seemed she was at death's door, also suffering from pneumonia. 'This machine is totally different from an iron lung, which applies pressure externally. This one applies a pressure internally, and enables the patient to get oxygen into the lungs.'

I say, 'Oh yes,' but I still do not fully appreciate the difficulties associated with the machine. The machine is available only at the Florence Nightingale private hospital. Nicholas will have to have the tracheotomy, then be rushed to the Nightingale, where he will be attached to the respirator.

Gerson continues to caution us: 'Because the machine has not been used on an infant as small as Nicholas, we shall have to experiment. We're not sure of the pressure that will have to be applied.' But that is not all: 'Tracheotomies are traumatic, and experience has shown that when performed on very young babies their chances of survival are slight.' He is, if nothing else, quite honest, and has been from the word go, always pointing out the near-hopelessness of Nicholas's illness. 'At least we'll stop the daily X-raying.' By way of comfort, he adds that the results of putting Nicholas on to the respirator could benefit other sick children.

We agree to the tracheotomy. At least there is an outside chance. I have passed out. I seem to be doing this with regular monotony. I have never fainted before, but it keeps happening. Perhaps this lapse into unconsciousness is my way of keeping myself from screaming out loud.

Both Marlene and the night nurse are to accompany Nicholas to the new hospital. We follow to the Nightingale and see our tiny baby lying on an adult-sized bed. It looks ludicrous. Three tubes from his tiny chest drain into bottles on the floor, and now a fourth tube is attached to what we hope is his life-saving machine. I do not understand the mechanism of this machine. On top of what looks like a massive cabinet are two large inverted bottles which, somehow or other, are an integral and necessary part of forcing the oxygen into his lungs.

The next day, a fifteen-month-old girl is in the room next to Nicholas, also on a respirator. At least his short life has already proved of use, I try to console myself. If he dies, his life won't have been in vain.

Nicholas's coma ends. His dark unsmiling eyes move from the bottles to the machine, and in between he watches the nurses, he watches me, but most of all he watches the great machine. The machine has become his surrogate mother. I can't pick him up and cuddle him. He can't be moved. He simply lies on this adult bed, in a nappy and nothing else, racked with fever, attached to the bottles and the machine, immobile, except for his big eyes. He seems to anticipate the vibrations of the tubes. He never smiles, but then there is not a great deal for him to smile about.

It is a Friday morning, a little over two weeks since the drama began. Harold has just walked in to see Nicholas, who suddenly seems quite agitated and starts to go black. 'Marlene, for Christ's sake, what's happening now?' Harold cannot believe it. Nicholas looks as though this time he will surely die. Harold feels completely and utterly helpless. There is nothing he can do, nothing at all except stand there helplessly watching this little child engaged in a desperate struggle.

It is the only time Marlene has been seen to run. She is looking for a doctor. As if by magic, Gerson appears. Gerson never goes off on his rounds without seeing how Nicholas is. Nor, for that matter, does he ever go to bed without a final check for the night. During the course of the day he pops in to check on how his patient is doing. The strain of keeping this up is beginning to tell on Gerson. I have heard him say, wearily, shaking his head, 'Nicholas, Nicholas, you need a full-time doctor.' The fatigue shows in the additional stoop of his large frame, and the rings which have become even darker under his almost black eyes.

Nicholas struggles desperately. The machine is working, but something else has gone wrong. Gerson diagnoses another ulcer. With a deft movement he cuts into the lungs and inserts yet another tube into the infected area. Again the hiss of air escaping into the tube is audible, followed by the thick, foul, yellow pus. Now both lobes are infected. Each lobe has its lifeline going into a bottle. The blackness leaves Nicholas's face as the oxygen is pumped into his lungs. He has survived yet another major hurdle. Harold finds himself shaking, but has to hurry to the office. He has a trial in the magistrates' court, and he can't brief anyone else to do it.

I also try to fit in a visit to my father, Hooks, from time to time. He has been ill with piles, and has had an operation for it. He was so uncomfortable that we hired a hospital bed for him. I wonder if that is where Nicholas picked up whatever dreadful virus he caught? Hooks is tired, and seems to have lost the will to live. He is not one to indulge in self-pity at all. He shakes his head and says, 'How ironic it is to keep an old man like me alive. Why can't they ensure that Nicholas gets better?'

A few days later we get a phone call from Jimmy. Hooks has died. Apparently his aneurism burst and he died instantaneously, just as his GP was leaving the bedroom after a routine call. I go to their home, and sit with my mother, Polly. We leave all the arrangements to Jimmy, who has already got the religious men to sit and say prayers through the night. We donate the corneas of his eyes. I do not go in to see his body. I am afraid of death.

Jimmy arranges the funeral, and it takes place within a day. I take time off from the hospital to go. My mother does not go to funerals, so I deputise for her. The custom of women sitting still and having people come up to us to wish us long life I find strange. My mother looks stunned.

My father had always been a dapper man. He had been nicknamed Hooks, a name we used once we were all adults, from playing the hooker in rugby. It is strange to think of him as a formidable rugby player because he was small of stature, yet very strong. Even as an old man his muscles retained the elasticity of youth. He did not talk much about himself, and we never thought to enquire. Occasionally he would talk of his youth, and tell how he would often be driven home in a horse and carriage after a rugby match with some severe injury. Each time his father would thrash him for what he regarded as his son's carelessness, but finally, on his deathbed, he entrusted the future of the whole family to Hooks, whom he acknowledged as 'the pick of the bunch'. This sentiment was shared by my mother, who always insisted that it was the Russian wet nurse who had made all the difference. She disliked her mother-in-law.

Hooks had kept a watching eye over all his brothers and his sister, and had supported two of his nephews through medical school in England. He had extended his concern to my mother's family as well, and when her sister Bessie and brother-in-law Simon Ritchken fell on hard times, he had sold them a farm he owned in Rustenburg for a token sum. Hooks was generous, kind, and a strong man who did such things quite quietly, never expecting any gratitude.

We never did learn why his father had selected Pretoria in which to settle. Our dinner-time conversation was always of the present; the past did not appear to have a place at all. All we knew was that there were pogroms in Russia and his family, like so many others, fled. In Hooks's case, his mother had travelled by cattle ship and then ox wagon finally to reach Pretoria, a journey that must have been hazardous and extremely difficult, particularly given the large size of her family. Of twelve children, several died, and only four were left by the time I was born.

Hooks was educated in Pretoria. There was one story he was fond of telling after a great deal of prompting and cajoling, his eyes twinkling in a totally mischievous way, unlike his usual serious demeanour. He graphically described his knock-out blow on a teacher who had dared to make an anti-Semitic remark in the classroom. 'It was me or the teacher – one of us had to go,' and he had marched to the headmaster's office with that in mind. The teacher was fired. My father's indomitable spirit was apparent at an early age.

He was involved in South African politics through his association with Tielman Roos, a leading politician. Together with Tielman Roos he spent endless hours in Turkstra restaurant in Pretoria plotting the fate of the country and laying plans for the time when Tielman would become Prime Minister, while the note pinned on the office door said 'Back in 5 minutes'. But Tielman had died suddenly, and that was the end of Hooks's involvement in politics. He met and subsequently eloped with Polly and came to live in Johannesburg, pursuing his legal career.

Was it his marriage that spawned the desire to make money? Was it the period – the late 1920s early 1930s? Whatever the cause, Hooks remained a silently restless man, always seeking the pots of gold that would make his children wealthy and secure. He fretted over this all his life, but never did succeed.

He looked much older than most of the other children's fathers when I was at school. Not only was he twelve years older than my mother, but he had been grey-haired since the age of twenty, and by the time I knew him he had a shock of silver hair. He looked Jewish: square jaw, large hooked nose, grey-green eyes and shaggy eyebrows. He was impeccably dressed, and wore spats always in winter – the very epitome of what I imagined an English City gent would look like. He had his shoes handmade in London. He had had a last made when he was there in 1933, and ever since then he had ordered four pairs every eight to ten years. This all had persisted even after World War II, because the firm had evacuated its clients' details and was able to maintain their service. His walk was jaunty, and he would raise his homburg hat when he greeted a woman. Of course he knew just how to slip the train porter the right amount of money in order to ensure us a good compartment when we went on our annual summer holidays to Muizenberg on the Indian Ocean side of Cape Town. He was a man of presence.

Hooks was a dreamer and a silent man, with ever-changing

schemes for making money – real money. He had turned down the options on a fabulous diamond mine in, I think, Tanganyika, where one of the world's most famous diamonds was found. He had had a gold mine. He had owned racehorses. He had started a company that manufactured cardboard boxes. But it was his partners who miraculously made the money, never Hooks, although there were times when we seemed to be quite wealthy. He did not do what other lawyers did: invest the very high fees in property. Hooks's legal practice never developed, because as soon as some proposition came up he would be off again on yet another new venture.

He was not a communicative man. My father belonged to that generation which never did acknowledge emotions – either his own or those of his family. My mother Polly, on the other hand, was totally different. She had been a renowned beauty, and had eloped with my father. She changed for dinner every evening. She amused Hooks. And even though she was unfaithful, I don't think he ever knew of this, nor did it diminish her regard and love for him. She met her lover for afternoon picnics, and when I discovered this I accepted it uncritically. I recognised her need for the adoration and attention which my father could not give her. This did not mean that she loved him less, or minimised his importance in her life. Their relationship was a quiet one, and she appeared to be the perfect wife.

But Polly could not cope with problems or disaster. Nor did she like babies, and she made it absolutely clear that she could not be relied upon to babysit or help us in that regard. 'After all,' she would say, 'I had nannies for you lot and I didn't do it then and I certainly don't intend to start doing it now.'

Almost immediately after Hooks's death, there is a dramatic change in Nicholas. He is visibly getting better. It is as though my father's indomitable, fighting spirit and strength have entered Nicholas's body. I cannot admit these beliefs to anyone. How can it be? When Betty and a group of nuns she was in contact with prayed regularly for Nicholas, I thought it was a lovely idea, but not one that could have any real effect. When

Betty confessed to me one day that she had brought a priest to baptise Nicholas but had refrained from doing so at the last moment because she thought I would have been offended, I again thought that it was touching, and would have welcomed it more for the comfort that it gave Betty than for Nicholas's sake. But now something different is happening.

After the first few numbing days following my father's death, I return to the daily visits to the nursing home. The mood has changed. Nicholas is responding positively to all the medication and treatment. 'You know, we have finally isolated the nature of Nick's illness,' Gerson Katz tells us one evening. 'He has had Friedlander's pneumonia' – apparently a rare and normally fatal pneumonia which strikes its victims down within forty-eight hours. The virus normally lurks in hospitals, and this confirms my suspicion that Nicholas picked it up from visiting my father when he lay in his rented hospital bed at home. 'And it is by chance that he has been given the correct drugs for it,' Gerson adds. Well, everything has been chance as far as I am concerned.

The tracheotomy tube is removed, Nicholas gulps for breath, and then breathes normally. The tubes from the lungs are removed. Already two have been taken out, and there are still three to go. Finally it is decided that he no longer needs to be in the intensive care unit and can be moved to a general ward. But Gerson is unhappy about this. 'Hospitals are such unhealthy places,' he complains. 'We really need to get Nicholas home as soon as possible. Let's get him out of here.'

Such excitement! Nicholas is to come home. To make things even better, Marlene agrees to come and spend the first few weeks with him just to oversee him and to keep an eye on the last tube, which is still in his chest but not connected to any bottle.

There is an air of excitement at home, and Angelina works hard to get everything ready. 'Why don't you go away for a few days?' Harold suggests to me. 'You really could do with a break before Nicholas gets home. You should go and join your mother, if that's possible, at the farm.'

Boekenhout Farm

AFTER THE funeral my mother accepted her sister's invitation to visit. Bessie lives in Rustenburg, as does her daughter, Tiny Polly, and her family, and her son Herbert and his family. Each of them has their own establishment far from each other. The farm is huge.

Tiny Polly, as she is affectionately known, is really very small. It is a bit confusing because my mother, as the eldest, is big Polly, then there is a niece of hers, Little Polly, Annie's daughter, who is the tallest; and then Tiny Polly, Bessie's daughter. Tiny Polly's size is not commensurate with her will and determination to farm successfully on her own. She had been given this portion of the farm when she was still unmarried, and she had planted trees on the site which would surround her future house. She cared lovingly for those small trees, carrying bucketfuls of water to ensure that they would survive the continual drought conditions which seemed to mark life in Rustenburg. She had visualised the type of home she would have long before she was married, and planned the planting of the trees with her future home in mind. And then, when she did marry, her dream was realised.

Mike, her husband, is of German descent and speaks English with a harsh Afrikaans accent. He is accepted uneasily into the family. He is not Jewish. His manners are rough and ready, and are markedly different from the gentleness of Polly, whose love of classical music leads her to practise for hours on a grand piano she bought herself. She is a small-scale dairy farmer. Mike, on the other hand, has brought his ingenuity and chemistry training skills into full effect. He runs a jam factory with a small black labour force. It seems to be a highly profitable business which requires minimal effort. They have three children, who are growing up on the farm playing with the black farm labourers' children.

Harold and I have visited them from time to time. It was Mike who counselled Harold soon after our marriage. 'Never move furniture,' he said. 'You come home from work and they say, "Oh, would you just move this table here, and let's put the settee there", and then you always have to do it. And not only that. When you are asked to carve the meat, do such a terrible job that you are never asked again.' I have never known whether Harold took Mike's advice to heart, but I do carve the meat.

Tiny Polly is always hospitable, and welcomes my suggestion of a four-day visit with Peta and Tessa. The three of us set out on Thursday midday for the long drive to Rustenburg. I decide to go via Hartebeestpoort Dam, a slightly longer route, but rather beautiful.

The drive is almost eighty miles, but the Volkswagen Beetle keeps up a steady 60 miles an hour. The distance seems nothing at all. Very different from my childhood memories of dirt roads filled with potholes and the smell of the dust heavy in the car. It is a perfect Transvaal winter's day. The sky is blue and clear – not a cloud in sight. The veld is brown; the small shrub trees are bare of their leaves. The contrast between the brown veld and the blue sky is wonderful. I have forgotten what the countryside can look like. I have spent so much time in hospitals, in concrete buildings, that the sight of the space and the endless vistas lifts my spirits. Oh, it is so good to be alive. It is so wonderful to contemplate the few days' break, and spend some time with the girls. They play in the back of the car, and I try 'I spy' games, which are hilarious because of course they cannot spell.

Tiny Polly will be welcoming and warm. Mike will be his usual brusque, teasing self. And my mother will be reassuring. I have not spent time with her at all since Hooks's death, and this will be a good opportunity for all of us.

The sight of the brown lawn leading to the reservoir which doubles up as a swimming pool, the thatched house with its country look of chintz curtains, chintz-covered settee, large open fireplace and old wooden Cape Dutch furniture, oozes a sense of well-being. It is a relaxing atmosphere, and a caring one. I savour the thought of a few days' peace and quiet and relaxation.

Polly and Bessie join us for dinner. We all retire early. It is going to be a good few days.

I wake on Friday morning to a perfect day. The sun is warm. Peta and Tessa have been remarkably undemanding. They are intrigued with the farm and rush to the stables to watch the cows being milked, then enjoy a huge breakfast with home-baked bread. The jam factory is their next stop. They have been rejected by Frankie, the middle child, who is closer to Peta's age but totally engrossed in what he calls his 'tip-up rolly'.

I feel relaxed. As usual, not a cloud in sight. The lawn and garden are ringed by the now large blue gum trees with their distinctive smell and dappled smoked-grey trunks. The house, the garden and the large reservoir are an oasis in this otherwise brown, parched bushveld. When I look out, the veld stretches endlessly, unbroken – no trees, just the dried heads of the long golden-brown grass swaying ever so slightly. The *hoo-hoo-hoo* sound of the blacktipped crested hoopooe bird breaks the silence of the morning.

The sitting-room is empty. I don't want to read, yet I can't sit doing nothing. I start working on the bright-red cardigan I am knitting for Peta; she always looks wonderful in vivid colours, which contrast with her curly mop of dark hair and her hazel eyes. The quietness is somehow oppressive, so I turn on the radio. I am lucky. There is a piano recital of Chopin *études* – all the pieces my mother used to play when I was a child and she still had her grand piano.

My reveries are interrupted by the news. I get up to turn off the radio when I hear the modulated tones of the announcer saying that a farm in the northern suburbs of Rivonia in Johannesburg had been raided the previous evening by the Security Police and a number of arrests had been made: banned ANC leaders and six white people. The police claim that they have smashed the underground headquarters of the ANC. The arrests took place at the home of Mr and Mrs Arthur Goldreich.

I gasp. This short, terse statement heralds the beginning of the collapse of my world. I turn off the radio and stand there, still and shocked. What I have feared for so long has now happened.

My mother walks into the room, followed by her sister Bessie, who has a comfortable homely waddle. It is hard to reconcile the difference between these two sisters – my mother beautiful, sophisticated and elegant; Bessie homespun in appearance, with short grey bobbed hair, sensible shoes and a funny accent.

'I just heard that Arthur's house was raided yesterday, and that he and Hazel and others have been arrested,' I say, trying to sound nonchalant.

'Yes, I heard the news this morning,' replies my mother, 'but I didn't want to bother you with that. I thought it might upset you. But isn't it astounding?' Her voice has that special edge she reserves for salacious gossip.

Arthur's wife is a niece of my mother's best friend, Dora Rosenberg, well known in Johannesburg Jewish circles because of the eminence of her barrister husband.

'What on earth is all this about? Why should they have arrested Arthur and Hazel, and who are the others who have been arrested? What about their sons?'

I fob off my mother's more immediate questions. 'Well, I dare say we'll find out. I'll phone Harold soon, and see if he knows anything about it.' My heart is racing, but I conceal my panic. I take up my knitting again, and say, 'Look how much I did last night. I'll get this thing finished before the end of winter' – and try to laugh. Aunt Bessie is not interested in politics; consequently, she pays no heed to this momentous news. She is more concerned with her trip into Rustenburg, and wants to know if I will go with them.

As soon as they leave, I try to contact Harold. I have to assume that he isn't among those arrested, because otherwise Jimmy would have let me know earlier in the day. But I still have to make sure. I try phoning him at his office. The lines are engaged. I dial again and again. Finally, the cheery voice of the receptionist answers. 'Yes, Mrs Wolpe, how are you this morning?' Her voice rises at the end of the sentence. 'Mr Wolpe is out of town, but I'll get hold of Mr James for you.' It all sounds so normal, as though nothing has changed.

Jimmy's reassuring voice comes on the line. I always feel safe with Jimmy around. He is a fixer. He knows everyone. He knows what to do in a crisis. He is able to take over and make decisions. We exchange meaningless pleasantries. 'Oh, by the way, Harold asked me to tell you that he has had to go out of town for a couple of days, and will phone you. Not to worry. We had some urgent case come up, and he has had to go to interview the client.'

Now I have to wait to hear from Harold. My thoughts turn to Hazel. I am horrified that Hazel has been arrested. It isn't so long ago since I had learned about the role of Lilliesleaf Farm, and why the Goldreichs had moved there. At first I shared everyone else's amazement at the move Arthur and Hazel had made. My admiration for Hazel increased even more. At the time I never questioned her role. We women did what we had to do, and accepted our husbands' actions. We might have felt panic, unease, disquiet and fear, but what could we do? Nothing, short of separating from them and going out on our own. In a way, even this option was not open to us. Our voices were not heard. We were the mothers who mothered, who cared for the children, who organised the home, who provided love and companionship for our husbands, and who could have fears, but they were not likely to be heard. What would have happened if Hazel had said: I do not want to move out of Yeoville. I do not want you mixed up with an underground movement? It was the movement which made the decisions. It was the movement which determined actions. What could we do about it? Not a lot. And as we were not part of any organisation, we did not have the right to speak out. So Hazel and I agreed that we would never be involved, because we would be there to look after the children. She has two and I have three. We could not engage in actions that could endanger ourselves because of our children. But this was not the only reason I did not get involved. It was more complex than that. There was the element of fear. I am frightened of police. I am frightened of fascism. I am frightened of violence. And I never learned to stand up and shout back. I had been brought up to conform and agree. We had never witnessed shouting, anger or violence at home; arguments were muted and infrequent. And then, of course, there was the movement itself.

Neither Hazel nor I realised that by virtue of our compliance we were involved. We had both been naive to assume this, as we were both to discover. It takes more than passive acquiescence to protect oneself.

My thoughts are interrupted by the phone. It doesn't ring that often, and I hope it will be for me. It is: Harold calling from a phone box, asking whether I have heard the news. I say, 'Yes.' There is silence. Then he says, 'I will be in touch with you again today.' Nothing more. Nothing.

Waiting for Summer

L ATER HAROLD told me he had woken on Friday 12 July feeling relaxed and happy. Nicholas was due to come out of hospital. He was enjoying the luxury of the solitude and the absence of demands from Peta and Tessa. He had read the morning paper in bed and smoked the obligatory cigarette, inhaling the warming smoke deep into his lungs. Might as well enjoy it, he thought, because he would have to give up once Nicholas returned home. When he drew back the curtains, the day looked bright and promised to be warm. He soaked in the bath.

'Miss Molly is here,' Angelina called out to him. Excellent! He was looking forward to the party that night; it would be the first social event since Nicholas's illness.

Molly Fischer, no doubt, was coming to tell him where the party would be held. People were cautious about giving any details on the phone, even if it was in connection with a social gathering. If banned people were likely to be present, then extra precautions had to be taken. Nobody knew whose phone was being bugged. Harold went into the small sitting-room, smiling. The minute he saw Molly, he realised there was something dreadfully wrong. She was pale; she looked drawn and haggard. 'Is Paul OK?' Harold asked immediately. Everyone was worried about Paul, her youngest child, knowing that he was living on borrowed time, suffering from cystic fibrosis. She nodded. 'Anything wrong with Bram?' asked Harold. Both Molly and Bram were long-time members of the Communist Party. What distinguished them from most of the other members was that they were both Afrikaners, with impeccable backgrounds. Molly was a niece of Mrs Smuts, wife of Jan Smuts, the famous

premier; Bram's forebears included the Judge President of the
Orange Free State. 'Die appel het ver van die boom geval' (The
apple has fallen far from the tree), one Afrikaans newspaper
had said of them. It was an anathema for an Afrikaner to join a
political party associated with the ANC.

Molly was holding a copy of the morning's Afrikaans
newspaper, *Die Transvaler*. Pointing to the headlines, she
blurted out, 'Oh, Harold, it's a calamity. They got them all at
Rivonia yesterday – Walter, Rusty, Kathrada, Arthur, Hazel,
Govan . . .' Her voice trailed off. '*Die Transvaler* is the only
paper to cover the story. There's nothing about it in *The Rand
Daily Mail*. Nobody knows about this yet.'

That evening the English newspapers carried the story.
Their headlines blazoned out the success of the police who had
smashed the banned ANC. The names of the arrested people,
including the white people, and photographs – mostly of Walter
Sisulu, Secretary-General of the banned ANC, and Ahmed
Kathrada, a well-known organiser of the South African Indian
Congress – were printed.

One report described how, at 5.30 in the afternoon on the
11th of July, a dry cleaner's van drove into the private driveway
of Lilliesleaf, a large homestead in Rivonia, where Arthur and
Hazel Goldreich lived with their two sons. A florist's delivery
van followed closely. Near the house both vehicles came to a
halt. The back doors swung open, armed police poured out,
and within seconds they were swarming through the house and
the outbuildings and, supported by reinforcements, scouring
the surrounding fields.

The police, the story said, were acting on a tip-off that
Walter Sisulu, Secretary-General of the banned ANC, was in
hiding on the farm. Their raid had been delayed because at the
last moment someone had realised that there was no warrant for
a search of Lilliesleaf Farm, and a rushed visit to a judge in
chambers had produced the requisite document. What they had
stumbled on inadvertently was a meeting of the top leadership
of the underground movement. They had hit the jackpot.

Sisulu had been sentenced to six years' imprisonment for
political offences earlier in the year. Harold had successfully

applied for and got bail for him. No one thought his appeal would be successful, so the ANC had decided he should go underground. He had been on the police wanted list.

'The tragedy is,' Molly said, 'had the police not muffed the whole bloody thing and carried out the raid when they had meant to, earlier in the afternoon, they wouldn't have caught anyone at the meeting.' Both she and Harold knew that plans were afoot to rendezvous elsewhere. The feeling was that too many people knew of what was happening at Lilliesleaf, and that this was to have been the last time the top leadership would meet there.

Lilliesleaf Farm in Rivonia had been bought as the head-quarters of the underground movement, and Harold had been responsible for the legal work involved in the purchase. The property had numerous outhouses in which people like Govan Mbeki and Walter Sisulu could live undetected, as had Nelson Mandela, then subsequently Ahmed Kathrada and others. The place housed many of the documents relating to the developing armed struggle, maps of the country, Roneoing machines. Everything. Even a radio station. Harold had been involved in acquiring detailed maps and planning possible areas suitable for guerrilla warfare.

To the outside world, it was the Goldreichs' new home. Arthur Goldreich had a flamboyant personality. He was an attractive man, with dark curly hair, a quick smile and an eager forward thrust of his head. His features were sharp but regular. His eyes sparkled. He gave the impression of always being in a hurry. Nothing in his life appeared to be mundane. He seemed able to inject a little magic into the most ordinary situations, and when he told a joke people were spellbound. His eyes would light up with the sheer pleasure he got from his attentive audience. There seemed to be no end to his talents. If he was at a party he would play a tune on the piano, or strum one on the guitar. He did not have a repertoire, but then he did not need one. He was a competent artist, and sold his paintings without any difficulty. His creativity seemed to know no bounds. And he was utterly charming.

He had never completed his studies in architecture, because

he had gone off to fight in the Israeli war, but this did not seem to have made a great difference to his career. He had begun by being a designer of anything and everything, and formed a partnership with a friend of his. This enterprise foundered, and he next became resident designer for Greatermans, the large department stores, soon designing store layout, store displays, even furniture for the director. Arthur was on a career spiral that could only take him upwards.

He and Hazel had married when they were both quite young. She studied teaching, and was the complete antithesis to Arthur. She was quiet where he was rumbustious. She always dressed impeccably in tailored outfits, and kept herself out of the limelight. I liked her enormously. Her unobtrusiveness masked a resolute quality and an inner strength.

Their move from their small Yeoville house, with its minuscule garden, to the grand ranch-style house in Rivonia had been unexpected to say the least. Lilliesleaf Farm differed totally from their Yeoville home; it was a sprawling ranch-style thatched house, with mock Cape Dutch gables and large curved windows, set in vast grounds which included stables, and acres and acres of garden. Their friends had speculated about this change in their fortunes. It took money to make that sort of move. People conjectured that Arthur must be doing really well at Greatermans.

Harold was no stranger at Lilliesleaf Farm. He recognised the devastating effect this police coup would have. He held his breath for a moment, in utter shock.

Molly started reading the newspaper report out. Harold exclaimed, 'My God, Molly, what the hell are we going to do?' People had to be warned. Molly gave him a number of names to be contacted, and mentioned those she would do herself. There was no time to be lost.

He walked her to the car. There was nothing more to say, not even a goodbye. They were both too stunned to talk. He was not to know that he would never see her again. She would die most horribly in the swirling waters of the flooded Orange River, trapped in a car which had plunged over the bridge. Bram was to survive that accident.

As Molly's car pulled away, Harold was overcome by a feeling of deep foreboding. His sense of alarm was for himself, for his family, for the movement, for his friends. He struggled to collect his thoughts and arrange what he should do first. After warning the people he had been asked to contact, he would have to consider his own actions. His situation was catastrophic. Apart from handling the legal purchase of Lillies-leaf Farm, he had only just completed a document on disciplinary procedures to be adopted by Umkhonto we Sizwe. It was in his handwriting. And of course his fingerprints would be everywhere – on the Roneoing machine, on the documents, everywhere. There was no knowing whether the Security Police were already aware of his involvement. It was only a matter of time before he would be arrested too. He could feel panic and despair welling up in him; such feelings were to be his constant companions for some time.

Questions tumbled around, one after the other: the fate of the movement, how safe individuals would be, how long it would take for the police to identify his part. All these problems crowded in on each other, edging each successive thought out. It was no good. He simply was not functioning coherently.

He used the first phone box he came to and made the necessary calls. The next step was to go to the office. Every move he made felt weighted like a sleepwalker's desperate struggle to escape some impending doom in a nightmare.

His pallor evoked a caustic comment from Doreen, Jimmy's extraordinary secretary. 'Not feeling well this morning? A hangover? Playing while AnnMarie is away?' she said teasingly when he asked her to get George Bizos, a colleague at the Bar, to substitute for him.

Harold had never been happy as a barrister. Although he enjoyed the intellectual challenge of legal argument, he found Supreme Court work nerve-racking. He had welcomed my brother Jimmy's offer to join his firm of attorneys a few years earlier. Jimmy, despite his youth, was one of the leading criminal lawyers in the country. Jimmy and Harold were very different, but they got on well, despite – or perhaps because of – their dissimilarities. Jimmy was politically naive. He believed in the rule of law. He was a lawyer by day and a playboy by night. His girlfriends were all glamorous. His future wife Barbara was no exception: tall, dazzling, large grey eyes – one slightly drooping from a nerve impairment – hair dyed a striking auburn colour and an ability to laugh easily. But she was different from the other women in his life. She was the only girlfriend Jimmy had had who hadn't tried to curry favour with members of his family.

Jimmy counted among his friends some of the country's wealthiest men – including Johnny Schlesinger, who had inherited the vast empire of the Zebediela estate, the entertainment world and other ventures from his father, David Susman of Woolworth's. Although he mixed in fashionable society, it wasn't only wealth and status that he sought in his friends. He liked people, from no matter what walk of life, and he had absolutely no racial prejudice at all. This was obvious in his relationship with Nelson Mandela, who had not long been admitted to the side-Bar as an attorney. Nelson had followed the custom of introducing himself to his colleagues at their offices. These white men were prepared to shake his hand in private, but pretended not to notice him in the corridors of the magistrates' court. Not so Jimmy. Whenever he encountered Nelson, whether publicly or privately, he was delighted to see him and greeted him enthusiastically.

It was amusing to go out with Jimmy at night. He would be eagerly accosted by dishevelled, rumpled little black boys who were the lookouts for the receivers of stolen goods, all of whom Jimmy knew because he had defended them at some time or other. 'Hello, Mr Kantor, all right, Mr Kantor?' they enquired solicitously. 'You need anything, Mr Kantor?' But as I've said, Jimmy was not political. His clients also included Colonel Klindt, head of the Special Branch in Johannesburg.

On that Friday morning, Jimmy realised that caution was called for. While he and Harold sat in the office, Arthur's sister Doreen phoned, asking him to act on behalf of Arthur and Hazel. Harold and Jimmy thought it advisable to leave the office, and headed for a run-down café not far away, safe from any police search. Harold said, 'I've got to go into hiding immediately. The police are likely to arrest me fairly soon following the Rivonia arrests. There is sufficient evidence at Rivonia to incriminate me.' Jimmy displayed no emotion in response to this bald statement. Although he might have been politically naive, he knew of Harold's connection with the Left, and this came as no great surprise. 'I need to establish contact with people before deciding what to do,' continued Harold. 'I must, though, avoid being seen by the police. I must not be arrested.' He could not tell Jimmy how grave the situation was because this would lead to Jimmy questioning him, and he wanted to protect his brother-in-law.

Jimmy, with his characteristic spirit of generosity and humanity, immediately offered sanctuary. 'Go out to Hartbeespoort Dam. You'll be all right there.' Hartebeestepoort Dam was Jimmy's weekend retreat. He had lovingly refurbished an old thatched house overlooking the dam, which was nudged into one of the valleys of the Magaliesberg Mountains. When Barbara came into his life, she too shared his enthusiasm. This was an ideal place. Harold would be able to use the phone there, establish contact with Bram and others, and come to some decision about what he should do – whether to go underground or leave the country.

Harold arrived at the cottage after lunch. There was nothing to do except wait. He had managed to see Bram before leaving Johannesburg, and arranged for him to come out to Hartbeespoort Dam the following morning. The sun set quite early, and the night was quiet. He could hear the jarring *kwiet-kwiet* of some night birds, but did not know what they could be. He was unused to being at the house at night, and he found the silence oppressive. He wondered who it was who had betrayed the movement. He would have to wait until the following morning to hear what plans Bram had.

Bram arrived early in the morning together with Ivan Schermbrucker. It did not take long to establish that the movement was in complete disarray. 'We've taken a helluva beating. There's nothing we can do to help you survive and work underground at this stage. You'll have to leave the country, and immediately. Sorry, old chap.' For a *ware* (true)

Afrikaner, Bram used quintessentially English expressions every now and again, a hangover from his days as a Rhodes Scholar at Oxford and London in the early 1930s. 'You're on your own. We just have no resources available to help you at the moment.' It was stark, and to the point. Bram looked sad. The three of them shook hands. The meeting was over barely ten minutes after their arrival. Harold was alone once more.

He could not think of any viable plan. He had no passport. He had no ready cash. He was well known to the police – not only through his detention in 1960, but more so through the innumerable political trials he had handled – for Nelson Mandela, for Duma Nokwe, for Walter Sisulu, for Ben Turok; and he had represented groups of people arrested for pass offences, or for putting up illegal posters. The list was long, and the police did not like him. He had never contemplated organising his own escape, although escape plans weren't new to him. It was only the previous year that he, Joe Slovo and one other person had planned Nelson's escape. Nelson was then being held in the cells below the magistrates' court while he was on trial. Harold and Joe had managed, through a black warder, to get hold of the key to the cell, and taken a wax model of it during the day. The next step had been to get a duplicate key made as well as a latex mask to disguise Nelson. It seemed so simple and straightforward. The key was ready, the mask had been made. It seemed foolproof. The mask was a masterpiece. Nelson would just unlock his cell and walk out with a new face. But they hadn't foreseen his unexpected removal to Pretoria.

It was different getting a person out of the country without any assistance. That took organisation and co-operation. Harold had been entirely dependent on the movement, and without their assistance he felt momentarily paralysed.

There was one person he thought he could approach – Stan Goldstein, a close personal friend, who was in no way connected to the movement but was clearly sympathetic to the struggle. Stan had offered help in the past. Now was the time to test this offer. 'I need to see you urgently,' Harold said on the phone. Stan's response was wonderful. He asked no questions beyond getting directions, and was at the dam within a few hours.

Harold felt some of the loneliness lift. Here was a man willing to put himself at risk, and he was not even a member of any organisation.

The two of them sat on the paved terrace, looking out over the dam. The stillness of the heat, even on a winter's day, was punctuated by the call of the birds, but even they were lulled by the warmth. It was an idyllic setting perched up above the water. Its tranquillity did not match the tumult in Harold's head. 'Look, Stan, I'm in real shit,' he said tersely. 'I've got to get out of the country, and quickly, but at the moment I don't know how the hell to do it. It will take some organising, but I will need to go into hiding in Johannesburg for a while. I can't stay here because I don't want to put Jimmy at risk. Frankly, I haven't a bloody clue at the moment. I just don't know what to do.'

This was not the sort of problem that Stan was accustomed to dealing with, and he was more than somewhat startled by the request. 'Listen, man, I don't know what to suggest. If you need a place to stay, you can have my flat. I've got a small place now since my separation from Mickey. The building is insignificant, rather tatty, and I don't know anybody there. You're not likely to bump into anybody you know. The flats are cheap, and it's not the sort of place that our friends would choose.'

Plans for Departure

I HAVE WAITED a day and a half before seeing Harold. When he arrives, the sun has already set. The air is still warm. The crickets seem to be everywhere. The comforting farm-yard sounds have a drowsy effect. None of this soothes my inner turmoil. Peta and Tessa, though, are delighted to see their father. It is nearly dinner time, and we will not have time to talk to each other in private.

Dinner is a nightmare of pretences. It is like an elaborate farce. None of us is talking about the issues that we each know the other thinks important. We don't talk about Rivonia, or the arrests. It is odd, and I feel uneasy. Nor is it like Mike to resist a dig at the Left – far from it.

Mike is at best a cynic. He epitomises the arrogance of the self-made man. He mocked his mother-in-law for never having electricity installed in her home; he mocked her for the primitive pit lavatory situated some distance from the main house; he mocked Polly's piano-playing; he mocked her dairy farming. He pointed out time and again how successful his jam factory was in comparison with her dairy, which barely covered the veterinary fees and took far more of her time than the jam factory took of his. He mocked other people. He was impatient of what he saw as human frailties, and justifed his lack of charity on the grounds of his own success story. His mother, a German immigrant, had been widowed when he was very young, and his childhood had been difficult. He had worked his way through university, and become a chemist. He and Polly are a curiously matched pair. Polly deals with his caustic comments laughingly. She turns her head, gives a big warm laugh and says, 'You don't really mean that. You are a one!'

I have to pretend that I am not worried. Harold has to pretend that he is not worried. Both of us have to pretend that all we are thinking about is Nicholas's homecoming in a few days' time. The stilted conversation focuses on this neutral territory.

Anxiety is gnawing at my stomach. It is difficult to swallow the food. I can think of no plausible excuse to enable us to get up and leave the table, but finally the meal ends and we move into the sitting-room.

The sitting-room looks warm and comforting. No overhead lighting. The glow from the two table lamps casts just sufficient light to make the open thatch visible. A huge log is burning in the fireplace, turning the copper hood to burnished gold. The heat from the fire warms the cold night air. Polly sinks into the engulfing comfort of the large settee covered in a dusty rose chintz. Behind the settee is an old oak table on which stands a vase filled with a variety of magnificent Cape flowers, dominated by the three king proteas with their outer stiff pink bracts, and their massed tiny florets like soft cone-shaped cotton wool, which dwarf the smaller proteas. Mike sits down at the desk under the window with a mass of papers in front of him. It is the moment to excuse ourselves.

In the privacy of our bedroom, I begin pouring out questions: 'What happened? How on earth did the police come to raid Rivonia? I can't believe they arrested Hazel. She hasn't been involved at all. We always said neither of us would get involved because we had to look after our children. Nobody else would. And now look what's happened to her. My God, it's awful.' I am close to tears.

Harold shakes his head wearily. 'There was fantastic security,' he answers. 'God knows – there must have been a traitor. The tragedy is that this was scheduled to be the last meeting there. We've been worried for some time, and everything was due to be moved away from the house.' He sighs heavily. 'The police don't know just what they have stumbled on. It'll take them a bit of time to realise how big their find is. It's the death knell of the movement. They've got the lot. And it won't be long before they get on to me. There are too many documents in my handwriting. I'll have to get out of the country as soon as possible. Even Bram says so.'

None of this comes as a surprise, but anticipation does not ease the shock. Harold has always masked any doubts he may have had, and insisted that he would be all right. Maybe you can't do the things he does if you worry about their possible consequences.

'Well, what's going to happen? How will they get you out? Or maybe I shouldn't ask?' Knowledge under these circumstances can be dangerous, and Harold avoids telling me things. He works on the principle that the less I know, the less vulnerable I will be. Every now and again, though, this has broken down.

I want to hear something tangible, something I can grab on to. Bram himself had convinced me that in times of trouble I need not worry. During my pregnancy I constantly raised the possibility of our leaving the country, even though Harold's whole life was so wrapped up in the liberation movement. I was frightened of moving. I was frightened of staying. No longer did I feel smug about sticking it out in South Africa. I had become more and more pessimistic, convinced that it was only a matter of time before Harold landed up in jail. His continued political activity no longer seemed worthwhile. My forcing him to leave could have disastrous effects on our relationship. Nor would it be easy. We were restricted in where we could go – America would never grant him a visa. England seemed the obvious choice, but work there would be difficult. His legal degree would not be recognised.

After one of the periodic rumours that Harold's name was on the list of those who would be taken in under the Ninety Days law, my nagging seemed to have some effect. Perhaps Harold was feeling vulnerable. Perhaps he had begun to recognise the problems I and the children would have. But he gave way and arranged for the two of us to discuss the whole matter with Bram Fischer – a man of impeachable integrity and gentleness, a man who commanded respect and love from all.

Bram came out one Sunday afternoon to Jimmy's Hartbeespoort Dam retreat. I had wanted Jimmy to be part of the discussion, because of Harold's partnership in the firm. Bram listened sympathetically to all my fears about Harold's safety. I did not raise my needs or anxieties. After all, I was the non-active wife who was not at risk.

Although he did not minimise the stress and strain of the type of life we were leading, Bram painted a realistic picture of what people like himself and Harold were likely to face in the future. 'I don't for one moment underestimate the difficulties we all face, yet it is crucial that people like Harold continue with their work. And I'm not only talking about the political cases.' Harold was one of the few attorneys who took on political cases. It was not lucrative, and attorneys were frightened of doing this work. 'Obviously they are important. He is playing an extremely significant role in the struggle – the more so as there are relatively few whites prepared to join with the blacks in their struggle.' Bram emphasised this last point. It made me feel proud of what Harold was doing. He convinced me that we should not contemplate moving yet. 'If the time comes for Harold to leave, the movement would provide every assistance, as it has done with other people,' he reassured me. It sounded as though there was no prospect of Harold going underground, which was some comfort, as I felt that white people, in particular, were even more vulnerable because of the small numbers involved in the struggle. Bram himself was later to go underground in 1964, only to be caught 290 days later. He was subsequently imprisoned for life, and died in jail.

Now I repeat my question: 'What's going to happen?'

'Nobody can help me. It's up to me to arrange my escape,' is Harold's response.

'What do you mean?' I almost yell. 'You always told me not to worry – that something would be done if necessary. What are they doing about it?' I can't believe what I've heard, and I don't want to believe it.

'Nothing,' is Harold's reply.

'Nothing,' I repeat pathetically, adding: 'But they said they had an escape route all worked out. I was convinced of that. Bram told me not to worry. I believed him – I did.'

Harold shakes his head. 'This arrest has been absolutely

catastrophic.' He is not a person given to superlatives. 'We don't know what has hit us. They've got our radio transmitter, they've got lists, they've got extraordinary incriminating documents. They've got the whole fucking works. It's just a matter of time before they start with other arrests. Nobody is able to help me at all. I've been told that I've got to make my own way. Every man for himself.'

I feel overwhelmed by panic. My worst nightmare is unfurling. We can't just wait around for Harold to be arrested. He can't remain in hiding at Hartbeespoort Dam. That would put Jimmy at risk. Johannesburg seems to be out – the more so as people who have been sympathetic in the past are becoming more and more apprehensive about putting themselves in danger, and some, unfortunately, are prey to the government's insidious and continuous propaganda. People are beginning to think the 'Communists' are a threat to peace and progress. The political climate has altered considerably. And the Rivonia arrests have added a new dimension to an already fraught situation. The stakes are even higher than before. Treason – and that covers an absurd range of acts – is now punishable by death.

Rustenburg is not far from the border of Bechuanaland, and Lobatsi, one of the towns there, is just under a hundred miles away, Harold thinks. I don't have a map, and I have no idea where Bechuanaland is in relation to Rustenburg or how he could get there. In fact, neither of us knows the area at all. Harold decides he will have to take a chance and try to cross into Bechuanaland, and then find his way to one of the towns. He has spent the past year learning to read maps to identify areas suitable for guerrilla activities. But does this give him the expertise to find his way to Bechuanaland? He is an amateur tinkering in war games, with no experience in soldiering. How can he cross the border? Is it heavily patrolled? What demarcates the two countries from each other – is it a fence, and if so, what sort of fence? Harold thinks that since the Rivonia arrests there is likely to be heavy surveillance, but the border is long. It seems that we should drive as close to the border as possible, and Harold should simply cross over it. It all sounds totally inadequate, and I can't imagine such a plan succeeding at all.

Then I have what I think is a brain wave. I remember talk of a wealthy, somewhat eccentric Jewish farmer in the area who has his own light two-seater plane. He could fly Harold to Bechuanaland, and there would be no danger of border checks. I have never met him, though I assume that as a Jew he cannot possibly be a supporter of the government – after all, so many of the ruling party are known anti-Semites. It does not follow, however, that he will stick his neck out to help Harold, a banned and named man.

I will put this suggestion to Mike. I don't want to involve Polly at all, because I think she will be petrified by all this. Mike, on the other hand, is tough and fearless. And he is family by marriage, and families stick together. In the back of my mind is the memory of talk of how my father had helped Bessie and her husband when their children were very small by virtually giving them the farm. True, my father could not have known then that the farm, with its platinum deposits, was to prove a treasure trove. I assume that Mike knows this, and will help repay the debt. I will speak to him in the morning, as Harold plans on leaving at the crack of dawn and returning the next afternoon.

I find an appropriate time to talk to Mike on his own. I say that Harold is in danger because he has acted for so many of the people arrested at Rivonia, and that we have decided he should leave the country, and put our suggestion to him. I watch to see what effect this has on Mike, but Mike has a poker face. 'What do you think?' I ask.

Slowly and deliberately, he says, 'I'll talk to him, but I'm not too hopeful. You see, there is the question of having the right papers – you know, a clearance for a flight. And he's probably going to raise all sorts of problems about that. But don't worry, I'll check this morning.'

Neither of us had thought about such mundane bureaucratic formalities. We just thought you got into a plane and flew where you wanted to, no strings attached. 'Well, can't he just say that he's going off to Pretoria to visit his aunt, or something like that?' I suggest hesitantly.

It is late in the afternoon when I hear the distinctive chug

of the Citroën drawing up outside the house. I rush to greet
Harold. It is already dusk. The darkness seems to be playing
silly tricks. There are two men – Stan and . . . It can't really
be. Harold is transformed. His beard is gone, and his hair is a
glorious ginger. 'I don't believe it,' I burst out. 'Let's look at
you.'

He looks totally different. Momentarily, at least. Why has
he done this? Before he can answer, Stan says he has to get back
to Johannesburg, and leaves. The girls are playing out in the
garden and I have a short, precious time alone with Harold.

He tells me how he stopped at a phone box on the way back
to Johannesburg, and arranged to meet Jimmy at Stan's Hillbrow flat. While he was waiting, paging through a *Time*
magazine with unseeing eyes, he heard a key being turned in
the lock. He could not move. Even his breathing was halted.
The door opened. It was Barbara, glamorous as ever in a tight-
fitting skirt and high heels. She greeted Harold warmly, and
said laughingly, 'I've come to give you a new look,' brandishing
some bottles. 'We've decided you should have a disguise. Your
beard has to go, that's the first thing. Then I'm going to dye
your hair. Jimmy thinks you had better change your image.'

Harold agreed. He had thought of various disguises in the
past, but had not contemplated dyeing his hair. Off came the
beard he had first grown while he was in detention in 1960.
Next came the bottles. Barbara had sought advice from her
hairdresser, and was going to give Harold a watered-down
version of her own startling red auburn colour. First the
peroxide, to bleach the natural colour. The smell was revolting.
Then the application of the dye. Barbara was enjoying the
situation, and she listened to him sympathetically. She was
extraordinarily supportive during the worst parts of Nicholas's
illness, and we had grown close to her.

Two hours later, Harold examined his new image. His hair
was verging on ginger, but the colour was good. Jimmy arrived
during the colouring process with a hundred Rand and a
compass. They had little time to talk. Harold's absence from
the office had added an additional burden on Jimmy. They all

agreed that Stan should drive out with Harold and return the Citroën to our house later that evening.

Harold has come armed with a compass, not much money and some walking shoes. He is prepared for his departure from South Africa.

Breathlessly I bring him up to date: 'Mike came back mid-morning with what we expected to hear. Margo feels he can't help us. With his wry, crooked smile, Mike comes up with a solution. He says to me' (and I attempt to mimic Mike's accent) '"There's this bloke and his wife, friends of mine from Norway, visiting here as guests of the Round Table, you know." I didn't know Mike was active in this, nor that he was the local chairman. Anyway, he told me that he had planned to take them on a long drive in the country, which he could do tomorrow. He also said that he's got a good friend who has a lovely farm not far from the Marico River, wherever that is. Apparently it is just on the border of Bechuanaland. He said that you would all have a braaivleis [barbecue] there, and then you can simply wander off on your own and cross the border.'

This sounds almost too good to be true, but I am excited and I feel that Harold will be safe and away from the clutches of the police by tomorrow night. What could be easier? At last some relief. I have become almost paralysed by fear for Harold's safety. I am no longer able to think coherently. I am so relieved that Mike has taken charge. He is firm, efficient and confident, and I trust him.

We both take deep breaths, and for the first time in what seems ages Harold actually smiles. Time now to face Polly and Mike at dinner. What will be their reaction to Harold's transformation?

Polly and Mike are astounding. There is absolutely no sign of surprise, and no questions, when they see the transformed Harold. They appear to have taken it all in their stride. Surely this should call for some comment, but none is forthcoming. At dinner Mike keeps the conversation going. He is relaxed, even witty. He spends time reminiscing about his student days – how he courted Polly, and how her family resisted their marriage. On this occasion he is the butt of his own barbs. Only after dinner is the question of the barbecue raised. We are in the sitting-room, sipping excellent KWV brandy. Mike starts talking nonchalantly about the next day's plans.

Harold immediately raises the question of whether Mike is sure that he should join them. 'I don't want to intrude at all,' he says pointedly. Mike brushes all this aside with a wave of his arm. 'Ag no, it's all right,' he says. Polly looks less happy, though, and she starts to question him about whether it is really all right. He ignores her, and speaks instead of the next day's arrangements, saying that they should leave early. This gives Polly an excuse to do something. She insists that she prepares the picnic basket tonight rather than leaving it to the servants to do in the morning. 'You know how they always manage to forget something really important.' 'Make sure you put in lots of boerewors,' Mike calls out. She rejects my offer of help, saying I will only get in her way, and that she prefers to do these things on her own.

Personally, I prefer to sit in front of the fire and drink my brandy. Mike says that his two guests will be dropping in shortly for a drink, and it will be nice if we can all meet. He repeats the caution that he won't say anything about Harold's venture across the border, and when I ask how he will account for it he says that Harold should leave a note somewhere in the car explaining his absence and telling them to return to the farm. It sounds as though he has thought of everything.

The couple are in their early thirties. He is an engineer, she is a schoolteacher. He tells us how much he has always wanted to visit South Africa, and how pleased he is to see for himself what life is like. He is quite expansive: 'I've visited quite a lot of farms round here, and I must tell you that I am really impressed with the way the natives are looked after.' It is clear to me who his informant has been. 'Look at the food rations they all get.' I know all about them. I recall as a child, when I was holidaying at the farm, Bessie's farm workers queuing up outside the kitchen door on a Saturday morning for their ration of mealie meal and sugar. At that time I took for granted the miserable wages and the appalling conditions in which they sweated, sorting out the golden tobacco leaves in a subterranean room in temperatures even higher than they were outside, and a humidity rate almost as high. The heat and the stench of sweating bodies was unbearable. Mike's visitor continues: 'These people have a good staple diet. If they weren't given this food they would probably waste their money on liquor.' He continues to extol the virtues of what is being done for the 'natives'. His wife Anya – tall, slender, and very blonde – does not join in.

Harold does not relate easily to complete strangers, and is even less forthcoming with people who support apartheid. He contributes nothing to the conversation. We both sit there politely. Tonight he is not sleepy at all – far from it. Tomorrow is to be a historic day for us. We do not know what the future holds, except that Harold will be safe, and free from the threat of arrest.

It is strange how stilted our conversation is when we get back to our bedroom. The gravity of the situation has created a barrier between us. There is so much to say, yet everything sounds so banal. I have become conscious of a fear quite different to the fear I experienced at the height of Nicholas's illness. I am trying to suppress it, but it affects me. I am tense; I feel pity for myself and anger at the failure of the movement. Why has Harold persisted in being involved, when it has always been obvious to me that the police will catch up with him? I have no urge for lovemaking at all.

Crossing the Border

T HE NEXT morning the sun shone as brightly as usual. The
sky was blue. Nobody mentioned it.

The Norwegians had arrived bright and early, and
we all breakfasted together. It seemed like just an ordinary day,
and Mike was very jovial. The girls didn't seem to notice
Harold's changed appearance. They had been thrilled to see
him the night before, but did not nag to accompany him. They
were still intrigued with Polly's youngest son, Frankie, who was
infatuated with his lorry and feigned indifference to Peta and
Tessa, his two younger admirers. Outwardly, Harold behaved
as though this was a normal day. The only sign of his inner
turmoil was the surfacing of his old habit of raising his eyebrows
continuously.

The four picnickers were dressed for a day's outing in the
veld – Harold in a white open-necked shirt and light-coloured
sports trousers. He gave me a peck on the cheek, and got into
the car while Mike finished putting the day's food into the boot.
There were no histrionics – well, there couldn't very well be
any. He said afterwards how he had watched Polly and me
standing and waving them out of sight.

The flat veld stretched out for miles and miles. The fading
yellow of the long-dead stems of the grass was broken every
now and again by a doringboom with its sharp spiky thorns. No
trace of any leaves. In the distance were the hilly ridges of the
Magaliesberg. The road wound round to the west, and they
passed Swartruggens, a tiny little Transvaal dorp with its cluster
of small corrugated-iron-roofed shops and one or two offices
lining the main road. Out again on the road in the direction of
Zeerust. The early-morning chill gave way to the warming glow

of the winter sun. Harold rolled up his shirt sleeves, and felt in his pocket to make sure that he had his compass. He was sitting in the back next to Anya, who was babbling away, talking about herself and her country. After half an hour they all lapsed into silence; the straight, straight road, and the *ka-thup* of the car tyres, lulled Harold into a light sleep.

He woke quite suddenly. He was leaving the country. He would be walking to Lobatsi, where he would make contact with the ANC people, and then . . . He didn't know what would happen next. He had no illusions about the outcome of the recent arrests. Life imprisonment would be the best the prisoners could hope for, and capital punishment was certainly not beyond the bounds of possibility. It all depended on who the trial judge would be. In his experience the more liberal the judge, the harsher the sentence. He began to recall some of the political trials he had conducted.

Harold's thoughts were abruptly interrupted by Mike's cursing: 'I can't find the bloody farm!' Mike sounded quite angry. He drove up and down. Harold felt a surge of tension. He stiffened, shuffling around in his seat, and then he thought that soon he would be on his own, soon he would be walking his way to freedom. He looked around curiously, wondering what it would be like once he had set off. How easily would he be able to follow the compass? He was hopeless at finding his way under normal circumstances, so how would he manage in the open veld? He felt nervous, and the previous days' stress did not help.

'Ah, this must be it!' exclaimed Mike when they came upon a long, wooden, dirt-blackened farm gate. Harold got out to open it. Usually there were little children around who would willingly open the gates, smilingly holding out their hands for the pennies or sweets thrown to them in the dusty road.

Round the bend they came unexpectedly upon a group of black people with two white overseers. It was odd that they should be assembled there and not on the fields working, Harold thought. Mike stopped the car as one white man came towards them. In a thick guttural Afrikaans accent, looking first at Harold and then at both the visitors, the man said, 'I am

Sergeant Prinsloo, in charge of the border police station, Derdepoort.' They had driven straight into a police border control group, not an innocent group of workers. 'Have you got your identity books? What are your names?' The visitors replied.

Harold was taken aback. The question was not totally unexpected. He had thought about this fleetingly, but was overcome by a moment of panic. He gave a false name: 'Ronald Woolfson'. He wasn't sure why he had done this. How stupid! He watched the burly, suntanned man, with a thick neck and a pudding-basin haircut that left the lower part of his head almost close-shaven, laboriously write his name down, pressing on to a board. Harold wondered whether Mike and the visitors had heard him give a false name. He thought not.

'Youse people mus come with me to the police station,' the policeman added instructing an African sergeant to accompany them. This was totally unexpected. Mike swung the car around and they set off for the police station, followed by Sergeant Prinsloo. As they drove along, Harold touched Anya lightly on the arm, and softly asked her if she would mind keeping the compass and the money for him. Although she looked totally bewildered, she responded to the urgent note in his voice. He thrust them into her hand. Anya quickly put the compass and money into her handbag, and nodded in assent.

They drove along a rough country farm road which wound up the hill to a police station, a prefabricated building with three offices surrounded by a five-foot wire fence. They were on the border of Bechuanaland. All that separated them from it was the gate at the lower end. A small cluster of huts was visible in the distance.

The police seemed interested only in Harold. He foolishly repeated the false name and a fictitious address. When he replied that he was a lawyer, the policeman was somewhat taken aback. But by now Harold had completely undermined his position.

It was now wonderfully sunny. Mike, with his easy-going manner, set up a small braaivleis. 'Ag man, you don't mind if we make our lunch?' he asked the sergeant in charge. 'We're all getting hungry. We might as well have our picnic right here, hey?' he announced to whoever was listening. He squatted down next to the fire he had built quite ingeniously, using some twigs and newspaper. He started cooking the sausages and steak they had brought with them. He asked one of the policemen to take a photograph for him.

The fat from the meat spattered on to the fire, causing the flame to jump in great bursts and then die down again. The smell of the burning meat was delicious, particularly the spices of the boerewors. The sun was truly hot. Anya and her husband were treating the whole episode as an adventure, and the police were behaving towards them in a warm and hospitable manner. Mike seemed to be relaxed, even enjoying himself, unperturbed by the activity or the curious situation. He never attempted to question Harold about the strange turn of events.

Harold was silent. He could not believe what was happening. Ever since the arrests at Rivonia he had half expected to be picked up in Johannesburg, but not under these circumstances. He knew what was at stake, and not even the tantalising smell could whet his appetite. His mouth was dry. He kept going over and over his ridiculous behaviour in his mind. He felt sick thinking about this, thinking about his future, thinking about being so close to escape. How often had he advised his clients never, under any circumstances, to do anything other than give their names; they should refuse to go to a police station unless there was a warrant for their arrest. Otherwise the police could do nothing. Yet here he had gone along to a police station without any protest. And having done so, he had no documentation to prove his identity. It was small consolation to blame his stupidity on exhaustion, tension and fear. He was overwhelmed by a feeling of inevitablity, of having been caught up in something that was bigger than himself and over which he had no control. The prospect was bleak. He would be held initially under the notorious Ninety Days law, and then he would probably be joined with those held in the Rivonia arrests.

Things did not happen often at this little backwater police station. Now there was an incredible bustle. During the afternoon more and more policemen arrived, in uniform and plain-clothed. Each and every move of the four people was watched. The afternoon wore on; long shadows were being cast by the solitary tree that stood outside the police station. Conversation between Harold and the other three had petered out. Harold felt isolated from the others, who were engaged in desultory conversation. Still they waited. Harold did not make a fuss. Mike did not make a fuss. And the Norwegians did not know what to make of the situation. The four of them just waited and waited and waited.

At seven that night they were taken inside the building and given cups of strong sweet tea and some coarsely cut sandwiches. This time Harold ate and drank a little. He got up to go outside. Immediately somebody followed him. He stood outside, contemplating the scene. There, just beyond the fence, in the early darkness of the Transvaal night, was Bechuanaland and freedom. As he paced up and down, he considered the possibility of trying to make a dash for Bechuanaland. But he had no doubt that the armed police would open fire, and even if he did make it into the British protectorate he knew this would not deter the police from giving chase. There were no British police present. Harold would be entirely at the mercy of the South African police, and the place was seething with them. It needed more than courage to make a dash.

It grew cold. The contrast with the day temperature was noticeable, and he went back in. The break in the tedium came when the electric lights suddenly blacked out. The dim light was replaced with even dimmer paraffin lamps. The station was obviously well prepared for power failures.

There weas the sound of motorcars arriving. He could hear a gruff voice demanding, 'Waar is hy dan?' ('Where is the then?') He thought he recognised this voice. It had a familiar ring to it. He didn't have long to wait to confirm his suspicions. It was Sergeant Dirker, a man with whom Harold had often crossed swords in court. He was by no means clever, but he was dedicated to his job. In the years that Harold had known him he had not got promotion, yet this did not seem to affect his enthusiasm. Dirker appeared to have a great propensity to make minor errors, which Harold and others could seize upon in order to get various political charges dropped. There was the time, for example, when Dirker had arrested Walter Sisulu in the street, but the evidence he offered in court was inadequate.

For all his lack of acumen, Dirker was well aware of the fact that he had been made to look a fool in court by Harold on a number of occasions. Harold was the culprit. Dirker did not like him. But tonight the situation was going to be very different. He was in a position of power at last, and he was going to enjoy every moment of it.

With exaggerated gestures, Dirker bent down and peered into Harold's eyes, his face close to him. Harold realised for the first time that not only did Dirker have foul breath, but his teeth were irregular and stained from tobacco.

'Ag Herold, it's really you, man. Look at you. You're yellow, man. Trying to run away like this.' And he burst into loud, uncontrollable laughter. He called out to his colleagues that they should just come and have a look at 'Herold' with his red hair and clean-shaven face; he was looking really 'snaaks' (peculiar). He danced around Harold, savouring the moment. Never before had he dared to address him as anything other than Mr Wolpe. Calling him 'Herold' was obviously one tactic he could adopt. His delight at the change in relationships knew no bounds. He could barely mask his almost childlike joy.

Harold was tired, and in no fit state to respond or retaliate. Anyway, what could he say? He answered the few questions put to him as briefly and succinctly as possible, not deviating from his earlier statement that he was accompanying Mike and his Norwegian visitors on a picnic. Harold refused to answer any questions about when he had left Johannesburg, where he had gone, what he was planning to do. And his refusal triggered off angry responses from the other police.

Clearly they were getting nowhere. Then Harold was escorted out to a car flanked by plain-clothes police. He saw Mike and the other two going towards their car.

They set off in the enveloping darkness over the country roads. Harold was sitting on the back seat between two police-men. By now the temperature had dropped quite markedly. Winter nights in the Transvaal can be very cold, and that night was no exception. An old blanket had been thrust into his hands as he had got into the car, and he was thankful for this bit of warmth as he draped it round his shoulders. He had no jacket, and was certainly not dressed for the cold night air.

He had no idea where he was being taken, and he certainly wasn't going to ask. He felt himself dozing off in the car, soothed by the warmth generated by the bodies sitting close to him. His sleep was light and troubled. He kept waking up as his head lolled from side to side, trying to avoid touching either of the policemen next to him.

They seemed to have been travelling for hours and hours. Harold did not want to look at his watch as the car drove up to what was obviously a police station – he knew that watches were one of the things the police took away from prisoners. Instead he slid the watch up his arm – it had one of those metal expanding straps and it was quite easy to do this without drawing any attention to himself. They stopped briefly at Zeerust police station. No sign of Mike or the others.

Finally they reached Rustenburg. As they entered the building Dirker called out, for everyone to hear, 'Don't let him' – pointing to Harold – 'out of your sight! Nobody's to talk to him, you hear?' Harold was taken into a room, which was carefully locked. An African policeman stood guard. Five minutes later the door opened and Mike was escorted in. His hair looked as though he had just showered – it was damp and neatly brushed down. He was carrying a small suitcase. The two men sat at opposite ends of the table. No word passed between them. Harold felt acutely embarrassed at the thought of bringing Mike into conflict with the police; also, he did not want to talk in front of the policeman. Mike, for his part, was clearly in no mood to engage in his habitual bantering. Without any warning the door was unlocked and he was escorted out.

Harold remained in the dimly lit room – a single bare bulb dangled from a wire in the middle of the ceiling. The black policeman stood quietly to one side, looking on impassively. Harold was overcome by fatigue. He suddenly realised just how tired he was, and put his head down on his folded arms. During this long day he had not thought about his family at all. But now, as he drifted off once again into an uneasy sleep, he found himself thinking about Nicholas, the girls, and how we would all manage.

He soon woke with a start, unable to locate himself at first. He shook his head and looked around, not focusing properly, wondering what he was doing in this dimly lit room. Then consciousness came flooding back. Quite suddenly his black guard stooped down, picked up a basket that was standing at the side of the table, looked at Harold with a penetrating glance, walked silently to the door, unlocked it and closed it softly.

Was the man trying to say something to him? Harold wondered. Was he leaving him unguarded on purpose? Was it a sign to Harold that he should try to escape? Momentarily he thought that he would make a dash for it. At the same moment he realised how foolhardy this would be. What could he do if he did get out of the jail? Where would he go? Rustenburg was a small town, and with his red hair he would be conspicuous. There was nowhere to hide.

No. It would be plain foolhardiness to attempt to escape. Harold could see into the charge room. Mike was there. Mike glanced torwards the room where Harold was sitting, and clearly saw Harold, but his expression never changed, and there was no sign of greeting. It was as though Harold was a total stranger. Well, not surprising, Harold thought, given the anguish and embarrassment I have probably caused him.

The black policeman returned to the room with a cup of strong, hot tea in a large, cracked mug. Without a word he put it down in front of Harold, who drank in long deep gulps. It burned his throat, but it was warming and somehow welcoming. He fumbled in his pockets for his packet of cigarettes. He was down to his last five, and thought that he could allow himself the luxury of smoking one now – or perhaps only half of it, because he had no idea how long he would be permitted to smoke, or whether they would allow him to get any more. He had only a small bit of change, just enough to buy another packet – if he was permitted to do so. He inhaled deeply, filling his lungs with the smoke, feeling somewhat light-headed as the nicotine surged through his body. Of course, I've hardly eaten anything, he reminded himself as he gave himself up to the sheer pleasure that the first cigarette of the day always gave him. He decided to smoke it down to the very end.

He felt a little better after this. He got up and started walking around the small room. The door was still left open. Every now and again a curious policeman would poke his head into the room, and the sergeant at the desk kept looking his way.

There was a slight flurry at the door, and he wondered what was happening.

The Long Way Home

I CONTINUE TO stand on the gravel pathway long after the car has rounded the bend. I have an awful feeling in the pit of my stomach. I try to convince myself that everything will be OK, that Harold will cross into Bechuanaland. Once he is safe, I will work out what to do. At least Nicholas will be coming home, and I hope Marlene will help nurse him back to full health. I have no idea what I shall do for money. We have no savings. There is the mortgage, the girls' nursery school fees, the servants' wages and living costs. I am still on maternity leave. I had planned to return to work when Nicholas was six months old. Everything is too uncertain. I know how difficult I had found it during the three months of the Emergency in 1960 following Harold's imprisonment. Jimmy has come to the fore every time there is a crisis; he helped my parents out, and now there is my mother to take care of. She has no money and no savings.

I feel like an automaton going through everyday motions. There is nothing concrete to hang on to, yet no way to get myself out of what seems to be a maze which leads me continuously into a dead end. It's strange how numb I feel. I don't feel pity for myself; or sadness; or fear for Harold; just a nothingness. I have anticipated such an event for months and months, but I never anticipated how I would feel.

I wonder what work I can do. I am a fully trained social worker, but I worked in that capacity for only one year after graduation, before I went to live in London for two years. The state is unlikely to give me employment. The job at the Institute is only part-time, and not all that well paid anyway. I will have to find something else, but I think that will be difficult. I will be seen as a security threat for no reason except that I am married to Harold. I am guilty by association.

I wait. The girls divert my attention somewhat, but not sufficiently to banish the thoughts that keep intruding. As the temperature changes with the dipping of the sun, I strain to hear the sound of an approaching car. When will Mike return with his Scandinavian guests? He said, when he left, that they anticipated being back late in the afternoon. It is that now. Where are they?

Polly begins to fret, speculating about the possibility of an accident. I know better, but do not know how to say I am sure that isn't what is causing a delay, although secretly I wish it were. I do not know how to assuage her fears.

Supper that night is grim. Neither of us makes much attempt at light conversation, and we eat in silence. Thank goodness for the children. Polly remarks from time to time: 'I suppose the car has broken down, got a puncture or something like that.' She pauses, then adds, 'It is so difficult to get help in the middle of the bundu' – but we know that a Mercedes is an exceptionally safe car.

We go to bed early. I sleep.

It is still dark when there is a knock on my bedroom door. I am already awake. Strange – it is my Aunt Bessie standing in the doorway with two men just behind her. Why Bessie? But I need no introduction to the two men. I recognise them as members of the Special Branch.

'We've arrested your husband and he's being held under Ninety Days. We want to look through your things,' one says, straight to the point. There are no qualifying statements, no preliminaries.

I feel both exposed and threatened. Covering myself awkwardly with my dressing-gown, I wonder if they have any sense of embarrassment at what they do. 'We're going to look through your things, Mrs Wolpe,' the second policeman says, just in case I hadn't heard.

Don't the police need a search warrant to do such things? Do I have any rights? Even if I do, I am unlikely to invoke them as I am, quite simply, frightened. Previously, when the police raided the house in the early hours of the morning, there was nothing that could be done except for a silent and sullen accession to their demands. Except, of course, that one occasion when two of these thugs advanced towards Peta and Tessa's bedroom and I said rather feebly, 'That's my daughters' bedroom, you can't go in there.' They ignored me until Nanette, our small poodle, who was sleeping on Peta's bed, stirred and growled at them.

I have very little in the small, rather austere room. Their search is rather perfunctory, although they do go through my small suitcase. I am hiding nothing.

'Where was your husband going, Mrs Wolpe?' I am asked rather politely. This is new. Special Branch seldom seem polite people, who talk in such a mild way. 'They were going on a picnic. It was such a nice day and they thought it would be nice to take the foreign visitors to see the countryside and have a braaivleis.'

My response sounds false. Perhaps I should protest, ask some questions, and demand to know why Harold has been arrested. But they are not at all communicative, and do not seem particularly interested in my replies. My immediate concern is for Mike, and whether he is being held as well. 'Where is Mike?' I address the question to Bessie. The tall policeman replies: 'You needn't worry. Mr Michaelis is home now. We're not bothered about him.' I am relieved to hear this.

'Can I see my husband? What are you going to do with him?' I need to know if Harold is all right, and hasn't been harmed in any way.

'You can come and see him, but it won't be for long. You'd better come now.'

I have to dress quickly. No time for any ablutions. But I do not leave without applying an eyeliner. Without that I feel naked. I can even apply it without a mirror.

Bessie stands aside, looking flustered and frightened. She has not forgotten the stories her mother told her about pogroms in Russia, and has held the police in awe since. But like everyone, if there is a problem with a servant or a farm worker she calls them in to settle the dispute.

I see Polly and Mike in the kitchen as I walk out with the police. They both ignore me. I feel an overwhelming sense of guilt for having got them mixed up in our affairs, but I don't have a chance to express my regret. Clearly they are angry, but there is no time to say anything as the police are striding out in front of me and I have to half-run to keep up with them.

I drive behind the police car to the local jail, and am ushered in to see Harold. He seems like a stranger with his dyed auburn hair, standing up in places, and the grey shadow of a stubble. He looks unwashed and unkempt, and quite despond-ent. We hug each other momentarily. I am consumed with a desire to know what happened yesterday. He sketches the bare facts fleetingly. We don't know how long we will have together, and how free he is to talk, so he speaks quickly but softly. He lowers his voice even more when he speaks about giving a false name, acknowledging his crass stupidity, and says that they are holding him for giving false information, and are taking him back to Johannesburg to charge him and detain him under the Ninety Day law. He urges me to see Jimmy as soon as possible, to tell him what has happened.

That is all. Our brief communication is over. A group of men come into the room in which we are talking. 'Come on now. Say goodbye to your wife, you won't be seeing her for a helluva long time,' says a young man with a smirk on his face. He is savouring the moment. They are gone, Harold with them.

I return to Boekenhout, where I am met by a cold wall of hostility. Polly and Bessie stop talking as I come into the room. There is no sign of Mike. No one asks me anything, not even about Harold. Quite obviously I have to leave, and leave quickly. I have always anticipated animosity, even ostracism, from white people, but somehow I have excluded my family from this category. After all, family is family, and I have been taught that no matter how much you squabble and bicker and fight, family sticks together.

'I'm so sorry for the trouble. We didn't think this would happen. I must get back to Johannesburg,' I say to these silent women.

I feel an emptiness. I have lurched from one trauma to the

next: Nicholas's illness, Hook's death, Rivonia, and now Harold's arrest. Although there is no end in sight, the fear, anxiety, pain and tension seem to have reached their zenith.

Polly and Bessie are clearly relieved that I am leaving. My mother arrives, and she and Polly come out to the car when I finish loading it. The girls sit in the back. My mother does not suggest that she returns to Johannesburg with me.

By now it is mid-morning. The winter veld is dramatic with its soft, earth-brown grass and the vast blue sky. But speed is all that matters. I want to get home. My paranoia knows no bounds. I am convinced that a man standing next to a solitary broken-down car stuck in the middle of nowhere is really a member of the Special Branch monitoring my movements. Peta and Tessa sense my tension. They remain silent, and don't nag or groan or moan about anything.

I stop the car outside the house. The girls get out and rush to see Angelina. Tessa, in particular, has missed her, and can barely wait to throw her arms out towards the big warm friendly woman. Angelina picks her up and gives her a big hug. She puts her down, not forgetting that Peta, quieter and less demonstrative, is waiting patiently for her hug. Nanette jumps up excitedly, wagging her tail furiously.

Both Angelina and Isaac look tense and worried. Isaac also works for us; he has been with us for more than a year.

'Nina, you look awful. What's happened?' Angelina replies: 'The police have been here all yesterday. They searched the house and they searched my room and Isaac's. They shouted at us. They said that we were just as bad as the master, we're rubbish and they will arrest us and take us to jail. They said how can we work for such terrible people as you. They said that the house is full of bad things and they are going to find them.' We both sit down at the dining-room table. It has to be an extraordinary occasion for Angelina to sit down at the same table as myself. But today is different. Today we are on a different level than that of mistress and servant.

I have never entertained the idea that Angelina and Isaac could be subjected to police harassment because they work for us.

Isaac comes into the room. He is wide-eyed and his mouth seems to be dry – he keeps licking his lips. I inherited Isaac from a part-time gardener who pleaded with me to give his brother a job. There was no work in his rural area. I did not want a second servant. The house is so small, and the garden doesn't require that much upkeep. But what could I do? Everything was new to Isaac, including electricity, but he learned quickly. He referred to all our friends by their first names, but Nelson was always called Mr Mandela. Perhaps it was more a mark of respect than an inverted form of racism. He bought a forged pass after he started working for us, the only way he could get one. There was strict control on men's entry into the urban areas, and they needed a passbook. Without it he could be summarily arrested, sentenced in court and then dumped at a farm to work out his sentence as a farm labourer, living in appalling conditions. We'd seen pictures of men dressed in hessian sacks with a bit of rope around their waists, and heard stories of their abuse by whipping and urinating into their mouths. Such stories confirmed our worst fears. Songs were being sung by the movement about passes: 'Nanti pick-up van; l'yeza pick-up van . . . Waar's jou pass jong, waar is jou pass jong . . .' (There goes the pick-up van . . . where's your pass boy?)

But it isn't the forged passbook that has frightened him, it's the police themselves. He has been pushed around; his bedding has been turned upside down, and his paltry possessions hurled on to the floor. 'There were so many police here . . .' he says, his voice trailing off. 'And all the time they searched there was one man standing guard outside the house.' Harold was also brought to the house, surrounded by Security Police, who searched through papers, documents and books.

'I don't know what we're going to do. It just looks very bad. I think that they will keep Harold in jail for a long time – I don't know when he'll ever get out. Oh, I'm so sorry you had to be troubled. They didn't hit you or anything, did they?' I ask.

Angelina shakes her head. Angelina is not political as far as I know. In fact I realise I know very little about her. Her mother farms somewhere in the Transvaal, in an area called Hammanskraal. I would not blame either of them if they wanted to quit. Angelina could find other domestic work quite easily. But Isaac is young and relatively inexperienced, and I am not sure that a reference from me would be good news for him.

I feel a desperate need to know that they will continue working for me for the moment, particularly Angelina. The girls adore her, and with Nicholas's imminent return home I will need her more than ever before.

'Nina, Isaac, it's going to be really tough and I need you more than ever before. I'm sorry, and I will understand if you want to leave, but I just hope you'll stay and help me. Please . . .'

Angelina dismisses my question. 'Of course I will stay,' she says unhesitatingly. Isaac also nods his head in agreement. My relief is great.

I am feeling very lonely. My mother is not around. Betty, my sister, who would have been a pillar of strength, has moved five hundred miles away, to Umhlanga Rocks, near Durban. She is courageous and, unlike me, able to speak out and take on the world. I wish she were living round the corner still.

During the 1960 Emergency I learned a whole range of new 'skills': smuggling, saying one thing but meaning another, pretending I wasn't aching inside, I wasn't hurt and frightened. But I wonder if my apprenticeship equips me fully for the days ahead. The political climate now is very different to that of 1960. The government means business, and is hell-bent on eradicating any opposition by the foulest means possible. In the security force there is a completely new breed of men, young university graduates, bilingual and poised. They are no longer dominated by bumbling, clumsy people, and have ceased to make stupid, crass errors that have cost them their convictions in court. Our Security Police are quickly learning the art of torture, and how to be harbingers of fear. And the Ninety Day law has provided them with the means of circumventing the rules.

But if anybody can do anything in the face of all this, it is Jimmy. After all, he is friendly with the police. Jimmy has never even had a whiff of politics. It is totally outside his experience or interest. He seems untouchable, and immune to any intimidation. I go to his office.

He jokes and laughs. 'Well, what do you expect? If Harold insists on being a bloody Communist then he will get into trouble. He should expect to be arrested.'

'Listen, James, I'm really worried about Harold. I'm scared they will torture him.' 'Don't be ridiculous,' is his response. 'They wouldn't do a thing like that. Look, I'll phone Klindt – you know, the head of Security – now, and find out what you can do. You know I went with Harold to Marshall Square and he was fine?' He is trying to reassure me.

He dials, and soon he is speaking to Colonel Klindt. I can't believe it. 'Hi, it's James Kantor. How are things? Listen, man, there's some problems with the will.' I am stunned. Jimmy is handling Klindt's intimate affairs. He discusses various technicalities, then he moves on to the arrest of his brother-in-law. What I hear is not very encouraging. He cradles the phone and turns to me. 'You will be allowed to take Harold a change of clothing every evening and some food as well, and you will be allowed to bring home his dirty washing for laundering. He's also allowed a Bible. Klindt says that if you take one up to him at his office in Gray's Building he will see to it personally that Harold receives it. There's no chance at the moment of my being able to see him, Klindt is emphatic that he is being held under the 90 Day Act.'

At 7.30 that night I am armed with a basket of food – some sandwiches, fruit – and various toilet requisites, clean underwear, and a shirt.

This is very different from the days of the 1960 Emergency, when I would visit Harold in jail in Pretoria. Then he and the thirty-four others who had been held following the Sharpeville Massacre had been transferred to a communal cell in Pretoria. It sounded almost jolly. Because of the large numbers involved, I never felt alone or isolated. Those of us on the outside constituted an informal support group, particularly while we sat in the waiting-room before being called in for the brief visit. We would chatter away, exchange experiences, and compare notes, no different from any people who regularly visit jails.

This time I feel virtually on my own; there is every likelihood that not only people from the movement but erstwhile friends will steer clear of me. Indeed, nobody has contacted me today, nobody.

It is dark when I arrive at Marshall Square. This in itself sets it apart from 'normal' jail visits. Marshall Square jail is small, in the heart of big office blocks which house the financial and business world of Johannesburg. At five o'clock, when the offices close and the high-heeled secretaries take to the street, followed by the black 'office boys', this part of town empties. It is unwelcoming, even frightening. The only lights that show are the braziers of the nightwatchmen.

There is a large old-fashioned bell at the side of the large studded wooden doors with big black bolts. It is like ringing the front-door bell of a stately home, not a jail. When the doors swing open I am confronted by a young warder who looks at me questioningly, and asks in Afrikaans what I want. I cannot summon the right words, and in my most Anglicised English accent I say, 'I have been told that I may bring some food and clothing for my husband. He's being held here under the Ninety Day law.' I can hear my voice ring out; it seems too loud for the occasion, but I have no control over it. 'My husband is Harold Wolpe.'

I feel quite shaky and powerless, but I do not want any warder to see it. I am told to come inside and directed to a small room with several warders sitting around. The warders are all Afrikaners. In my formative years I never mixed with any Afrikaners. The only ones I ever knew were the cases I had in my student days as a trainee social worker. A fifth of all Afrikaners were classified as 'poor whites' thirty years ago. The effects of their eviction from farms, the burning of farms by the British during the Anglo–Boer War, the sustained drought from 1903 to 1908 had all contributed to the creation of a demoralised, impoverished group of people, riven with social problems. The police force and the prison force, though ill-paid, always

ABOVE *Polly, my mother, with my brother Jimmy, my sister Betty and me in the foreground around 1934.*

LEFT *My father – Hooks – was always debonair. This was taken in 1935.*

BELOW *Our conventional wedding in 1955. I'm intrigued to see I even wore long gloves. My dress though was a pale grey number.*

ABOVE *A rare family photo of all the Wolpe family. Harold with his father, mother, brother Joe (who's lived in America since 1959) Mickey and Margery, in 1963.*

BELOW *Angelina and Tessa at six months.*

ABOVE *Tessa sitting on my lap, taken on a weekend at Jimmy's Hartbeespoort Dam retreat, 1960.*

ABOVE *Harold in 1963, just before Nicholas was born and a few months before he was arrested.*

BELOW *An obliging policeman captured the moment of the 'braaivleis' close to the border while waiting for the police interrogation.*

Daily

Registered at G.P.O. as a Newspaper
Established 1902

JOHANNESBUR

**THEY ARE
STILL ON
THE RUN**

ARTHUR GOLD-
REICH—5 ft. 10 in.
tall, has thick black
hair, is slightly built,
walks with a mild
stoop, had a full
black beard. Aged 33.

M
5
a
th
is

ESCAPE: PO

90-

at

W

POLICEMEN
the sensati
detainees fled.
there had beer

Threater

but not

by poli

—Mrs. W

Staff Reporte

IN a statement mad
Wolpe after her n
night she said there
a misunderstanding

ADDULHAI JASSAT — 5 ft. 7 in. tall, very slightly built and has a light complexion and long black hair. Aged 27.

HAROLD WOLPE — 6 ft. tall, has natural black hair, which is discoloured slightly red (he dyed it earlier), and a prominent nose. He is aged 36.

CEMEN HELD

men still
ge; Mrs.
is freed

ME REPORTER

d for questioning in connection with Square escape in which four 90-day ers declined last night to say whether

hroughout yesterday senior police officers arefully investigating every aspect of the which was obviously well-planned and to the minute. The theory of an impulsive has been ruled out.

Maj.-Gen. R. J. van den Bergh, chief of the .D., said that the escape was considered in an remely serious light and that a full inquiry uld be held. Police believe that the escapers y have had negotiations with outside contacts r some time.

e missing men are Arthur Goldreich, a Johannestist, who was held with 17 others in last month's swoop; Mosie Moolla, chairman of the Transvaal Youth Congress; Harold Wolpe, an attorney; and ai Jassat, a member of the Transvaal Indian Youth ss.

The day after the escape the paper published descriptions of the men on the run and showed me after my ordeal.

A happy reunion for Mrs. Anne Marie Wolpe and her baby son Nicholas, who lingered between life and death for seven weeks while Johannesburg doctors using a new respiratory unit battled to keep him alive by letting the machine breathe for him.

LEFT *The photo Harold regarded as his talisman and kept in his breast pocket throughout his time in jail and during the escape.*

BELOW LEFT *Harold photographed in his ' jail' in Francistown soon after his arrival. He looks so different without his beard.*

BELOW RIGHT *Arthur, also clean-shaven in Francistown.*

ABOVE *Harold in jocular mood with Nicholas in our kitchen in London in 1988.*

ABOVE RIGHT *Peta with her daughter Alicia born in June 1993.*

RIGHT *Tessa with her adored nephew Jonathan in November 1993.*

BELOW *A farewell for Peta and Tessa in our South African home in 1993 with all of us together.*

ABOVE *Me in July 1993 in London, thirty years after our escape, taken by Tessa in her garden.*

LEFT *Harold in February 1993 not all that far from our home in Cape Town. A magnificent view of the drive to Chapman's Peak.*

provided a source of employment to their descendants. Not surprisingly, these men are crude and rough.

They say they must look at what I have in the basket, because the prisoners aren't allowed anything but some food and clothing. I watch as they move the food around in a somewhat perfunctory way.

'Sit down here, lady,' says one of them, named Piet, 'and wait while we take this to him and bring back any dirty washing that he might have for you.' He laughs as though he has cracked a joke. I smile back politely.

Two men remain behind. I am subjected to the gaze of the predatory male. Apart from my obvious difference to the more usual jail visitor, who does not tend to be white, English-speaking and middle-class, I am female and well shaped. I am examined from top to toe in a way that leaves me feeling uneasy. I feel sickened. I am vulnerable, and depend on the goodwill of these men to get food and clothing to my husband.

My husband's jailers represent for me the evil of this country. They are able to be brutal, they are able to order other men and women around, for one reason only – because they are white. Momentarily I wonder about my own racism, my anti-Afrikaner feelings.

Before too long Piet returns with a small bundle of clothes, and leaves them for me in the basket. 'Here you are, Mrs Wolpe,' he smiles, 'some dirty washing for you.' Again I smile politely, thank him and say good night. I am escorted to the big locked gates and let out.

The night air is cold, and I gasp slightly to catch my breath. I feel nauseated. My Beetle is parked outside the prison. It starts up quite easily in spite of the cold night, and I ease the car round the corner. A block on I stop in order to look back at the cell windows on the first floor and wonder whether Harold is in any of these, and whether he can see the car. I am overwhelmed by exhaustion and depression. Warm, salty tears begin to trickle down my cheeks. I do not cry easily.

Home again. The house is quite silent. Nina has seen to both girls, who are sleeping soundly. 'Anybody phone?' I ask her. No. I want to hear from somebody. I think that I had better not phone anyone myself – the phone could be tapped, and my call could put that person on the marked list.

So many questions race through my mind. Will all this have any effect on Nicholas? Gerson Katz is bound to read about Harold's arrest; how will he react? Will Marlene come and help look after Nicholas once he is discharged? And will Harold's family be any help to me?

I flop into bed, wondering what pattern my life will take now.

Marshall Square

HAROLD SAT huddled in the back seat of the car, which sped in convoy to Johannesburg. On the long drive from Rustenburg to Johannesburg he turned over and over in his mind the events of the past two days. There was a nagging feeling that somehow, something was not quite right.

Why, oh why had he given a false name and address? Mike and the others would surely have given his correct name, as they were questioned before him. It just demonstrated how exhausted and tense he must have been feeling. And should he have risked all, and jumped over the fence, and run for freedom in Bechuanaland? He kept returning to these two points over and over again.

The first stop was home in Maxie Street. They arrived to a 'welcoming committee': three police cars outside and, inside, the small house was ablaze with activity. It all seemed so out of place in the quiet street.

Angelina's solid, tranquil presence gave Harold some solace. She stood in the kitchen with her arms folded over her ample bosom, waiting and watching. While he sat in the dining-room the police searched, looking frantically for evidence of his treachery. They even scrutinised the blotting paper. The phone didn't stop ringing. It was members of the Special Branch conferring with each other. After two hours they tired, allowing Harold to pack a small suitcase, and off they went to the sixth floor of the Gray's Building, the Special Branch headquarters.

Harold had been a fairly frequent visitor there in the course of acting on behalf of various political activists. Now he was there in a totally different capacity. He didn't like it at all. Like a common criminal, his fingerprints were taken and then he was led to a small office, where he was asked again what he had been doing near the border. There was a buzz of excitement, so different from the last time he had been there.

Detective Sergeant Dirker renewed his delight at the reversal of fortune. He could gloat again over Harold's detention. Dirker was a big, heavy man, ponderous in mind and body, and he relished this moment. He kept calling out for others to come and see his prized charge.

There was a continuous flow of Special Branch men, most of whom Harold already knew. He began to feel very angry, but he could do nothing. He felt dirty, dishevelled and ridiculous. Dirker prodded him yet again: 'Herold, I'm telling you, man. I'm investigating a very big case, and I'm warning you: if I find anything against you, you'll be for it.'

It was with some relief that Harold was escorted out of the building to go to his office. They drove past the barristers' chambers, the Supreme Court, the Carlton Hotel and the Coliseum Theatre. He tried to fix these images in his mind, wondering when next he would see these sights again. He looked with envy at the crowds of shoppers.

The receptionist didn't recognise him as he walked into the office. The police made it clear that no one was to talk to Harold. Jimmy, of course, ignored this. With his usual charm and aplomb, he said there were a number of cases which Harold was handling and they had to go through them. There were no objections. Jimmy had a way with the police. With all the files in front of them, Jimmy was able to pass Harold a note: 'The police believe you fled 'cos you'd discovered they intended to put you under house arrest.' Jimmy's source was likely to be impeccable. It must have been Colonel Klindt himself. This was good news, at least until the police were able to link some of the documents from Rivonia with his handwriting. Harold's spirits lifted momentarily.

The police continued their search. They confiscated a mass of material – some of no more than historical interest, like the file relating to his detention during the 1960 Emergency. He had amassed a motley collection of memorabilia: petitions to the Supreme Court, limericks, poems, plays, placards advertising their dramatic productions and a diary of events of the period in jail in Pretoria. He also had records relating to Nelson Mandela's latest trial and imprisonment.

The next stop was Marshall Square. Harold knew the place well; he had often had to arrange bail for clients being held there. As he was brought into the charge office, there was no immediate recognition of him by the desk sergeant. As Dirker spat the name out, the desk sergeant looked up, amazement on his face. 'Hell man, Mr Wolpe. I didn't recognise you.' Harold gave a wan smile. In a way this man's response was oddly reassuring; there was no hostility – just incredulity.

Harold was stripped of his tie and belt. His watch was still pushed up his sleeve. At least he had that, he thought. He was escorted to a cell after being told gleefully by Dirker that he was being held under the 'No-Trial Act'. The cell was small: only eight feet by ten feet with a high barred window that he could not even reach or look out of. The heavy cell door banged closed. As it shut, the darkness overwhelmed him. The ensuing silence shocked him into a realisation of the hopelessness of his position – the virtual certainty that he would face trial with the people arrested at Rivonia and that, like them, he would be sentenced to life imprisonment or to death.

There was a pile of blankets in the corner of the cell. It was now ice-cold, and dark in the early winter's evening. There wasn't even the narrow cot of a bed he had assumed was regulation furniture. Exhausted, he spread several blankets on the floor, covered himself with some from the pile, and made a pillow out of two or three of them. He lay there completely numb. He was too tired to mind that the blankets were filthy, stank of stale perspiration and fear, and were stained with the semen from previous occupants' attempts at poor comfort.

He dozed fitfully. He turned over on his back and looked at the bare bulb hanging from the central point in the ceiling. The light wasn't bright at all – probably only a 40-watt bulb, he thought. But then he did not anticipate being able to do much reading there. This was not going to be like the days of the 1960 Emergency, when thirty-five white men had all been locked up together in Pretoria Central, where they shared a large dormitory. They set up an entertainment committee, and their days were fully occupied. There was an extraordinary range of people with extraordinary talents. They held political discussions, they had classes on literary criticism, on archaeology, on political analysis. Whatever expertise any one person had was fed into the group. Vincent Schwartz was one of the prisoners. It was years since Vincent had been politically involved. His former association with the ultra-left Democrat of Content was sufficient grounds for him to be included in the wide sweep that had characterised the government's panic reaction to the intense disquiet following the Sharpeville Massacre. Vincent was a poet. In Pretoria Central he lectured on Dylan Thomas. He read his own poems. And he drank endless cups of coffee. Even now Harold chuckled silently to himself as he thought about the limerick Vincent wrote at the end of their hunger strike.

> There was a young man called Vincent
> Whose thoughts were all towards democracy bent
> When at the last he broke his great fast
> It was for democracy of course not the content.

They were able to cook their own meals. Monty Berman and Percy Cohen were reputed to be good cooks, and these two men were in charge of the evening meals. Requests would go out for particular foods. He even recalled how he had asked for Calamata olives.

His reveries were suddenly interrupted by the clinking sound of keys, a sound he was to become very familiar with. The cell door was flung open. There were three uniformed policemen crowding in the opening. One was a constable, the second the commandant of the prison and the third, judging from his uniform and the scarlet band around his cap, a high-ranking officer. The latter glanced round the cell, and then addressed Harold.

'Everything OK, Mr Wolpe? Do you have any complaints?' That was pitiably laughable. 'I want to be moved. This cell is far too small. I want one with a bed and I want a cell with toilet facilities.' He knew his rights, and his previous stint in jail had alerted him to the improvements that calls for better conditions could achieve. The police left.

It must be quite late now. The afternoon light had faded. Surreptitiously he glanced at his watch: 5.30. He began to feel some pangs of hunger. His cell door swung open and a tin plate, covered in a layer of dried grease, a potato, boiled cabbage and the tiniest morsel of gristly meat, was thrust into his hands. There was only a tin spoon. No other cutlery. He couldn't eat.

A little later the first contact with the outside world occurred. A basket of food and clean clothing was brought to the cell. He eagerly opened up the food parcels, wondering why on earth they were wrapped in newspaper. Then it clicked: some precious reading material, and even a stump of a pencil. He scrabbled through everything, hoping for a written message. There was nothing. He ate the food hungrily, and realised that he was indeed famished. The smell of the home-made meat balls set his saliva glands working. He ate the meat and the salad with relish. He even ate an orange, and found that he enjoyed that as well. He realised that it was the first time he had eaten in days.

His sleep was restless. Over and over again in the wakeful periods he tried to recall what incriminating evidence against himself would be found at Rivonia. There were the maps he had worked on. Those would have his fingerprints on, so would the Roneoing machine. He had negotiated the purchase of Rivonia. Worst of all was the draft for disciplinary code for guerrillas which was in his handwriting.

Early the next morning, black coffee and a slice of dry bread were brought to the cell by a warder who refused to engage in any conversation. Prison routine was beginning: breakfast at 5.30, lunch would be at 11.30 and supper at 5.30, if one could use these terms to describe the food that was doled out. He peed into the bucket that stood in the corner, washed his face using the bowl filled with cold water that stood on the table and shaved.

There was nothing to do. He paced up and down. Up and down. Who the hell was singing 'Poor Old Joe' and 'Swanee River' so badly? he wondered. An old meths drinker, most probably. He felt distressingly lonely. In the past he had occasionally taken off and gone away for a weekend on his own. He would go to a mediocre hotel in Warmbaths in the Transvaal and luxuriate in the solitariness, just reading a novel, basking in the sun and talking to no one apart from the waiters at mealtimes. This solitariness was quite different. The mind had to function within its own self. No outside stimuli, minimal human contact. Solitary confinement was a highly effective technique for breaking the soul.

He tried looking out of the window. That was no good; it was too high. He tried to visualise what he would do day after day. There was nothing to do. He was bound to think of all his past mistakes, lost opportunities. It was almost impossible to conjecture how anyone handled solitary confinement. Did he have sufficient inner resources to withstand that, and the police questioning? He recognised the dangers involved in answering any questions, and knew that that was to be avoided at all costs. But what would it be like? Would he eventually welcome the human contact with the police? That, too, could happen.

That day he heard nothing, saw no one, and could not even eat.

Later – it must have been about 3.30 p.m. – there was a sound of keys, a clanking, and his cell door opened. He was told by a black warder that he was being moved to another cell. He was led to the next floor, to what appeared a luxury suite by comparison: a large room about twenty-two feet by eighteen. There was a bench beneath a barred window through which he could see the world outside. There was an office block opposite, and if he turned his neck he could just see a typist sitting near a window. He even had his own *en suite* bathroom! Partitioned off from the room by a low wall was a toilet. Even though it had no seat, and the bowl was heavily stained, it was a vast improvement on a bucket. There was a shower – cold water, of course – and a small hand basin. The toilet had a cistern high on the wall, and a chain for flushing it. There was another window just to the side of this. The room was painted in regulation grey, and the names and dates of previous occupants bore testimony to their stay. No other graffiti.

He felt a little better here. At least he could see outside and it was not as claustrophobic as the first cell had been. His thoughts were interrupted by the unexpected silent appearance of a large and handsome black warder. He was at least six feet tall, with a smooth, unlined, golden-coloured skin that seemed to gleam in the dull light. The man held a packet of cigarettes and a few matches in his outstretched hand. Harold could not believe it. 'They're for you,' the stranger said. 'They've been sent to you from some other prisoners.' He added a cautionary note that Harold should hide them somewhere so that the other warders would not see them.

As silently as the man had appeared, so he disappeared. The cell door closed again. Harold felt his spirits mounting for the first time. He lit the cigarette, and drew deeply and with immense pleasure. He had not smoked for more than a day, and as the tobacco smoke filled his lungs he could feel the heady, pleasurable tingling sensation as it coursed through his veins.

He knew then that it would be only a matter of time before he would communicate somehow with the other political detainees. As he did not know what to expect from the interrogation that was bound to come, it would help if he was somehow able to make contact with Arthur and find out what he had said.

He carefully flicked the ash into the palm of his hand, not minding the slight burn. He would have to be careful not to leave any telltale trace of the illicit cigarette; he didn't want them confiscated and didn't want to be subjected to any interrogation about how he had acquired them. He cherished every puff, and then suddenly thought he had better not smoke the whole thing – he would have to ration them. But he thought that he would give way this once and treat this first cigarette as some form of reward – no, hardly a reward, maybe as something to compensate for the nightmare of the past few days. Only seven days had passed since the Rivonia arrests, and two days since his abortive attempt to leave the country.

Where best to hide the precious cigarettes and matches? He paced round the cell, examined the lavatory, hand basin and shower. He found that he would wedge them into the space between the cistern and the wall.

A food parcel arrived yet again, this time accompanied by a Bible. He realised that this was to become a routine event – food and clean clothing, something to look forward to. And the Bible would at least provide some reading material.

His appetite did not match the previous evening's. He forced himself to swallow some food. The rest could be taken to the black prisoners, who were unlikely to receive food parcels. There seemed nothing else to do but try to sleep, although he thought there was little chance. The cell door opened again. This time it was much quieter than before. The same black warder stood there and beckoned to Harold. Harold followed him, puzzled.

In the corridor, just outside the cell, stood Arthur, and beyond an iron grille gate stood Abdullah Jassat, Mosie Moola and Chiba. He hadn't seen Abdullah and Mosie since he had appeared for them shortly after Nicholas's birth, when their charge under the Sabotage Act had been withdrawn. They had immediately been rearrested, and were now held under the Ninety Day Act. Chiba, similarly, was being held in solitary.

Harold was stunned. Arthur looked equally shocked. 'My God, it's you, Harold! What the hell are you doing here? I thought you'd be on the other side of the border by now,' he whispered. The two men embraced each other.

Mosie beckoned Harold closer to the grille. 'Gee, I can't believe it's you. Yesterday I heard the steps and lay down on the floor of my cell. If I do that I can just see under the crack of the door to the staircase. I saw this red-haired man coming up between the two cops. Hell, man, I couldn't recognise you. Last night I asked the others if they knew anyone with red hair, clean-shaven and wearing glasses.'

Harold's reply was brief and to the point: 'I was caught trying to get across the border near Zeerust. We drove straight into a bloody border guard. My bloody luck!' He barely paused before he asked, 'But you guys, what plans have you got for an escape?'

Abdullah said, 'We've been thinking about it, you know. It's helluva difficult.'

Mosie said, 'Although we've been talking about it a lot, so far we haven't come up with anything.'

They stood there talking to each other for a full thirty minutes. Harold learned that not only could he get cigarettes for a small offer of some money to the warders, but that it was possible for the three Indians to get out of their cells.

Chiba explained it all to him: 'You know we're not like you chaps. We've got to call for the warder if we want to go to the lavatory. The cell doors have locks on the outside. So when one of us gets taken down to the lavatory we can just slip the cell door open of one of the others. It's easy. You can't notice it at all. From the outside it looks locked. Anybody walking past the corridor and looking in couldn't tell that the cell wasn't securely locked. Anyway, they're not that careful. You know they can be quite lazy. If they hear us bang the cell door after they've escorted us back to our section and they've locked the dividing iron grille gates, then they're not bothered. So whoever's door's been unlocked can open up and let the others out. It's amazing, man. You could do the same with Arthur's cell.'

Harold was anxious to try it out. It worked. With just a flick, the catch on the cell door could be released. At the slightest sound of footsteps, he and Arthur could be back in their own cells in a moment.

'You must be careful, man,' warned Arthur. This little bit of freedom could not be jeopardised by carelessness. 'Sometimes the others have done this in the daytime, but you've got to listen carefully. Luckily the Special Branch always ring three times. If that happens, man, you'd better move like hell. We don't want to be caught.'

Their meeting terminated all too soon. The black warder came up and cautioned them: 'You'd better get back into your cells now.' Harold returned to his cell; his spirits were lifted. At least he wasn't on his own. His thoughts turned to escape.

Basically, there were only three chances. The first was to bribe one or more warders to let them have the keys, and either have duplicates made or simply utilise them in a walk-out. The second was to shoot their way out. They would have to get some guns. But none of them knew the first thing about guns, and even if they did, how could they get hold of one? This option sent shivers down Harold's spine. He was not an aggressive or a violent man. He had had his share of fights as a boy and a youth, but violence was anathema to him. The third possibility was the oldest one of all: to cut their way out of their cells. It would take ingenuity, determination and time. Time and determination were certainly resources they all had.

The next day Harold interrupted his pacing and stood at the window next to the toilet. He discovered that if he twisted his neck he could just see a little courtyard below. It was on the third day that he realised that there was a woman there. It was Hazel, Arthur's wife, detained at the same time as the others. She was totally isolated. There were no other white women in the jail.

The window was covered with a fine mesh which had been broken away in several places. Harold discovered that he could just get two or three fingers into the hole. By coughing loudly and wiggling his fingers, he finally caught her attention. For both of them it was a wonderful moment.

'Hazel, can you hear me?' he said, in a soft, low voice. She responded immediately. They did not dare talk for long, just long enough to bolster each other's morale. He realised how Hazel must be fretting over her arrest and worrying about her children. Her mother worked full-time, and could not help out there. 'Doreen is helping, I know. The last I heard the boys were fine and Doreen was being wonderful,' Harold was able to tell her. Harold hardly knew Arthur's sister. He had heard that she had stepped in and taken Arthur and Hazel's sons to live with her and her family. From then on Harold and Hazel spoke every day. 'You know that Arthur and I are able to talk as well,' Hazel told him. That was to prove very useful in the future.

Harold now had contact with Hazel, Arthur, Mosie, Abdullah and Chiba. There was a glimmer of hope. And what was even better was the newspaper picture of Nicholas's homecoming that arrived that night in the foodbasket. He gasped with delight at the sight of Nicholas being held. He sat for a long time gazing at the picture, and did not stop the flow of tears. Solemnly he held the picture up and folded it carefully, putting it into the pocket of his shirt. Each night he would ceremoniously put the picture next to his bed, and each morning he placed it in his pocket. It was his talisman, a symbol of hope.

Prisons, like hospitals, schools, the army and factories, are designed to regularise and control every movement of the inmates, throughout every moment of the day. Harold could soon tell the time of day according to the mealtimes, exercise time, lights out. He would be awakened at 5.30 in the morning with a boiled egg, some bread and what passed for coffee. He didn't eat. Instead he would get up slowly, do some stretching exercises, though not for long because it was rather cold. Next he would shower. Even though the water was exceedingly cold, it was invigorating. He would wash painstakingly and meticulously, making sure that no part of his body was overlooked. After rubbing himself dry he would, with care and precision, fold the towel and hang it up. It had to hang smoothly, the ends meeting each other exactly. Next was the shave. Not a bristle of hair was to remain on his cheek or chin. He would stop and touch his face lightly. The slightest trace of a hair was sufficient cause to start all over again. He hadn't shaved for years, and certainly he had never taken this amount of trouble when he had been clean shaven. The battery shaver would start whirring. It was a welcome noise. The towel would have to be refolded. The last chore would be to clean the hand basin thoroughly.

The bed. This could really be strung out because the sheets had to be folded exactly right so that not a crease or a wrinkle could be seen. There were the corners. If you folded the bottom sheet in and then held the side part up in the air with one hand, you could then slip your free hand under the corner and tuck that in neatly. The piece of sheeting that had been held up on high was carefully folded over, and – great, it looked just like the professionally made hospital bed he had looked at so many times during Nicholas's illness.

The morning routine took him at least fifty-five minutes.

Breakfast followed. This consisted of various items that had been brought in the previous evening, which he would chew very slowly, prolonging the meal. He would ceremoniously drink the coffee from a Thermos flask. Whatever was left over would be packed away in neat little parcels, every last little crumb cleared away. Then came the ritual of washing the breakfast dishes. It was only a tin plate, a tin spoon and a metal mug. That chore was done in the same slow-motion movement that characterised the others.

The climax of the morning meal would be a cigarette taken down from its hiding place. He would pace up and down, smoking.

The hamper of food was the lifeline with the outside world. It was home-cooked food: fruit, bread, and something to drink in a Thermos. He would scan the newspaper in which so many items were packed for snippets of news or the bridge puzzles.

Eleven o'clock was exercise time. For half an hour he would be accompanied by the warder on duty in the courtyard which was surrounded on the one side by the walls of the prison cells and on the other sides by thirty-to-thirty-five-foot walls, covered with barbed-wire netting.

He could look up at the secretaries perched on their typing chairs, bashing away at the typewriters. 'Are you never curious?' he would muse. 'Do you never wonder who it is walking round and round? How can you resist a little peek at these people?' But they never seemed to move. He walked up and down, up and down. How many times did he do this in his precious half hour? What distance did he cover each day? He knew that it was not difficult to calculate the distance. He preferred to delay doing so, because then there would be something to do tomorrow or the next day. And he could talk to the warder who walked up and down by his side when he exercised. 'Have you had any prisoners who tried to escape?' he would ask casually. He was told with great feeling that that chap Van Niekerk had tried to cut his way out of the cell. 'That must have made a helluva noise?' came the next innocent question. 'Ag no, man,' the naive warder replied. 'It's easy, you know. All you have to do is put dry soap on the blade and that cuts down the noise a helluva lot.' What were the procedures adopted by the warders to secure the jail? What type of locks were used? What is the layout of the jail? How secure is the quadrangle where the police park their cars? Only once was his walk spoiled by the sudden appearance of Dirker who spat out at the warder: 'Is it safe to leave him here just with you? You must make bloody sure that he doesn't escape.'

Every day he added to his little treasure trove. The yard seemed to be strewn with straightened paper clips. Like a hamster, he picked these up and carefully stored them on the windowsill, thinking: You never know when they could be useful.

After exercise he was confined to his cell. The tedium of the hours was broken by the delivery of the prison food during the day and the hamper at night.

While he paced up and down, he would try to recite some of his favourite monologues from Shakespeare. 'Damn it! I've gone and forgotten that bloody line,' and he would curse himself for the lost hours of schooling when he was playing football instead of memorising chunks of poetry or prose from Shakespeare. He even tried to sing. He was particularly fond of the songs Eli Weinberg, an old comrade, had sung with such gusto on their walking holidays through Basutoland, which had become the firm favourites of the detainees in 1960. He was too shy to sing out loud, even in the solitude of his cell. His teacher had triumphantly humiliated him when he was only eight. 'There's somebody quite, quite out of tune,' she thundered to the whole class, 'and whoever it is will ruin our summer concert. Continue singing, children,' she instructed the class, and marched between the rows of children until she came to Harold. She stood for a while, then her voice rose by several pitches in her excitement at discovering the culprit. He wanted to shrivel up and be swallowed by the floorboards. Instead, he was instructed to mime to the music and not to utter a sound.

Every fifth day the bell at the entrance to the cell block would be rung three times, and shortly after this he would be visited by two members of the Security Police, who came to interrogate him. They were not heavy-handed – quite the contrary. Their routine never altered. 'What do you have to tell us?' Harold's reply was equally routine: 'About what?' They would say, 'You know, about subversive activities,' emphasising the *you*. He would then ask, 'What do you mean by subversive activities?' and they would say, 'You know what we mean by subversive activities.' Harold would slip into the role of interrogator, and they would respond. It would take them five to ten minutes to recognise what was happening, and they would stop. Every time they recorded: 'He has nothing to say.'

They were always pleasant and polite. There was no attempt at any form of intimidation.

The other regular visitor was the magistrate who, under the terms of the Act, was obliged to visit Ninety Day detainees in order to determine whether they had any complaints about their treatment. It was always the same magistrate, Mr Clarice, a short, bent, middle-aged man. For many years he had sat in the traffic courts listening day after day to drivers trying to defend and justify themselves for having parked too long in a parking lot or failing to keep within the speed limit, or committing some other traffic offence. This new task was promotion for him. Harold was taken to the office, where Mr Clarice sat and timidly asked if Harold had any complaints. Harold, like the other detainees, would say, 'Yes, I want to know why I'm being held here and why I'm in solitary confinement. I want to be able to have books; I want newspapers and a radio. Why am I being locked up without a formal charge being laid against me?'

It was Sunday, time for exercise. This time the warder on duty was young and inexperienced. Whether it was because it was Sunday or whether the warder preferred to be out in the sun, Harold didn't know, but the time stretched out. A full two hours was spent walking slowly round and round the perimeter of the exercise square. There were no young secretaries to distract them. Harold was able to keep up a constant chatter. 'Where do you come from?' was his opening ploy. The young man replied, 'My father has a small farm near Louis Trichardt, but things don't go too good for him.'

'Do you have to carry around all these keys all the time? It must be quite difficult to know what is what.' Harold's innocent comment led to a detailed discussion on which keys the warder had and what doors they opened. 'I've even got the key for the back door,' he boasted to Harold.

This was the kind of information Harold needed. Where did the back door lead? A few days later he learned that this back door led into a courtyard where the detectives' cars were parked. From there a gate led directly on to the street, and this gate was never locked.

That night the five of them were huddled together, Abdullah, Chiba and Mosie separated from Arthur and Harold by the barred iron gate. Harold said, 'I wonder if there is any chance of our getting hold of the keys.' He reported on the conversation he had had that morning. Unlocking themselves seemed the simplest solution. It meant getting the key from the warder in charge of the cells at night. With that, they could just open the door and walk out. Simple! But – and this was just one of the many buts – the warder would have to have the keys not only to the door which gave access to the cell block but also, presumably, to a back door which opened on to the yard where the detectives' cars were parked. There was no possibility of going out through the front door – they would have to pass the charge office. They needed to know more about the layout of the building, and what surveillance was maintained at the back. And they needed a friendly warder.

There was one possibility. His name was Greef. Mosie, Abdullah and Chiba had all struck up a close relationship with Greef. Greef was a young Afrikaner, only eighteen at the time. He had come from a small dorp in the Northern Transvaal. He had played with Indians as a child, had smoked his first cigarette with his Indian friends. He was an intensely physical man. He was very strong, and regaled the prisoners with stories of how he had successfully fought four or five other people simultaneously. He had two consuming passions: motorcars and girls. He really wanted little from life except to possess a car and have a girlfriend. He was warm and friendly.

This was his first job, and he couldn't understand why these men should be held in solitary confinement without any charge being brought against them. They didn't appear to have committed any crime: they hadn't stolen or cheated or beaten people up; they weren't bums who drank themselves into a state of insensibility. As far as he could make out, they were men who had ideas about the rights and wrongs of people, and he couldn't see why they should be locked up in what he considered inhumane conditions. He was not all that articulate, and found it difficult to express these thoughts: actions were easier for him; so at night he would unlock some of the men when things were very quiet, and let them meet and talk together. He even did this with some of the black prisoners, which – given his background – indicated a deep-seated sense of fair play which defied all the prejudices that seemed to characterise his people.

Greef was most friendly with Chiba, the oldest of the three Indians, who was able to converse easily with him. The two of them could sit together talking for hours. They would talk about the countryside, which they both knew well. Chiba would discuss the café owned by his uncle – the café which stayed open all hours of the day and night, and was the only place where the local farmers could be assured of getting credit and finding what they wanted. Greef knew it well.

If anyone could help, it was Greef. But Chiba ruled out any possibility of implicating him in any escape project.

'It's out of the question,' he said. 'We can't do anything that could harm Greef. He's too nice a guy to let him get into the shit. As long as I'm around, you're not going to do anything like that.'

'It's all very well for you,' Arthur tried to reason. 'You're just being held under the Ninety Day law. We,' he said, pointing to Harold, 'are going to be charged with treason. It's life, man, at best. Maybe even the death sentence.' Chiba would not budge from this position, no matter how hard Harold or Arthur argued to the contrary. 'There's no hope of our getting off,' Harold protested, lending his legal knowledge to their plea. 'No,' said Chiba. 'Involving Greef is out of the question.'

They had to think of another strategy. It would be weapons or cutting their way out. Either way, they needed contact with the outside world.

Harold sat on his bed. He paced up and down. He took out his white linen handkerchief to blow his nose. The cold weather made his nose run. At least he didn't have any hay fever. That was something to be thankful for. He turned the hanky over and over absentmindedly, running his fingers along the edge. 'Oh my God,' he said quietly. He had a potential solution. This was an inspiration. The handkerchief had a quarter-inch hem, one end of which was actually unstitched. Wasn't that the perfect place for hiding a note? Feverishly he got a piece of toilet paper, tore it very carefully into a small square so that there were no ragged edges, then folded it meticulously. With a certain amount of coaxing he could just get it into the seam of the hanky, and it didn't show. There was no telltale bulge. Oh, how ingenious! He was delighted. Now the question was how to convey this to the outside world.

Luck was on Harold's side.

On the fifth morning, he was taken down to the commandant's office. 'I'm sorry to tell you, Mr Wolpe, that your aunt was killed in a road accident yesterday,' said the commandant solemnly. 'Your brother-in-law, Mr Kantor, has pleaded on your behalf, and you'll be allowed to attend the funeral. Mind you, no monkey business. You'll be under strict guard.' Harold seldom saw his aunt, and his feelings of pity for her and her family were overtaken by jubilation at the prospect of getting out of Marshall Square. 'I've spoken to Mr Kantor about this,' the big man said, 'and told him to arrange for you to get a suit to wear for the occasion. You can't go to a funeral looking like that,' he added, eyeing Harold's appearance disparagingly.

Harold tried not to look exalted at this news. He tried to adopt the appropriate demeanour. It was hard to contain his excitement at making contact with the world outside.

The day arrived. His morning was fully taken up with the preparations for the afternoon's funeral. First he had to get the message written and inserted in the hanky for the night-time collection of dirty washing, then he had to put on his suit. He carefully prepared a small piece of paper, folded it painstakingly to see that it would fit into the space of the handkerchief seam, then pulled it out again. He was going to write the simplest of messages: 'Try to get a copy of *Macbeth* in for me. I need reading material desperately. Love you.' He needed to know that the system worked before he could trust himself to write anything about an escape attempt.

He dressed with even more care than usual. Still there were hours to wait. He paced up and down, up and down, waiting. Three rings heralded the arrival of the Special Branch. There were two of them, detailed to escort him to the Jewish cemetery.

I don't even mind being squashed between these men, he thought, as he revelled in the sight of a normal world outside prison. He looked hungrily at the life in the streets as they drove to the cemetery. The momentary respite disappeared on their arrival. He felt not only conspicuous, but unsure about how to behave. Flanked by the two policemen, he was acknowledged by some of his relatives, but nobody came up to him. How could they, when he was so obviously under guard?

The Funeral

NICHOLAS IS coming home today. My worst fears that Marlene would reject us and not return with him were unfounded. I had gone to the hospital fearful of the reception I would get from her and, indeed, from Gerson. Harold's arrest had been blazoned across the front pages of the newspapers. They had to have seen it. Marlene hadn't. Her impeccable smile did not alter when I told her about the events. 'I suppose you won't want to come back and nurse him now,' I said, and continued almost incoherently, words tumbling out one after the other, no break at all. Did she realise that we were undesirable people, and I could fully appreciate it if she changed her mind; the police are likely to keep me under surveillance; I don't want to jeopardise her position at all, and don't want to put her under any pressure at all about looking after Nicholas. I watched her perfectly made-up face, lipstick in place, hair neatly tied up in a French knot. Her smooth skin, lightly covered with panstick make-up. She laughed outright. 'What on earth have Harold's exploits to do with me?' was her response. 'You don't really think that I would desert him now, do you?' She smiled at the baby, who looked so different now. He was no longer attached to any machine or bottle. He looked like a normal baby.

I hugged her, and I felt tears welling up. I didn't want to cry. Gerson, on the other hand, looked absolutely shocked, and avoided discussing the matter with me beyond saying how dismayed he was.

Angelina has everything ready. Gerson is keen that Nicholas's recovery should be given some publicity, to inform the medical world of the possiblity of using a respirator on a tiny baby. The press is informed, and as Marlene and I arrive home, they are there. Pictures are taken.

It is so thrilling to see Nicholas looking normal. He is put in a pram outside in the sun for a while. Marlene takes his clothes off; and he kicks his legs and gurgles and laughs. My baby is laughing. My baby smiles. My baby is alive.

The next morning a picture of me holding Nicholas is there on the front page of the *Daily Mail*. Machine Saves Rand Baby's Life, is the caption. I must get a copy of this cutting into the prison for Harold. That night I don't beat about the bush. I don't cover any of his food with the clipping. I am direct: 'Our baby has been terribly ill,' and I tell the warders about the problems we have had. 'Look! He's home now, and I know that Harold would be thrilled to see that Nicholas is all right and looks so wonderful. Won't you give this to him when you take in his food?' I plead with them. Their response is wonderful: 'Ag yes, man, of course we will.' I could have hugged those jailers.

Marlene and I soon slip into an easy routine. Outside the hospital Marlene is very different. When no one is around she does not take any trouble with her appearance. She is anguished about her personal relations. She is in love with a doctor. He is Jewish, and will not commit himself to her. But she can't find a way of telling him to go to hell either. She has some simple rules in life. Never exert yourself unnecessarily is one of them. She leans up against the sink, taking the weight off her body as she cleans out Nicholas's bottles, to demonstrate her homespun philosophy to me.

The phone rings. It's Jimmy, who says, 'Harold's aunt died, did you know?' Of course there was no way of my hearing about such things. There's a note of triumph in his voice as he says, 'I've arranged for Harold to attend the funeral. At least you'll be able to see him.' I do not normally go to funerals – I find an excuse for not attending. My father's was the first I had been to. This is one funeral I look forward to. I have never met Harold's aunt, but nothing will keep me away.

It is a bright, crisp, typical Transvaal winter's day. There is a slight sting in the air. Transvaal winters are exceptional –

warm, dry, bright and cheerful. I put on a tan-coloured jersey suit; the jacket is a short box one with a large round collar, buttoned at the waist. The knee-length skirt is straight. I am really proud of it. It doesn't look at all home-made, I think. The wide collar was tailored, and I had even been careful with the finishing off. I am due to meet Jimmy and go with him to the cemetery. I can't face this ordeal on my own. 'Do you think everybody's going to stare at Harold and me? They'll probably try and avoid having anything to do with us,' I say to Jimmy in the car.

I shrink away from the two possible reactions: pity or ostracism. I can just imagine people muttering to each other: 'Do you see her? Poor woman! She's married to Harold – you know, Sarah's son, who has just been arrested trying to cross the border. He must be one of those Commies!'

We are early. I stand aside waiting for Harold's arrival, nodding to some people who look familiar. In my anxiety I recognise only immediate family: the other figures blend into a sea of faceless people. Harold's mother, Sarah, is standing next to his father, Michael. I have a typical daughter-in-law relationship with her, exacerbated by her increasing loss of short-term memory.

Harold suddenly appears, flanked on each side by a policeman. I am still surprised by his changed appearance: no beard, red hair. The policemen stick to him like two leeches as he goes to greet his parents. Harold's father doesn't recognise him at first. When he realises who it is, he starts to cry. His mother has no problem. Her short-term memory has disappeared, and the clean-shaven man with his light hair must have reminded her of a youthful Harold. She greets him, blissfully unaware of the trauma surrounding her youngest child.

Harold comes up to me. We can do no more than hug briefly, and then hold hands momentarily. The policemen act like a human barrier between us. I stand by, stiffly waiting for the ceremonial walk to the graveside to begin. This was to be a traditional burial. Neither Harold nor I can talk.

Then Jimmy, with a stroke of genius, manages to divert the attention of Harold's police escort. Without any warning he is walking between the two policemen. 'Have you ever been to a Jewish funeral before?' he begins. Then he launches into a detailed description of the customs. Harold and I find ourselves able to fall behind the three men as the funeral procession walks slowly to the graveside, while Jimmy retains their full attention.

Harold starts whispering urgently. There is no problem about anyone else hearing. The other people in the funeral procession seem to have shunned us completely.

'Listen carefully. I'm able to send messages to you at last. This is how I'll do it' – and he tells me of the system he has devised. There's no time for any explanations, and I can't even express my amazement. The important thing is that we will be able to communicate. He is anxious to hear how I am managing, how the children are, particularly Nicholas. 'That picture of you and Nicholas is wonderful. I never let it leave my body,' he says, patting his shirt pocket. This is so unlike him. 'I keep the picture in the front pocket of my shirt. It is so marvellous seeing Nicholas and how wonderful he looks. Some of the warders are OK, you know, and probably will let you send in a book for me.'

The policemen take up their position again. There is no more chance to talk. Too soon the whole ceremony is over, and Harold is whisked away. The community manages to ignore me.

That night I resume my usual jail-visiting routine. This time I hope to find a message. On my way home from Marshall Square I steer with one hand, fingering the seam of the handkerchief slowly and methodically. Sure enough, there's a slight bulge in one seam, away from the corner. I can't wait to get home to read the message. My heart pounds slightly.

Home again. I go straight to the bathroom and fling the washing down, closing the door as though I am going to use the toilet. I sit on the toilet seat with the handkerchief in my hand, and ease the note out. I straighten it out carefully, eagerly scanning the tiny writing. I don't know what to expect. Perhaps a love letter, a note to say how much he misses me and longs to be back. That is unlikely. Harold is not a demonstrative man, and finds expressing his emotions in such a way difficult, if not impossible. The request for Shakespeare's *Macbeth* makes me feel quite disappointed.

I flush the note down the toilet, postponing at the same time the thought of how to get books to him. I certainly won't tell Marlene about this new development. Instead I join her to catch up on the day's news. This is my other world, my real world, away from prison, jail, fear and anxiety. I barely see the girls, and the only time I am able to handle Nicholas myself is when he wakes for a bottle about two or three in the morning. I cherish this time. I slip quietly out of bed, trying not to disturb Marlene, and warm the bottle of milk. We share the big double bed, and she manages to sleep through Nicholas's waking for this feed. The night is mostly quite still and peaceful. I can play noiselessly with Nicholas. The light from the street lamp shining through the fanlight above the door leading to the strange little courtyard provides a soft glow, sufficient for my needs. It is the only time I experience any tranquillity; it is a gentle time when nothing matters except the needs and joy of the baby. I cannot credit the pleasure I get at being wakened at that hour of the morning! Just me and the baby. There is no one else who can get my attention, no one with whom I have to make conversation. No one. Just Nicholas and me. He is so good. Apart from the scars on his body and in his neck, there are no visible signs of any adverse effect of the trauma of the past two months. He is a living miracle, and delightful with it – smiling, gurgling, and quite contented.

With daylight, harsh realities return.

Tonight will be the testing time for my first serious attempt at smuggling. The basket is neatly packed with the clean laundry and the food parcel with *Macbeth* tucked away beneath the food. My note is brief. I feel absolutely restrained by the extraordinary limitation in space, and struggle to find just the right words to say that I am fine, the book is going in, the girls seem to be coping all right, Nicholas is making amazing progress. In the end I think: God damn it, it doesn't matter how I say it. I resort to key words and nothing else. There is no space to begin to say what I really feel – how betrayed I feel by my belief that we would be helped if anything befell us, how I hadn't really bargained for a life which involved smuggling things into jail, a life of being ostracised by family and friends alike, of being on my own. Even worse than that is the feeling that I really have no right to complain. Harold is in jail and I am free. Anyway, I never have doubts about helping him. It is quite simple. It is my duty.

I go to visit Di Schneier, one of my closest friends, who is due shortly to join her husband Felix in America, where he has an appointment at the prestigious Johns Hopkins University. When I arrive, she says, close to tears, 'Things are in a terrible mess.' I don't know whether she is referring to her departure, the Rivonia arrests, or the desolate state of her home.

She is finishing her packing, and has reached the stage where she is discarding things that won't fit into her suitcase. She carelessly flings on to the thick-piled bedroom carpet a voluminous black leather bag with a suede lining. I protest, tell her she is crazy to discard such a wonderful bag. 'Have it if you want,' she says. I don't need any persuasion.

'How are they?' she asks, referring to Harold and Arthur. 'Is there any news of them?' I can tell her nothing, and I stumble over my reply. 'Look,' she says, with an urgent tone in her voice, 'I've got £3,000 in trust. Jimmy is holding it for me. If you could use it to help Arthur or Harold, then you must do so. I will arrange to see Jimmy before I leave, and tell him that this is what I want.' I am overwhelmed at yet another example of her generosity, and thank her profusely. 'I can always tell Jimmy. You're too pressed for time now.' Her face darkens. 'My bloody relatives have given me a whole load of diamonds.' She laughs mirthlessly. 'Of course they're not for me. It's their way of smuggling money out of the country.' She is clearly contemptuous of them. We are interrupted by the children's return from the garden.

At eight that night I ring the old-fashioned bell at Marshall Square. My heart starts beating rapidly, and I wait for the big door to be opened, shaking slightly, not knowing what will happen if the book is confiscated. Would that land me in trouble?

I know the warder who opens up. It seems he is often on

night duty, a very young man for such a job. His name, I subsequently learned, is Greef. He is pleasant, and isn't part of the ribald male chatter that usually takes place with a group of warders. As I am escorted into the anteroom, I say casually, 'There's something special in there for him.' I am not sure whether he hears me or not. Is this a cue to which he will respond? I never did understand how this matter of signals works; is it better to be explicit, or do some words hold a key that is sufficiently lucid? I will soon know. The usual perfunctory search doesn't occur. Instead I am shown into another room. The young man says, somewhat curtly, 'Sit down here. And wait for his clothes. I'll bring the basket back with me.' The book remains at the bottom of the basket, which is whisked away, presumably *en route* to Harold! I cannot believe my luck, and relax my taut muscles as the warder disappears. I wait for the dirty washing, the Thermos flask and a container from the previous night's food to be returned to me. It's worked. If I wasn't feeling so drained by my tension, I would be jubiliant. I wonder what the next message will be.

There is no message the following night, or the night after.

On Sunday night there is another message. I can feel the tell tale bulge in the handkerchief. Tonight I'm not going home directly. I have arranged to meet Ruth Slovo for a showing by the film society after going to Marshall Square. She has managed to get a message to me, and we both acknowledge that this is a safe place for us to meet. The Special Branch are unlikely to keep watch on this cinema. This is an outing to which I have looked forward with great anticipation. I realise as I see Ruth in the foyer that I am going to touch normality tonight. 'Hang on a moment Ruth, I need to go to the loo,' I say cheerfully. I have the handkerchief securely in my pocket, and I don't let go of it for a moment.

It is getting to be a habit, I think, this sitting on a lavatory seat reading illicit messages. I flatten the small piece of paper carefully, wondering what Harold is going to ask of me this time. Surely not another Shakespeare! This time the writing is even more cramped and difficult to decipher. I read and reread it:

Contact D whose cousin
A will give you information
about gas guns we're going
to try and escape get as much
information as possible about
guns. This must be done quickly

There is no time to digest this. I have to get back to the foyer, smilingly responding to Ruth's questions about what has been happening, how Nicholas is, while my whole being is in a state of turmoil. I sit in the darkened cinema, my eyes focused unseeingly on the large screen. Even if my life depended on it, I could not have given a description of the film. This is my first intimation that Harold wants to escape. To do so using a gas gun sounds an utterly desperate measure. It is almost impossible to contemplate.

I can't think of anyone with the initial D. As the big figures on the screen go through various motions, and the sound crashes out, I go over and over all our friends, and then people who I think are in the 'movement'. The key to all is D. Without D I can't contact A. And there is the imperative about speed. And then my mind switches to their attempt to use a gun. A gas gun must be harmless, otherwise why suggest a gas gun? How can they blast their way out of a jail using a gas gun? I don't know that I want to be associated with anything as ghastly as this. It's one thing smuggling in a Shakespeare play, but quite another smuggling in a gun! Can I, in all conscience, do it? These questions race round and round, and each time I come back to who the mysterious D is.

Ruth and I part company outside the cinema. We haven't had much time to talk at all. She is clearly anxious about her own safety. I don't have the reserves to offer her much comfort. The future looks particularly bleak for her, but at least Joe is out of the country and she has parents who give her every support, particularly financial.

Luckily, Marlene is asleep when I get home. I lie in bed, staring out through the pane of glass at the top of the door, alternatively thinking what I will do if they do try to escape and who the mysterious D is. I pull the blanket tight round me for extra warmth. Sleep doesn't come. There is so much to think about.

Oh, how stupid! D is obviously Doreen, Arthur's sister. She isn't someone I know at all well, although she came to see me shortly after the arrests to talk about the Goldreichs' boys. She was worried about them. They had seen their parents arrested, and were very disturbed about everything that had happened. We had walked in the garden discussing this, and she said how frightened she was about the turn of events.

I must have slept after Nicholas's two o'clock feed. As soon as I am up, I phone Doreen. It's not long before she is with me, and we stroll in the garden away from Marlene's curiosity and any bugging devices. 'Listen, Dor, I've had a message from Harold asking me to contact your cousin to get some information from him. I haven't a clue who he is, except that his name begins with A. Apparently it's really urgent.'

She listens attentively, with her piercing dark eyes fastened on my face. She is a slight woman, even shorter than I am – and I'm only five foot three and a half – very attractive, with jet-black hair cut in a *gamin* style, and almost equally jet-black eyes. I notice lines of tension around her face. She tells me how I can contact A, and suggests I go to his home.

I have difficulty finding the house, missing the turning in my haste to get there, cursing my stupidity all the while. I am now overly cautious, and won't stop and ask anyone for directions. Then suddenly, there it is, and I'm driving up a long curved pebble-covered driveway. It breathes affluence. I experience doubt that someone living here will be prepared to help, particularly given the circumstances. The lawn looks manicured. Not a weed in sight. Although it's midwinter, there's a lot of colour in the garden. I catch myself thinking enviously of what such gardens signify: neat homes with husbands who provide the wherewithal for gracious living. The wives' problems probably centre on the children's progress and what to do on Saturday nights and whom to invite for a dinner party and what to cook and whether Sarah or Rebecca or Lucy is a good nanny and whether to have burglar-proofing put in and should we build a swimming pool or a tennis court.

The door is answered by A's wife. I never did find out her name. It is still relatively early in the morning, but her appearance matches the garden: every hair in place, and looking as though she has just stepped out of the hairdresser's. She is well-groomed down to her manicured red fingernails. No doubt she is one of those highly efficient housewives who know what to tell the servants to do, who supervise their work, and whose children don't leave their toys lying all over the house. I don't go beyond the front entrance hall, but I am sure it is well furnished. I can't acknowledge my jealousy of this type of living. I never have. I always dismiss people like this, partly out of envy.

I probably look tense as I say I need to contact A urgently. 'It has to do with Arthur, you see,' I add. I try not to sound too anxious. I watch her face as I talk, and there is no visible sign of any perturbation. Maybe she plays poker.

She seems to take it all in her stride, even such an odd request from a woman whom she has never met asking for a rendezvous with her husband. 'I think it is advisable to meet somewhere like Braamfontein,' I suggest to her. I am vague about why my home is not a good idea. I don't have to elaborate. She has clearly made the right connection. We agree that I will meet her husband in a small café in the heart of Braamfontein. 'I'll see to it that he is there at 3.30 this afternoon. I'll tell him what you look like.'

It really is becoming more and more like a B-movie. At 3.25 I'm sitting sipping coffee in a small coffee bar in Braamfontein. On one side is a bar with high stools; and opposite, against the wall, a row of small pub tables. The place is austere: no decorations, no pictures on the walls. A coffee house with no pretentions. I wait for the arrival of a complete stranger whose advice is likely to alter my life.

A man in his late thirties sits down next to me and smiles pleasantly, as though we know each other well. 'AnnMarie, isn't it?' he says. His voice is soft and low. 'A cappuccino,' he tells the person behind the bar. I have always enjoyed the dramatic, but this drama is almost more than even I can savour. I am frightened, yet at the same time part of me is fascinated by the cloak-and-dagger atmosphere. Each of us is talking out of the side of our mouth, not engaging in eye contact at all.

'I've had a message concerning Arthur, and a few others, about trying to get a gas gun in order to break their way out of Marshall Square.' I don't know how else to tackle the topic except by being totally direct. I have never been very good at subtleties.

A doesn't have the same composure as his wife. He looks startled. After the initial shock, he starts to talk about gas guns. 'Listen, I can make some enquiries about this, but I'm pretty sure that it won't work. I'll find out and meet you here the same time tomorrow afternoon.' I nod. 'I'll see you.' He rushes out after paying for both our coffees. I sit a while longer.

Home again, and I am able to spend some time with Peta and Tessa. Outwardly everything appears normal, as I play ball with the two girls on the lawn outside and Nanette goes crazy chasing after the ball, competing with them. Marlene now treats Nicholas as her own during the day, and I feel I have no part in his day-to-day care. He is being kept in isolation from his sisters to avoid picking up any infection from them.

Tonight I am due to meet Jimmy and Barbara for dinner at a Chinese restaurant, and at Jimmy's suggestion I will take in a Chinese meal, so I have no need to prepare anything for Harold at home.

The restaurant in Bree Street is relatively new, the decor is bright: chrome and plastic, with tables close together. Barbara is late, and Jimmy and I are having a desultory conversation. She sweeps in, looking more than usually glamorous. Her big grey-blue eyes are outlined with thick false eyelashes, her skin is smooth and skilfully made up, highlighting the contrast with the autumnal russet colour of her hair. Her blouse is open sufficiently to reveal the cleavage of her full breasts, her belt is drawn tight to emphasise the curved hips and the long legs in high heels adding to her height.

She has been at an advertising agency all day modelling, and clearly enjoys the attention she receives. She is conscious of the impression her late arrival creates, enjoying the admiring glances cast in her direction. She prattles on and on, seemingly unaware of my silence. I am intrigued with the false eyelashes, which I have never before seen at such close quarters. They seem to drag at her eyes, and I catch myself wondering how actresses cope with this appendage. Jimmy looks tired.

I decide that I should tell Jimmy that Harold has intimated that he wants to escape. Jimmy is quick to respond to my request to talk to him privately by an 'Oh, I've got something for you in the car. Come and collect it, otherwise I'm likely to drive off with it.' All ingenuous, yet when we got into the car he immediately turns on the radio at full blast to foil any attempt at bugging. Jimmy is clearly learning fast. There is no way of knowing how sophisticated the police have become or how widespread their techniques of surveillance are.

'James, Harold has been in contact with me and says that he is going to try and escape.' No details. Jimmy is quite taken aback. 'My God, he's crazy. He must stand his trial like a gentleman.'

I am stunned by his response. Does he really believe in the rule of law? Does he really feel that anyone who transgresses and is foolish enough to be caught should stand trial? Does he really not know just how vicious the state can be? I know that he has a streak of puritanism in him, and that he holds distinctly old-fashioned views that reflect more my father's generation than his own. Does he really think that political trials are conducted in a gentlemanly fashion, and that political prisoners will receive a fair hearing? Has he no idea of what has been going on? In 1961, when I was in London, Jimmy was there for a brief business visit, and we dined together with some mutual friends. He had joked then about his brother-in-law, the Communist. Later that night in the taxi I remonstrated with him, pointing out that there was an underground movement in South Africa, including the Communist Party, and that careless words could have serious implications for Harold. He seemed to listen to me then, just as he is listening to me now.

'You know if he escapes, or even tries to do so, you will land up in jail.' My God! I haven't thought about that at all. I have never considered the possibility of my becoming a victim as well. What would happen? What would happen to the children? The familiar feeling of tension mounting in my neck flows back, and I can feel my head throbbing. I decide then not to tell Jimmy anything more about any plans whatosever. If I could be arrested, then Jimmy's safety could also be in jeopardy if he knew anything. We go back into the restaurant, and Barbara continues to chat until I collect the food Jimmy has ordered for Harold.

I pull up in Fox Street, round the corner from the entrance of Marshall Square. I park the car and look up at what I believe to be Harold's cell window. The feeling of total desolation overwhelms me, and tears start coursing down my cheeks – not for long though. I have to go through the nightly ritual of getting the basket of food checked.

Yet another surprise: in place of the warders I have become accustomed to, a tall black guard with finely chiselled features curtly tells me to follow him. Down a dark passage painted in the regulation khaki colour of state institutions, past a cubicle where the young guard, Greef, is talking in soft earnest tones on the phone. He looks a little distressed – his chin is resting on his left hand and his voice sounds pleading as though he is talking to his girlfriend. Up a flight of stairs.

I cannot believe it. There at the top stand Harold and Arthur. How is this possible, if they are being held in solitary confinement? I hug them both quickly. I cannot even give Harold a special hug or kiss. The black guard moves discreetly to the side and says, 'You'll have to be quick. You can't have long up here.' I give him a weak smile, and turn back to the two men.

Our hurried exchange focuses on a gas gun. I have no time to explain the difficulties of trying to decipher the message. I have no time to find out how Harold is coping with his incarceration. I can only manage to say, 'Your cousin is not enthusiastic about a gas gun.' I can't think of any other word to describe his reaction that afternoon. Nor can I think of saying that I'm frankly terrified about all this. 'Gas guns,' I tell them, 'are extremely noisy, apparently. I'll have more information tomorrow.' I have no idea what a gas gun is or how it differs from ordinary guns. Are they big or small? Are they lethal? Can they kill? Or do they just knock people out for a short while?

I am begining to feel as if I'm playing a bit part as a gangster's moll in a Damon Runyon story. I want to talk about the 'bust-out'. I have no language that deals with this type of thing, and lapse into the American phrases that are typical of the thrillers I read. I have visions of the two shooting their way out and opening up the whole of Marshall Square and letting out hordes of black prisoners. As an afterthought I say, 'Oh, by the way, Di has left the country.' There is only one Di in our life, and we have watched her flirt with Arthur at parties. 'She told me that she has three thousand pounds in trust, and I can use it in any way I see fit if it helps either of you. It's with Jimmy.'

There isn't time for any conversation. What we say is hurried. 'Listen, Annie! Find out about blades. Try and get the strongest blades available and get them in to me,' says Harold, adding, 'Perhaps we'll have to try and cut our way out if we can't use a gun. Let me know. Say in your note tomorrow night that Peta isn't getting on well at school if the gun is no good. They'll never know.'

I feel momentary relief. Filing their way out of jail sounds infinitely preferable to shooting their way out. It sounds less hazardous. There are all sorts of questions I want to ask, but there is simply no time.

I promise to send a note the following night.

Our time together is over. The guard indicates that I had better leave. Another hug, down the stairs and out into the cold air. This time I find myself shaking. The surprise meeting has overwhelmed me completely. I cannot believe it yet. I also know I cannot tell anybody about this encounter. It would be too dangerous.

I go to my rendezvous with A in the same café the following afternoon. We meet as though we are old friends: broad smiles and a handgrip. This time we drop our conspiratorial air and try to give the impression of lovers meeting for a clandestine tryst, not plotters talking about the merits and demerits of gas

guns. A confirms what he thought yesterday: 'It's a hopeless
idea. The bloody things are noisy, they're dangerous and really
difficult to use. They wouldn't get very far with them.'

'Well, they've also suggested that they could try and file
their way out. File through cell bars,' I add lamely.

'Well, that's a different matter altogether. They would need
the strongest possible blades. It would have to be tungsten
blades,' he says. Ironic, I think – tungsten is the one mineral I
know something about, because my father had struggled to
make a success of a tungsten mine during the war years. A says
he will bring both a pair of cutters and some blades to the house
later, so that I can try and get them through to Harold and
Arthur as soon as possible. I don't discuss the mechanics of all
this with him at all. He clearly doesn't want to know any details,
and I equally clearly don't want to give him information.

A is really efficient. By the time I get home after doing
some shopping, Angelina tells me that someone has come to the
house with some things for me. She shows me a pair of steel
cutters and a whole load of blades. 'Marlene hasn't seen these,
has she?' I ask. Angelina shakes her head. There is not much
love lost between them. Marlene treats Angelina very much as
the servant who is to do her bidding, and will not let her
anywhere near Nicholas. Nor does Marlene come near the
kitchen, except for doing Nicholas's bottles at night.

There is not much I can do about disguising the cutters:
they are fairly large and have bright red handles. The only thing
I can think of is putting them in the cavity of a cooked chicken.
I rush out to buy a chicken, and ask Angelina to roast it. When
it is done, I carefully wipe the cutters to remove any trace of
fingerprints and stuff them into the bird. I do the same with
some of the tungsten blades. If there wasn't so much at stake, I
think I would laugh. I look at the ends of two bright red handles
sticking out two inches from the bird's backside clearly and
plainly for all to see. I wrap the chicken in several layers of
paper, each time making sure that there can be no fingerprints.
I'll send in the rest of the blades tomorrow night, if all goes
well. I have an excellent plan for them.

I have read enough thrillers to know that one needs some

alibi, and this applies to myself as well as to Angelina and Isaac. They have already been questioned by the Special Branch, and I don't want them put in a position of not knowing what to say should they ever have to answer questions about cutters and blades. 'Listen here. If anything happens to me, or you're asked about cutters and blades, you must say you haven't any idea. If you're shown them, say you don't know what they're for and you've never seen them before. If anything goes wrong, I'm going to say that somebody came round to the house today and left this chicken and bread here as a present for Harold. OK? You say nothing,' I emphasized.

They are remarkably relaxed about it all, and if they think it is at all odd, they give no indication. We are all learning quickly how to respond to these remarkable situations.

That night my visit to Marshall Square is filled with foreboding. Messages in handkerchiefs is one thing; a Shakespeare play another; but cutters and blades are of a totally different order. I can feel my heart racing as I ring the bell and wait, basket clutched tightly in my hand.

I have already had one bad experience a few days ago, when I had two books in the basket and an unknown warder opened up the gate. I couldn't risk taking the basket in. I smiled at him, said, 'Gosh, I am stupid – I've left something behind. So sorry, I'll be back in a minute', trying to sound flighty and little-girlish. I didn't dare try smuggling with a total stranger. Quickly I tossed the books out, and went back to the gate breathing more freely.

My luck is in: the tall black guard opens up. What immense relief. I babble on about how kind some people are and look – they brought me a whole chicken for Harold and isn't he lucky and he will really have a good dinner that night and I haven't had to cook at all. It all goes like clockwork. I wait and receive the usual dirty washing. I don't even bother to feel round the edges of the handkerchief on the way home as I drive. I don't much care. They have their cutters and some blades; the rest will follow tomorrow night.

By the time I get home, I am absolutely exhausted. I am not devious by nature. I don't take to such escapades. There is too much at stake. I can't even contemplate the dangers that all this holds for me. I don't even stop to question what I see as my duty to help Harold in whatever way I can. I am beginning to ache with fatigue. I have hardly seen the girls since Harold's arrest. I find myself longing to creep away quietly on my own, even find myself thinking that a spell in jail can't be such a bad thing. At least you don't have the incessant strain of running around! And then I realise that I am beginning to feel some anger and resentment.

Smuggling in the blades the next night is much easier. It was a Peter Sellers film, *Two-Way Stretch*, that inspired me. We saw it shortly after Harold's release from jail in 1960. Peter Sellers was always funny, his timing was perfect but it wasn't Peter Sellers who provided me with the answer for the smuggling. There was a scene involving a visit to some prisoners in jail. A big-busted blonde woman in a tight-fitting sweater and tight-fitting skirt, with exaggerated swaying hips, strolled into the visiting room in which the prisoners were separated from the visitors by a high wire fence. The blonde was the decoy. While the warders watched the woman, panting like randy dogs, the visitors threw a range of items over the wire fence. One of these was French bread stuffed with blades. Well, that is the perfect way to get the blades through to Harold and his friends: just stuff the bread full with blades. Hardly a problem, in comparison with the tension of getting the cutters in.

Plans Revisited

NONE OF the detainees had been particularly happy with the idea of a gas gun, but they felt it should be investigated. The news of its difficulties came as no big surprise. In any event, they had considered alternatives. They had already discussed cutting their way out. There were two possibilities – through either Arthur's or Harold's cell. Either way, this involved sawing through three steel bars and then a hazardous jump on to roofs which could result in their being seen. Or they could cut through the one bar in the passageway. There were disadvantages in working in the passage, mainly because of the noise, but this they decided to risk. Even if they succeeded in getting through, they still had other difficulties to face: they would have to jump over wire mesh and on to another roof. This seemed the easier of the two options, and Harold was determined to go ahead.

So the message had gone out for blades.

As he unpacked his food, Harold stepped back and let out a slow whistle. 'My God!' was all he could say when he saw the red handles sticking out of the chicken. He chuckled softly when some blades tumbled out when he withdrew the cutters. He even felt hungry in his anticipation of doing something concrete about getting out. For once he sat down and ate heartily. Normally he ate little of what was in the basket, sending the bulk of the food down for the black prisoners. That night was different.

Arthur and the others were jubilant when they met later. They began work immediately. It wasn't easy. They soon realised that it would take even longer than they had anticipated. The bar was thick and immensely hard. Nor could they risk cutting from the front in case a passing warder or even a policeman noticed the cut. It would have to be done from behind, and this meant that whoever was working at it would have to squat on a ledge, and put his arm through the bar. This reduced the amount of pressure that could be used. Neither Arthur nor Harold was particularly strong, and they found that their arms tired quite quickly.

The scraping sound seemed to reverberate through the corridor. Maybe if they whistled the grating noise would be masked. Contrary to what Harold had been told, soaping the blade and the iron bar didn't seem to reduce the noise at all. Although whistling was one of the forbidden activities, Arthur ignored the prohibition in an attempt to drown the noise. Harold couldn't whistle – he would sound like a cat's cacophony, which would surely bring Greef round to see what the trouble was. Every once in a while one of them would flush the toilet, again in an effort to muffle the sound.

Luckily, Greef spent a lot of time closeted in his little cubbyhole talking on the phone or listening to his radio. He did not seem to hear the noise.

After four hours of non-stop effort, little had been achieved: 10 for effort, 1 for attainment. One sixteenth-of-an-inch incision in the bar, which was three-quarters of an inch thick, was all they had to show for their labours, and several blades were blunted. This did not augur well for the future. Cutting their way out was going to be a very slow process.

'I reckon time is going to be against us,' Harold said gloomily, squatting on the cold floor. 'They're not likely to hold us here much longer. After all, it's really only a reception centre. They'll probably move us to the Fort or somewhere else in the country.'

That night, as they returned to their cells, their spirits drooped.

The next morning two Special Branch policemen arrived. Harold heard the bell ring three times. He knew what was in store for him. The questions were the same as they had been previously: 'We want to know about you and Communism.' 'What do you mean by Communism?' Harold turned the interrogation around. His interrogators became his witnesses on the stand. 'Ag, man Herold, stop asking us questions. You're here to tell us things, not ask them.' The questions would taper off, and then cease. 'You know, Wolpe' – sometimes it was Wolpe, sometimes it was Harold – 'you're going to stay here until we're satisfied that you've answered our questions satisfactorily.' There was no threat, no suggestion of any manhandling. The interrogation was quiet, and even civilised. It was a useless venture, and all three men knew it.

The usual distractions did not work for Harold that day. By nightfall he was overcome by a feeling of despair. He did not even open up his food parcel, and his lethargy was such that he also made no attempt to have the food taken down to the black prisoners. He and Arthur toiled again and again – the effort seemed fruitless.

He returned to his cell close on midnight. He sat disconsolately on his bed, the cell door firmly closed for the night. His stomach rumbled, and he realised he was hungry. He hadn't eaten since early afternoon, and then only a slice of bread and a cup of cold tea. He opened up the food parcel and perked up a bit when he saw a loaf of French bread. He tried to break off a piece. He held it firmly in his hand, but nothing happened. It was rock hard. He felt a rage well up inside. 'Why the hell can't she even see that the bread is fresh when she brings my food?' He stared angrily at the bread. Something wasn't quite right. His feeling of lethargy suddenly disappeared. Cautiously he managed to break the tip off the top. Then he saw something sticking through. It was a blade, and another and another. He pulled rather feverishly at the bread, thinking with horror what might have happened had he sent the food to the black prisoners. He felt cold all over at the thought. There were twenty blades in all. He would have to wait until the next night to tell Arthur. In the meantime, he hid them under the mattress.

They didn't talk much while they worked. Arthur's gift as a raconteur was dependent on his audience. He could keep everyone amused at a party, but he did not keep up light chatter in the jail. 'Do you think we should keep the blades and the cutter in the cell?' he asked, after a long silence. 'You never know. We might be searched, and then that would bugger up everything.' Harold agreed. He too had been thinking that he was chancing luck in keeping so much in the cell. 'What do you suggest, Arthur?'

They decided to put the blades and the cutter in the cell next to Arthur's which, they had discovered, only stored mattresses. Carefully they placed them under the last mattress but one in the pile. 'It looks quite safe,' Arthur commented. 'From the looks of things nobody's been here for a helluva time.'

Two more days of what was now beginning to look like fruitless activity, yet Harold still clutched at hopes of success. His pacing in the cell was disturbed by the sound of unusual activity in the corridor. He moved silently to the cell door, and with his eye at the peephole he saw, with horror, some warders going in and out of the next-door cell. Carrying some mattresses. Their supply of blades was at risk. It only needed a warder casually to lift the mattresses for the incriminating blades and cutter to clatter on to the floor. 'Oh shit! They'll find the bloody blades, and then we'll be searched.' He feared reprisals. Maybe no more food parcels, no clean clothing – this contact with the outside world, however slight, would be curtailed.

That night Harold learned that Arthur had seen the comings and goings too, and he admitted to experiencing the same chill of fear.

In the corridor on the wall opposite Harold's cell was a long old canvas fire hose which looked as though it had been there for decades and never ever been used. It fitted in with the stone and metal construction of the building. The hose was looped backwards and forwards in an S shape. Harold and Arthur agreed that this would make an ideal hiding place. They laid the blades in the folds of the canvas with ritualistic care. They were pleased with themselves but their pleasure was to be short-lived.

Harold's black mood surfaced again the next morning. He lay on his bed reading the Bible. It was the unexpurgated version that I had got for him. He was looking up all the references to sex in the index, but found that most of them were dreadfully uninteresting. His mind kept drifting back to the problem of cutting through that three-quarter-inch-thick steel bar. It can't be done, he had to admit to himself. We really will have to find some other solution. He drew a blank there – there seemed to be no other way out. Suddenly he became conscious of new sounds. He realised how sensitive one becomes to sounds in jail: normally he was far from observant, but in jail everything changes. He knew that this was related to the sensory deprivations of every kind: the absence of human conversation, the absence of different smells and the brown and grey of the building.

There were sounds of activity outside his cell. Once again he moved to the peephole. He was transfixed by what he saw. There were two white prison warders he recognised, kneeling on the concrete passage floor, next to a red wheel. A third man, an African labourer, was knocking a hole into the cell wall with a cold chisel. He realised, to his horror, that the wheel was the receptacle for a new fire hose, which would obviously be placed on the wall. What would happen when they removed the old hose and all those blades fell out? Not only goodbye to any chance of freedom but, more than likely, a massive search.

His first thought was to warn Arthur. Hazel could act as the go-between. On a small piece of paper he wrote a note telling her to warn Arthur about the fire hose, and he attached this to the chain of paper clips which he had so assiduously collected during exercise in the yard. He always knew they would come in useful one day. Through the cell window above his private 'lavatory' he could see Hazel sitting in a patch of sun in the small courtyard which seemed to be used exclusively by her. With the usual coughing and spluttering he managed to get her attention. He let down the note, carefully, through the break in the wire mesh.

His technique was successful. Hazel got the note, read it and then said, quite simply, 'He knows.' That night, if nothing untoward happened by then, they would have to consider what to do.

The next step was to safeguard his precious possessions: a small stump of a pencil, a blade, and matches. He carefully examined every aspect of the cell, fingering different places. Finally he selected a niche behind the broken mesh in the window. He could just manage to get his fingers through the mesh and put his belongings there. The books were hidden behind the lavatory cistern. There was a hollowed-out place into which they fitted quite snugly. Maybe previous occupants had also had similar problems. It is surprising just how inventive one can be. And as for the cigarettes, those slotted into the broken part of the framework of the window. He worked quite feverishly, becoming conscious of his own breathing.

There was no search. Nor was there any further activity outside his cell after the first initial spurt of banging on the wall. Silence. Nothing. The lunch break must have been and gone, and still no one came to continue with the work. The afternoon dragged into evening and into darkness. And still nobody. The day shift must have long since changed, and no further construction was likely to happen. They were safe for another night's sawing. They decided to risk putting the blades back into the cell under the mattresses. After all, there was still a huge pile of them, and it looked as though the old firehose would be replaced with the shiny new red one in the morning.

It was at that time, as Harold subsequently told me, that the two of them learned about Diane's magnificent gesture of help. As he made his way back to his cell, his mind turned over and over the possibility of using the money for a bribe. Up to now there had been no ready cash available. Now suddenly it had dropped into their laps. He had already given Greef a tobacco pouch, and Arthur had given him a pipe. Neither of them had thought then of trying to bribe him: these were simple acts of thanks for his humane response to them. Greef was pleasant. He had even let all the Africans out of their cells on a Sunday so that there could be a grand reunion.

One of the black prisoners was Andrew Mashaba, a tall, good-looking man who claimed to have been out of the country receiving military training. He was well known to Harold, and Harold trusted him – so much so that he had decided to try to involve him in the escape plan. Harold was sure that if they offered Greef a relatively small amount he would find it very difficult to refuse, he earned so little. His passion for cars and desire to own one would prove his Achilles heel.

As they were busy with the intransigent bar that night, Harold said to the three men behind the steel gate, 'I think we should seriously talk to Greef about letting us out of this place.' Arthur chipped in: 'It would be quite easy for us to make it seem that we had overpowered him and knocked him out.' He got off the ledge he was squatting on, and demonstrated a swinging arm movement to strengthen his point. 'No way,' said Chiba, emphatically and with great fervour. 'We're not going to implicate Greef in any of our plans. I absolutely forbid it. The man has been my friend. We can't take advantage of him. He's young, he's inexperienced, and he just doesn't know the ways of the city. And those guys' – referring to the Special Branch – 'will donder him [beat him up]. There's no way that I will be party to any such action, and I'll warn Greef about it if you guys go ahead with your plan.' Chiba was adamant, and no amount of argument would sway him.

Then, as suddenly as he had been arrested, Chiba was released.

At first the men thought that the police were simply repeating the treatment given to Mosie after his ninety days were up. On his eighty-eighth day of solitary confinement Mosie had been told to pack his bags, and he was taken away that evening. The others did not know what had happened. They did not have too long to wait. Mosie rejoined them again two days later. He had been taken to an outlying police station and released, and although he had no money, he was told to go home. He started walking down the road followed by the police. They stopped him and rearrested him for the second lot of ninety-day detention.

They waited for Chiba to return. Nothing happened. He did not come back the next day either. Chiba was definitely free.

With Chiba's release, the main obstacle to approaching Greef to help them escape was removed. Harold and Arthur were busy with what was looking more and more like pointless and endless filing. 'We'll have to ask Greef to help us. There really is no other way out of this. We're never going to get anywhere with this bloody filing. We may as well give it up.' Arthur was dispirited by the lack of progress. He paused to massage sore muscles. Harold was sitting for the moment on the cold floor. He shared Arthur's pessimism. That three-quarter-inch-thick steel bar showed no signs of giving way beneath their onslaught. He had thought about Greef quite a lot. He had considered the possible consequences for Greef if something went wrong. He did not share Chiba's highly moralistic view, but he did wonder what would happen to Greef if things went wrong and it was discovered that he had helped them. He felt the burden of implicating an innocent man. But would Greef help them? Being friendly and helpful was one thing, but it was quite another to participate actively in helping people like them to escape.

'I wonder what would happen to Greef if he was caught?' he said out loud. Arthur stopped rubbing his arm at this, and squatted down next to Harold. They were both silent, then they started talking simultaneously. 'We'll just have to approach him,' Harold said. 'We have no alternative.' This clinched it. Together they started to gather up the blades to hide them under the mattresses. With Greef's help they would be able to pursue their plan of action: getting the gates unlocked. As Harold had learned, it needed only one guard on duty at night to get the necessary gates unlocked and open the door to freedom in the back courtyard.

Joined by Abdullah and Mosie, the men began to discuss their plans. 'Who will ask Greef?' Abdullah asked. 'You're the lawyer,' he suggested to Harold. 'You could point out the problems, and also explain to Greef what will happen to us if we don't get out of jail now.' They thought about this. 'I don't think I'm the best person though,' said Harold thoughtfully. 'After Chiba, Mosie has the closest relationship with Greef. He seems to get on with him better than anybody else.' At first Mosie refused, but after each of the others had had a go at him he reluctantly agreed to act as the go-between.

'Hell, man, what will I say?' Mosie asked. Every one of them gave different suggestions. 'Listen: whatever you do, don't offer Greef the full amount of money. You've got to start at a much lower figure than the £3,000 to allow some room for bargaining,' Arthur suggested. Harold emphasised the point: 'Arthur's right, Mosie. Start really low down, like five hundred. Then, if Greef says it's too little, offer some more.' Mosie looked decidedly unhappy.

It was a Thursday night. Greef came on duty, and later he came on his round to greet them. Mosie said, 'I want to talk to you.' Greef promised to return a little later, after he had completed various tasks. He returned to Mosie's cell. Mosie, bracing himself, said to Greef: 'I want to ask you something. I'm not going to ask you, though, unless you promise on the Bible that if you don't agree you'll never mention that I made this request to you.' Greef put his hand on Mosie's Bible and made the solemn undertaking that he would never divulge a word of what Mosie asked him to do.

Mosie was really nervous. He blurted out: 'If you help us to escape, we'll give you £3,000.' In spite of their agreement, Mosie couldn't face bargaining with Greef. He explained the plan of the keys: 'All you'll have to do is let us take over your set of keys. Then we can unlock the gates and go out through the car park at the back of the station.'

Greef's reaction was guarded. He looked puzzled and worried. He frowned, shook his head. Slowly he said, 'I'll have to think about it and let you know, Mosie.' An hour went by. He came back, going straight to Mosie's cell. 'OK, man, I'll help you. I know what to do. What I'll say is that Arthur banged on his cell door and I went to his cell. Arthur wasn't in the main part of his cell and I went to look for him. He was in the ablutions section. I didn't see him at first, and I remember nothing from that moment. I suppose Arthur must have hit me over the head and knocked me out.' 'No, man,' Mosie replied, 'I don't like the sound of that at all. We're not going to hurt you, man. Let's go and talk to the others.'

Greef let Harold and Abdullah out of their cells and took all three to Arthur's cell, the largest one. Greef explained what he planned to do. Arthur thought it was a good idea. He did indeed have an iron bar which he had found on top of the cistern – an old lever, which had once been attached to it. 'I'll have a practice go,' Arthur said. He took the iron bar and swung it hard. 'My God, you'll kill him if you hit as hard as that,' Mosie remonstrated. Arthur blanched visibly. 'I can't do it,' he protested. 'I really can't go ahead and hit you over the head. No, Greef, no way man.' Greef encouraged him: 'Just have some practice goes, and you'll be all right.' Arthur nodded his head rather miserably. 'Then what will happen?' asked Harold. 'Well, you'll have to tie me up,' Greef responded. 'Then I'll use my glasses – I'll break them, and cut myself free, and then I can raise the alarm. I'll say that Arthur must have taken my keys, let you others out, and that's how you all got away.'

It sounded too easy. Secretly Harold thought that it couldn't be as simple as that. Nor was he too happy about the idea of knocking Greef out but he was sufficiently desperate about their future prosects to push all doubts aside.

'Can we get any of the others out as well, like Andrew Mashaba?' Mosie asked. Greef shook his head. 'No way, man,' he replied. 'It would be really difficult to get any of the black guys out. We would need a different set of keys, and it just wouldn't work. I can only help you four,' he replied, glancing at each one in turn.

They then had to discuss the money question. It was not a simple matter. Should they try to arrange for the payment to be made before the escape, or should the money be paid after the event? If before, there was nothing to stop Greef from accepting the money and then going to the authorities who might allow them to escape, thus setting a trap for them and the others. The four had decided that payment should be made only after the event. None of them would renege on such an agreement. They said as much to Greef. He agreed.

Now the next step had to be contemplated. What was to happen once they were out of jail? It was one matter getting out, quite another remaining free.

The Blue Moon

I AM BEGINNING to realise that as long as I have a project I am somehow managing to keep a grip on myself. I cannot begin to entertain an idea of what may happen to me or the children if an escape materialises. Part of me does not believe it can happen. I don't even know how many people are going to escape. I get the impression that it won't be just Arthur and Harold. I have a vision of Marshall Square opening up and disgorging hordes of people. 'Jail break,' would be the headlines the following day in the *Daily Mail*. I've seen too many American movies.

And even if they get out of jail, what then? I have little hope about the help the movement can give Harold and the others. I assume that it must be easier for black people or Indians to disappear. The white community is relatively small, and those on the Left are well known. What hope is there that they'll be supportive? Johannesburg cannot boast a large progressive community willing to put itself at risk.

The jail break is about to happen. I have been told to check that the money is paid over, and that a car must be available tonight. The first is relatively easy to do. A car! I don't have much time. I have absolutely no idea how to get one. Perhaps Mannie Brown will have the answer. Mannie is a confusing person. I know him through our tennis club, if one can call it that. It consists mostly of banned people. There was Joe (until he left the country), Mannie, Julius (he had arranged for us to have the use of the Houghton Junior School's tennis court), Ivan, and only a few women. From time to time one or two of them go off into a huddle, and at times of crisis the club suddenly ceases to function. Mannie is a schoolteacher, a person who seems totally unruffled. He was arrested together with all the others following Sharpeville, and proved how devious he could be with a broad smile on his face. He knew how to break the rules and appear totally innocent. He has chutzpah and, among other things, is an excellent tennis player.

I had a brief meeting with Mannie early this morning. He laughed when I said: 'I have to get Harold a car.' He said, 'Phew! Where can I get a car? I haven't got a moment today. You'll have to use yours.' 'But the escape is probably tonight,' I protested. He apologised, and off he went. 'I'll see you later tonight,' he said as he left, 'so we can make final arrangements.' 'Well, all right, but I'm going to the Blue Moon for dinner after the delivery of food.' I can't recall when last I went out purely for pleasure. Michael Gluckman has persuaded me to go out for a meal. He is one friend who has not been afraid to show his solidarity though he is not a member of the movement. That hasn't stopped him from coming up trumps when needed. He was the one Harold turned to when he needed semi-hiding just after Nicholas was born. 'You need a break. Let's go and eat somewhere. Any ideas?' I suggested the Blue Moon, a Greek taverna not far from Fordsburg. Mannie said he would see me there and find out what I had managed to do about a getaway car.

My fantasies surface again. Steal a car, I think. The problem is that I don't know how to go about it. Then I have what I think is a brain wave. I know that the *Rand Daily Mail* has a fleet of cars in the basement. I phone a woman I have met on only a few occasions in the course of my work. She is a practising Christian whom I trust implicitly. I ask her to arrange for me to see the editor of the *Mail*. We sit in a small office, and after quick introductions I come straight to the point: 'I am going to ask you a question, and then, please, you are to forget I have ever asked you, OK?' Both of them look puzzled. 'I have got to have a car tonight, and I don't know what to do. Can I steal one of your company cars?'

The editor looks at me for a moment, somewhat taken aback, but he responds calmly. He asks no questions. He just replies, 'No good. There is an attendant, and he would want to see a pass. You could never manage it.' I feel silly and sheepish, but at least I have tried. How did people manage in Europe during the war, I wonder? They seem to have done all sorts of things; they showed such initiative when it came to taking on the Gestapo. I am clearly out of my league. The two of them are superb. They both react as though it is the most normal thing for someone to ask. They know, and I know they know, that it is connected with the Rivonia arrests and Harold's, which have all been front-page news. We exchange some pleasantries and I depart, wondering what they are saying as I leave the small room.

It will have to be our car that is left there.

I meet Michael at the restaurant at 8.30. I can't tell him anything at all. The Blue Moon is one of our favourite haunts. It is unpretentious, and its popularity has increased since the film *Never on Sunday*, starring Melina Mercouri. A small band plays what we all assume to be traditional Greek music; and couples take to the floor between courses and whirl around, pretending they are in a Piraeus café. The food is always excellent. Inevitably we eat sardines that must have come from Lourenço Marques, grilled on an open charcoal fire with wild thyme and lemon juice. Until the Blue Moon I had thought that sardines came only jam-packed in tins of oil. Johannesburg had the ubiquitous Greek café, the corner shop which stocked everything and stayed open all day every day and late into the night. This is something new, and the smart young set go there regularly.

Michael is trying very hard to divert my attention; he is very solicitous. The fresh sardines are wonderful, as usual. The wooden-cask-like flavour of the Retsina is an excellent accompaniment, and soon the wine works its way into my bloodstream. I relax for the first time in days and days. We dance to the rhythmic music. He makes up for all my long silences by keeping up a constant chatter.

While we whirl around I suddenly notice Mannie making his way towards me. He comes on to the dance floor, taps me on the shoulder and says, with a broad smile, 'We'll be away a short while. I'm sure Michael won't mind.' I mumble something to Michael, who smiles in return and makes his way back to the table. At least we've eaten the sardines. I won't miss out on that. Michael is understanding, and knows better than to ask any questions.

We go outside and Ivan Schermbrucker, another tennis club member, is also there. I never know who is involved, although I have a shrewd idea. 'Mannie, I haven't been able to get a car. I really tried. It will have to be our car.' Mannie agrees. 'We'll take yours and leave it there. If nothing happens, Ivan will bring it back to you first thing tomorrow morning.' I get the feeling that Mannie doesn't seem to think that anything will happen. 'Here's cash for the jailer's bribe,' I add, and thrust into his hand an envelope with the money, which I got earlier from Jimmy. Luckily, Jimmy did not ask me any questions beyond saying that he thought Di wasn't quite above board.

The spell of the Blue Moon has been broken. The interlude sobers me completely. I feel tired, and Michael takes me home soon after.

I sleep deeply and soundly that night until Nicholas wakes and I am able to feed him. At about eight o'clock in the morning I have Nicholas with me in the front room. The sun is shining. It is another wonderful Transvaal winter day. The sharp early-morning cold has disappeared. I feel almost past caring. I suppose no escape happened last night, or I would surely have heard something by now. Or maybe they tried and got caught. I don't understand my feeling of distance from all this. Suddenly Ivan appears. He says casually, 'Thanks for the loan of the car. Here are the keys.' No indication of where the car was the night before. No knowing winks, no nudges. Nothing. Marlene is bustling around, and we have to be guarded. 'I think I may have to borrow your car again tonight, if that's OK with you,' he says. I reply sarcastically, 'Well, the only date I have is with prison. You can have the car after I've delivered the food. Let me know if you need it. I get back about 9.30 or so. You're welcome to it. And you needn't hurry to get it back to me – I plan to sleep in a bit tomorrow morning – if he'll let me.' Nicholas gurgles, and smiles toothlessly. It sounds as though

Ivan and Mannie are going to try and do something about an alternative car today. 'Could you ask Mannie to pick me up about four this afternoon? I have to go into town to see Jimmy, and I need some help.'

I arrange for Peta and Tessa to spend the weekend with one of their close friends, and after lunch the mother picks up both girls. I hug them and tell them to be good and enjoy themselves. Mannie comes round at four o'clock, and we drive around. He tells me of the plans for tonight, and that I am not to worry. We are all convinced that it will happen tonight. Mannie has organised another car. Our car won't be needed. We're driving down Sauer Street. He says casually, 'Oh, we've got a flat there' – pointing to a block of flats. 'Who's we?' I ask innocently. He laughs his infectious laugh, and says it's a safe flat. 'That's where we'll take them tonight.' This is my first inkling of the existence of such a place. The trouble is that such knowledge can be catastrophic. I would rather not be told about it at all. There's nothing to divulge if you don't know anything. Christ, Mannie, you're a bloody fool, I think.

I am less than careful about the food parcel. Some cold chicken, fruit and a few rolls. A slab of dark-brown chocolate. If Harold gets out tonight he can always pocket it, I think, and it might prove useful in full flight. This is the opposite of the condemned man's last feast.

I ring the bell. The large wooden doors swing open. There is the African warder – thank goodness! He ushers me into a waiting-room with a bright light without any shade, takes the basket with the food and clean clothes, and says, 'You must wait here for the dirty clothes.' I am puzzled. This is a room I have not been in before, and I don't know why he tells me to wait there.

Suddenly the door opens and Gordon Winter comes in – the last person on earth I want to see. Gordon is a reporter on the *Sunday Express* and nobody trusts him. He is a stocky man, with sandy-coloured hair. In his clipped British accent, which sounds more cockney than BBC, he greets me warmly. 'What's doing, AnnMarie? What's new? What can you tell me?' Ever the reporter. 'Oh Gordon, come on. You know what's going on.' I laugh outwardly. Inside, my heart thumps rapidly; I'm terrified that Gordon has got wind somehow of the impending escape. Why is he here? I wonder. 'I'd love to know what's happening. My life is just one long run of hauling to and from this lousy place. I'm waiting to collect the dirty washing and get my basket back.' Oh Gordon, if only you knew, I thought. What wouldn't you give to be able to lead with this story? I try smiling brightly.

I assume that the change of venue must have something to do with seeing Harold again, but nothing can happen while Gordon is around.

'Here, take tomorrow's paper. It'll give you something to do tonight,' and he hands me a copy of the *Express* which will hit the streets in the early hours of Sunday morning. More polite smiles and thank yous. He leaves abruptly.

I sit down on the hard regulation wooden bench, look at my watch, look at the bare bulb in the ceiling, get up and walk around. The door opens quietly. Ben, the black warder, appears. He beckons to me, tapping his lips to make sure I make no sound. I follow him silently, past the little office where I once saw Greef talking so earnestly on the phone, up the short flight of steps. Harold is standing there.

'Why on earth did you use our car?' he blurts out. 'It was crazy. I hope you aren't going to do the same thing tonight.' No time to explain my failure. 'Listen,' he goes on urgently, 'it's going to be tonight. We've sent out a message on the signals that we'll make. Just please make sure that the car is where it was last night, and that it will be moved round the corner if we're late for any reason. Got that?' No more time. Ben is hovering anxiously. A very quick hug, and then I go back downstairs, feeling quite dazed. What can I do? I ask myself. Some time tonight your husband is going to try and escape from jail, you are going to be arrested and your children are going to be left alone. I am caught up in a chain of events that have their own momentum. As I get into the car I realise that I am still clutching the *Sunday Express* under my arm. I throw it carelessly on to the back seat. It isn't my favourite paper and I don't like Gordon.

I drive home like a maniac. On the way I stop over and see Mannie to confirm what Harold has told me. I begin to think about the consequences. What will happen to Nicholas? He still has a tube in his lungs, he still requires nursing. Will Marlene walk out on him? And the little girls? They have been most hideously neglected by me since the onset of Nicholas's illness. My mother is now in Durban with Betty. No doubt it will all fall on Jimmy's shoulders again. Jimmy is like a rock. He seems untouchable and, like my father, simply shoulders other people's burdens. I realise that I don't entertain thoughts about Harold's chances. I have separated our lives. What happens to him from now on is no longer connected with me and the children. I am probably the one who will be there to look after the children and myself. I am on my own. There is too much uncertainty.

Home again. Marlene is smoking in the sitting-room. She is wearing jeans. She obviously doesn't have a date, because she has no make-up on and her hair is hanging loose on her shoulders.

I join Marlene. My concern now shifts to Nicholas. I must know that he is going to be looked after properly once I am carted off. I have no idea what is going to happen to me beyond going to jail. I know that the smuggling I did during the 1960 Emergency could have landed me in jail for three years. Now things are very different. In a split second I decide to take Marlene into my confidence. I put my favourite record on, Aretha Franklin singing, among other things, the 'Battle Hymn of the Republic' and 'Water Boy'. I feel that it will give me courage.

'By the way, Marlene, I'm going to tell you something, and I have to trust you completely,' I say, almost casually. 'You could do terrible things to me and everyone if you wanted to.' I look to gauge her response. She raises an eyebrow, waiting for me to continue. 'Harold's going to escape from jail tonight.' Well, there it is: I've told her. She could go straight to the phone and let the police know.

I wait for her response. She laughs. 'I don't care what the hell he does,' she says. 'It makes no difference to me at all. I'm not involved. I'm not interested in politics. And if he wants to escape, that's his business.'

'You see,' I say, letting out my breath – I am unaware that I have been holding it – 'I'm likely to be arrested as well. They'll be furious if it happens, and they could take me off to jail. I've got to know whether or not you will go on looking after Nicholas.' Her answer is immediate: 'After all we've been through – you're crazy to think that I would abandon him. He's got nothing to do with his father's politics. I would never leave this child. You needn't worry about him at all.'

It is as though I haven't just thrown a bombshell at her. She goes back to her drink and cigarette, and I listen to the music for a while. Suddenly I feel exhausted, and I'm asleep before she gets into bed. I wake for Nicholas's two o'clock feed. It is so quiet and peaceful, and this time I try to keep Nicholas awake a little longer, but as soon as he finishes his bottle he falls asleep. So do I.

I wake at seven o'clock. It's Sunday morning. The bedroom is bright. Nicholas is playing in his cot, kicking his legs and gurgling away. There is no trace of the thin, scrawny, ashen baby who returned home a few weeks ago. His face and body have filled out, and he has colour from the time he spends lying in his pram outside. Marlene is up and dressed. She has plans to go on a picnic, and is getting ready. I get Nicholas's bottle and start feeding him.

I hear voices. It sounds as though someone is with Marlene in the sitting-room. Marlene comes hurriedly into the bedroom, followed by a young dark-haired man with a big moustache. I splutter: 'What's going on?' 'Get your clothes on, Mrs Wolpe, and come with us.' 'Can't you see I'm busy with my baby? He's been very ill. I can't just come with you.' 'Bugger your baby. He can die for all I care,' he bellows out. A cold feeling pervades my whole body. 'What's going on?' I ask. 'Just come with me,' he answers. I protest that I have to have a bath. 'Get a move on,' he snaps back at me. So the escape attempt must have been made. Have they been caught? Are they going to be tortured? He is certainly giving me no clues. Marlene comes over and takes Nicholas out of my arms. She whispers, 'They've got away.' Thank goodness for that, at least. The bath is a quick top-and-tail job. I grab the first thing I can lay my hands on. That is a mistake. It is the grey shift dress I wore the day I rushed Nicholas to hospital, and I have never replaced the button I wrenched off in my anxiety to get there. I can hide the gap with the tie belt. I stuff a packet of cigarettes in my bag and swallow a strong Valium. Better calm yourself down, I think, you're going to need all your reserves.

Freedom?

A S SOON as he came back into the cell after seeing me, Harold took up his position on the bench next to the window to watch for the arrival of the car. He could then give the signal: switch the light on and off four times if it was all go, or on and off once and off for five minutes if there was to be no attempt. A car stopped one and a half blocks away; two men got out – one white, one black. They seemed to potter around. Immediately he became suspicious. Perhaps it was a trap for them. Had Greef betrayed them?

Eight-thirty came, and minutes later a car drew up and parked where our car had been the previous night. Harold had no doubt it was the escape car, and gave the signal. It was yes for 'Go ahead'.

Suddenly there was a flicker, and the lights in the lamppost on the corner of Main and Sauer Streets opposite the telephone exchange went out. This was followed by another flicker, and all three lamps went dead. It seemed that this had happened only on this corner. There was another flicker – they all went on, and finally out again. Harold felt suspicious: was this a trap, or a favourable portent? He took it as a good omen. If they failed to get out in time to reach the car, shortly after midnight, they would have to cross that corner to meet up with the car at the second assignation. And that was a busy corner – police would be driving past, coming into or leaving Marshall Square; this increased the chance of being recognised.

Harold had to wait to tell the other three what had happened. They listened silently. There was too much tension for any conversation. 'Let's get dressed,' said Mosie. And the wait until midnight seemed unbearable.

At ten o'clock the four of them were ready, and dressed in their warmest clothes. They waited. They paced. They anxiously tried to listen to sounds that would give them some idea of the level of activity in the charge office, hoping that not too many new prisoners would be booked in.

Eleven-thirty – only half an hour before they were due to leave. Greef rushed up the stairs. 'It's terrible, man,' he said. 'One of the men in the charge office sent the black guard to fetch him some cigarettes and he hasn't come back yet. He's taken a helluva long time to come back. I don't know when that guy will settle down for the night and be out of my way.' They listened, but said nothing. 'That's not bloody all,' he went on. 'Three young guys have been brought in. They're going to be charged with drunken driving. And you know what that means.' It was a rhetorical question. They all knew the routine well by now. Not only had the men to be formally charged, which was time-consuming in itself, but they had to be taken to the local district surgeon for a blood/alcohol test. Fifteen minutes later they were still in the charge office. Greef was getting edgy.

It was eleven-forty-five. The three young men had been taken off, and when they returned the bell would be rung at the cell block. This meant that Greef would have to be available to open up immediately and book them into cells otherwise the alarm would go off. There just was not sufficient time now for them to carry out their number one plan. The midnight departure was not possible.

Midnight. Harold kept watching the street from his cell. Mosie sat on the bed in Arthur's cell. Abdullah paced up and down, and Arthur stood at the door to the ablutions section. Every now and again one of them would suggest that Greef would be coming soon. The others barely acknowledged the remark. They were still full of hope, although not one believed that they would succeed.

Five minutes past midnight. Harold saw the car being moved from close to the back of the courtyard away out of sight, in accordance with the plan.

Twelve-thirty. Only forty-five minutes before their car would leave from the second position, and then there would be no transport. The adrenalin generated by anticipation was fast turning into a feeling of despondency. Greef had reported that the three young men were still not locked up. 'I don't know what we'll do,' he said.

The four conspirators started to consider contingency plans. 'If we don't go tonight I think we'll never get out,' said Arthur despairingly. 'I'm worried that they could move us to another jail,' added Harold. There was general agreement that it was tonight or never. 'What if we suggest to Greef that he should let one of us out so that the driver could be told to remain on beyond one-fifteen?' volunteered Arthur. It was a hare-brained scheme. They were feeling so desperate that they agreed to put this to Greef. They did so when he next reported to them fifteen minutes later.

'You lot are crazy to think that could work,' Greef responded. 'Just think what would happen if that one person was caught.' He paused for all of them to stop and contemplate the possibilities. 'It would only need that one guy to be caught, and then all of you would be in trouble. And what do you think would happen to me?' He did not need to elaborate. They realised that in their desperation they had become quite irrational.

Their anxiety was contagious. Greef came up with a change of plan. 'I tell you what I'll do,' he offered. 'I'll unlock the back door, let you out, then relock it.' 'But there's no way that we'll be able to go ahead with the plan of knocking you out and tying you up,' Mosie pointed out. 'You don't have to worry at all. I've thought about that,' replied Greef. His plan, he said, was quite simple. After they had been let out, he would take himself back to Arthur's cell and knock himself out. 'Once before, you know, I knocked myself out by banging my head against the wall. It was quite simple.' 'What the hell will you tell them about how it happened?' one of them asked. 'I'll say that Arthur called me into the cell and then knocked me out when my back was turned.'

Deep down, each of them thought that this could not work, in spite of Greef's renowned strength. They knew that their original plan was the best, but now they were sufficiently desperate to ignore the defects of this scheme. They agreed.

It was now ten past one on Sunday morning, 11 August. Greef came up quietly and beckoned them to follow him. The five of them tiptoed down the steps. One of them knocked over a milk bottle, which clattered down. Nothing happened. They came to a door which Greef unlocked, into a room that looked like a store room, to another door. This was the one that led to the courtyard. Even though Harold had spent so much time thinking about the courtyard, he was not prepared for the number of Volkswagens parked there. He stepped back in sheer amazement and fear, expecting at least one if not two men to open fire on them, from at least one of the twenty-five vehicles. Just outside the door was a dustbin. Harold dropped all their blades into it. He did not want to leave them inside. It could jeopardise other prisoners' chances in the future.

Each man touched Greef in acknowledgement of what he had done for them. There was no chance to exchange any words. They were free.

Harold had savoured such a moment. He had anticipated that he would experience an overwhelming emotion, he would feel great joy. Instead his mind conjured up an image of Detective Sergeant Dirker's face when he heard the calamitous news, recalling Dirker's warning to the warder one day while he was exercising outside. He smiled wryly to himself as he followed the others, struggling to keep up with them. Of all times to get an attack of gout! He could not believe it possible. He had not exactly been overindulging. The pain in his foot was crippling.

Four shadowy figures moved silently to the gate of the courtyard, walked down Main Street and across Sauer Street, passing the dark corner where the lampposts were still in darkness. The Viking Restaurant was in the throes of closing. The last customers had already left, and they could see the Indian waiters clearing up and getting ready for the next day. The waiters were too busy, and probably too tired, to notice anyone hurrying by. One more street to walk, and then into Fox Street.

They could see the car waiting for them. It wasn't exactly where they had anticipated it would be, but then that didn't matter. It could not be more than five minutes since they got out of prison. In one minute they would be speeding away to safety.

Arthur was the first to reach the car. He turned to look at the others, an expression of dismay on his face. There was no driver, and although there was a cap on the back window-ledge, the door was not open. They had arranged that if they were late the driver would leave the one back door open, and the keys of the car underneath the hat. Arthur tried every door. They were all locked. Something had gone terribly wrong. This could not be their escape car. They had no transport.

In their interminable reviewing of their plans they had discussed what would happen if their arrangements failed. They had all agreed that they would split up. It would look too suspicious to have two white people and two Indians walking together at that time of night. Abdullah and Mosie would make their way to Ferreirastown, an Indian ghetto not all that distance away. It was simply courting disaster for all four to keep together. They had to remain as inconspicuous as possible. The two pairs took leave of each other, with Arthur and Harold moving off first. There was no time for any farewells. Fear gripped all four of them.

At this point Harold started to take over. He realised that he functioned far better under such circumstances. Arthur, who inside the jail had maintained a calmness which Harold had never felt, was now quite panic-stricken. 'Let's go towards the station,' Harold said urgently. 'I can't imagine patrol cars coming down this road,' he added encouragingly. Arthur nodded, his throat too dry to answer. They strode out towards Rissik Street, which would be quieter than Eloff Street.

They were tempted to run. They resisted this temptation, realising that they did not want to appear as though they were running away from something. Soon their breath was coming in harsh steamy bursts, but they kept up the pace. Harold did not have time to think about the pain in his foot. Once on the go he felt better, the panic and tension oozing away.

'Watch out!' hissed Arthur. Coming towards them were four young white men, obviously drunk judging from their gait, and spoiling for a fight. That's it, Harold thought. We're going to be knocked out by these thugs and we'll bloody well land back in jail. As they came abreast of the group, one of the youths started cursing. Inexplicably, the others grabbed him, and they lurched on their way.

'What are we going to do?' Arthur kept repeating in his panic. 'Where the fuck are we going to go?' 'I've got two possibilities,' Harold replied. They had no cash on them, and couldn't even use a public phone to make contact with anyone. Harold thought of making their way to Stan Goldstein's small flat, where Barbara had shaved off his beard and dyed his hair. The flat was in Hillbrow, and they would have to pass Joubert Park. They could weave their way through back streets to get there. 'It should take us another twenty minutes.' Harold checked his watch. It was 1.35. They would have been gone less than an hour, yet long enough for the escape to have been established and a search begun. He was struggling to keep up with Arthur. They dared not slacken their pace.

Neither spoke as they hurried on. The streets were still and quiet. They put their heads down whenever a car approached, hoping each time that it was not a police car. Their journey seemed never-ending. Up Edith Cavell Street. There stood the building, one of those new, thoroughly jerry-built jobs, in which any sound in the long corridors would reverberate throughout.

Harold knocked on the door of the flat. It was a hollow sound. No chink of light from under the door, but then it was unlikely that Stan would be up at that hour of the morning. He tried again after a minute had pased, and there was still no response. It did not seem as though Stan was there, or else he slept so soundly that no amount of knocking would awaken him. The noise could attract the wrath of other tenants in the building.

There was one other possibility in the area. Barney Simon was a sympathiser, but no activist. From time to time he had made his flat available for occasional meetings, and Harold knew that the key was on the ledge above the front door. They could get in without any problem, and would be safe there for a while.

They made straight for the flat, taking side streets wherever possible. At this hour of the morning there was virtually no traffic and no sign of life. When they could they ran, although their speed was hampered by Harold's pain. Neither talked. They both conserved their breath for the task of getting there as quickly as possible. Harold was feeling exhausted, and walking as swiftly as possible up Harrow Road didn't help. This was a danger point. 'They must have discovered we've gone,' said Arthur. 'They've got to come this way in their search. It's one of the main roads out.'

They had to turn right, off Harrow Road. There were two possibilities, and they chose the one that would take them alongside Harrow Park. It was a dark street. They saw an old Renault double-parked. Its back lights had just come on and they heard the engine turn over, ready to drive away. 'I don't believe it,' Harold cried out. 'It's blood Barney himself! I don't bloody believe it!' Arthur reacted with amazing alacrity. Summoning strength from his inner resources, he sprinted towards the car.

They couldn't see the car's extraordinary pink paint. In the daylight it could not go unnoticed. The Renault was old; it got off to a slow start, and churlishly gathered up speed. Miraculously, Arthur reached it ten yards before the stop street, and banged on the window. Barney rolled it down. 'Well I never!' he said incredulously. He was a quiet person, not given to extravagant expressions. 'It's Arthur! I thought you were in jail!' Breathlessly, Arthur said, 'We've escaped. Harold's with me.' Harold caught up, and the two men got into the car. They were two minutes away from the flat. They all agreed that if tracker dogs were going to be used, this would break the scent.

The building was deserted, and no one saw the three men enter. Once they were inside, Barney made them a cup of tea. 'You know, I never ever drive up that road,' he said. 'It's sheer coincidence I was there. You wouldn't believe it. I went to see my girlfriend tonight. I was planning to spend the night with her. She got the curse and said she felt really rotten, so I left. Suddenly I felt the urge to pee. By the time I got to Harrow Road, my bladder was bursting and I just couldn't wait to get home. I turned off into this road because it's quiet and dark, and I could take a leak. So, you lucky guys, that's how come you found me there. I had just finished peeing.'

'Well, anyway, we would have come straight to the flat,' Harold added. 'Oh, but you don't know, do you, that I've had the front door repaired and a new lock put on. It wasn't closing properly. So now the key is no longer left outside,' replied Barney. Lady Luck seemed to be running with them.

The tea was finished. 'I'm desperate for a smoke,' Arthur said. Harold added, 'Me too.' Barney was a non-smoker. 'I'll go and try and get some fags,' he replied, and left. It took him half an hour, and when he returned he said, 'It wasn't easy to get you these,' holding out four cigarettes. 'None of the dispensing machines was working. I had to stop and buy a couple of cigarettes off somebody in the street.' The two men lit up and dragged deeply. Then discussions started about the next stage. 'We need to establish contact with our people,' said Harold.

First thing in the morning, Barney drove off to Mannie's house. It was too risky to phone or to go there in broad daylight. He was gone roughly an hour. Nobody had slept, and Arthur and Harold were beginning to get tired. The adrenalin was no longer flowing.

Barney's mission was successful. The two were to remain at the flat until someone came – within the next twelve to twenty-four hours. With that both men slept, one on the divan in the sitting-room and one in the spare bedroom. They slept the sleep of the dead, but not for long.

My Arrest

T HERE ARE at least five big burly bullying men, all
extraordinarily angry. I am hustled out of the house. I
can see Angelina and Isaac standing outside the kitchen
door, looking very frightened. I can do no more than nod to
them. There is a silent acknowledgement in return. I don't
want them implicated either. Marlene keeps very much in the
background, holding Nicholas.

I am squashed between two men on the back seat; there are
two in front. The front passenger keeps up a non-stop tirade
against me. He curses and swears at me. He isn't very imaginative, because he keeps saying the same things over and over
again: that I organised Harold's and Arthur's escape, that I
have ruined the life of a young warder, that I am wicked. I
protest my innocence. That only gets him yelling even louder at
me. 'You were running round Johannesburg in the early hours
of the morning, organising everything. Look, we found the
Sunday Express on the back seat of your car. You can only
buy it at two in the morning.' I am shocked that they have
searched my car – though they don't seem to have looked in the
dustbins where I had dumped the surplus tungsten blades that
night before I had gone on my visit. I protest my innocence
again. 'I was home, I was feeding Nicholas. You can ask our
nurse, Marlene. I came home straight after I had taken in the
food and things last night. I was given the paper by the reporter
Gordon Winter. I saw him at the jail.' 'You know where they
are, and you're going to tell us sooner or later.' There is an
explicit threat, and my stomach does a somersault.

When they talk among themselves in rapid Afrikaans, I
cannot follow what they are saying. My vision is blocked by

these men. I am terrified. I cannot believe what is happening to me. I am completely unprepared.

I have been to the Gray's Building, Security Headquarters, once before, when I saw Colonel Klindt to arrange for Harold to get the Bible. This time the atmosphere is very different. The corridors are throbbing with men, who seem to be rushing in and out of offices. There is a state of disorder. Some faces I recognise, most I don't. I am escorted into a long, narrow office and instructed to sit down on the upholstered chair in the corner near the open window. A small desk faces the wall, with a telephone on it; a filing cabinet stands in the corner. There are a few straight-backed chairs. The office is strangely bare, as though nobody really works in it.

Immediately the interrogation begins. Two men come in and start firing questions at me. The questions are similar to the ones I have been asked in the car. It is soon clear to me that there is a convention of teams of two men at a time. Mostly they yell at me, sometimes in Afrikaans and sometimes in English: 'We know exactly what you have done. That poor man Greef, whom you corrupted, has told us everything. You organised the whole thing . . .' Over and over again they ask the same questions, and over and over again they demand that I tell them where Harold and Arthur are. I am promised freedom only if I talk. I am asked to be sensible. I am told to be sensible. I am yelled at and I am cajoled: 'All you have to do is tell us, and you can go home again.' They complain that I refuse to talk in Afrikaans. One of them obviously knows Jimmy well, and says if he can speak Afrikaans, why can't I? Part of me is intrigued by these various techniques, but mostly I am quite simply terrified by the incipient violence. I anticipate that I will be assaulted. I keep protesting my innocence, and repeat the story about being given the newspaper by Gordon Winter.

Time is dragging, and they are not getting anywhere with me. Apart from the few men who have been gentle, the others exude hatred and hostility towards me. The tactics change. An older man, probably in his fifties, comes and sits down close to me. His hair is thinning, and his command of English is good. I relax a little with him, and suddenly realise that I am hungry.

'Well, my dear, we can go down to the café, if you want.' I am not his 'dear'. I say nothing. We leave the building, amidst a few raised eyebrows, and go round the corner to a café where tea is served from a huge pot and poured into massive utility chipped white cups. I order a ham sandwich, and he orders the same. Thick white bread sandwiches are slapped down on to the table, which is covered with a stained and faded oilcloth.

'You know I'm good to the Bantu,' he tells me. He avoids the more pejorative terms, like kaffir or native, which are commonly used in referring to Africans. 'I'm kind to them. They can talk to me like a father. I don't know what you and your lot want with them. We treat them perfectly well. Your husband and his lot are just causing everyone a helluva lot of trouble. You know it's Sunday, and I want to get back to lunch. My whole family comes for Sunday lunch, and I want to see my grandchildren. It would take just a minute if you tell us everything. Then we can all go home.' Fool that he is, to think that I believe him! I get the message that I am personally responsible for ruining all these nice men's Sunday off, and they resent that as much as they resent me. 'You just tell us where they are, and then you can get home to your kids.' I try to eat the food, but my appetite seems to have disappeared. 'I have no idea where they are,' I say, all the while thinking: I could kill you, Mannie, why did you have to show me your hiding place? I'm scared that they will do something horrible to me, and then who knows whether I will have the strength not to divulge it.

'You know,' he continues, 'your husband has ruined the career of a fine young man. Greef was doing very well, and you and your husband have come and poisoned his whole life. He has ruined the flower of the Afrikaners. His career is now in ruins.'

The waitress slaps down the bill; I take out my purse and pay for both of us. I won't ask him to pay for me; at the same time I am too polite to say to him: Pay your own bill. He makes no move to pay his way. Immediately I am angry with myself for not having said: Pay for your own bloody tea and sandwich. Pride and fear join hands. We go back to the sixth floor.

The questioning continues in the same way, except that they are becoming more and more frustrated, more and more threatening, and more and more insistent that I tell them something. My bladder does not stand up well under this pressure. I keep wanting to pee, and every time I ask to go to the toilet I am escorted by one of the men. It feels like running the gauntlet. As I pass a group of men, they sneer and stare. 'Sy gaan weer pis' (She's going to piss again), and then loud guffaws. Oh how I hate them and their crudity! I ignore these remarks.

They too are tiring. I am left with only one man guarding me, who was my interrogator in the car. He sits slumped over the desk, cleaning his nails with a penknife, looking quite despondent. His rage and frustration are dissipated. Suddenly I feel sorry for him. His demeanour now is quite at odds with his behaviour early in the morning. I reverse the situation: 'You have been so horrible to me. Why have you been like that? Why have you so shouted at me? I don't like it. Why do you hate me?' 'Ach man,' he replies, 'I have had a very hard life, a very hard life.' He seems unable and unwilling to elaborate. 'I've so looked forward to today. I was supposed to play rugger you know, and now it's all spoilt.' His Sunday game gone – no hooking into the scrum, no adrenalin through the sprint down the field, no splashing and fooling around under the showers with his mates, and drinking late into the night. He has been on duty since the escape was discovered, and that seems to have been in the early hours of the morning.

The Valium has been working, controlling all the tensions of the preceding weeks, although my shoulders are knotted up into tight bundles. I, who am usually as straight as a proverbial ramrod, slump down more and more into the chair. Suddenly the atmosphere of the room changes. My disheartened guard gets up to leave as two men whom I have never before seen enter. They stride, heavy-footed, over towards me with an aggressive thrust of their bodies. These men mean business. The violence I have always dreaded is imminent. One goes to the window to draw the curtains. The other shouts menacingly,

'I want to deal with her myself.' I have no illusions. This is going to be the real thing.

They are both thickset, stockily built, with biceps that bulge out from the short sleeves of their shirts. Their arms are hairy and their hands are large, with thick fingers. I notice that one has dirty nails. He turns out to be called Swanepoel. His crew cut accentuates his coarse features. He looks like a caricature of the thuggish, inarticulate, uneducated Afrikaner who has for so long been the butt of racist, anti-Afrikaner jokes. This is no joking matter. This is a team, and a menacing one at that. The other partner is a mirror-image of Swanepoel, darker and swarthier, with the same thickset wide neck, coarse features and well-tanned skin. I know instantly that they are likely to use violence. I have never before encountered anyone like either of them. They epitomise evil. Through the glass panel of the door I see the silhouette of a head poised to listen. Another ominous sign.

Smoking, I immediately bow my head down as they advance towards me. Swanepoel screams, 'Put out that bloody fag.' I stub it out nervously, burning my fingers in the process. My fatigue is overtaken by a sense of utter and total fear. Swanepoel screeches, 'Look at me when I am speaking to you.' I obey. Perhaps I manage to convey my feeling of repulsion and disgust for him and his partner, so that his immediate response is to screech at me, 'Don't look at us that way.' I don't know what to do, so I cast my eyes down again. Their anger is increasing. It seems to match the thick swelling of the veins in their foreheads and necks. They appear momentarily impotent with their suppressed rage. Neither is fluent in English. Nor, for that matter, do they seem fluent in Afrikaans. They know how to swear; they employ every kind of expletive in the book, and some I have never heard before. I fear torture. They demand that I speak in Afrikaans, which I steadfastly refuse to do. They curse my inability to 'praat onse taal' [speak our language]. They seem quite prepared to do anything to get me to tell them where Harold is. I say, 'You don't think I could organise anything as complicated as an escape, do you? You're obviously dealing with a highly organised group of people. I don't know anything about their activities, and have never known.' When I fail to reply to another question, they resume their screaming and swearing. Swanepoel shakes the chair in which I sit, while his partner has his hands poised round my throat ready to choke the very words out of me. They are ready to commit murder.

This session seems interminable. Suddenly I become aware that I am momentarily entranced, and everything moves into slow motion. I watch the saliva dripping down the sides of their mouths. I watch the thick purple veins throbbing in their necks and foreheads. I listen to their expletives and their spluttering. I recognise their inability to express themselves in any way other than physical violence. I feel pity for them. They are such miserable creatures, hardly human. What is happening to me? Am I really feeling sorry for them? I seem to float away from myself and go outside my body. I watch from the sidelines, and see myself slumped in the chair terrified by two subhuman monsters. Shame. They really need help.

This feeling does not last long. I become aware of a new kind of fear which I have never known before. It is quite different from the fear I experienced at the height of Nicholas's illness. This time I am frightened for myself. Fear that I might die. Fear that I might break. Fear that I will not be able to sustain the interrogation and last out long enough. Fear invades my whole being. I cannot control it. I want to cry out: Leave me alone, stop tormenting me. I am too scared to say anything.

Swanepoel suddenly gives up. He has shouted himself hoarse. His partner has shouted himself hoarse too. They are both sweating profusely. They have reached an impasse, and can go no further without resorting to violence. Clearly I am not going to talk without being made to.

Mercifully, they leave as abruptly as they appeared, and I am left feeling limp. From early childhood I have had a strong fear of physical torture, and abhorred violence. When I was about ten I found a book hidden in my mother's wardrobe. This was so untypical – nothing was ever hidden away. I asked what it was and she hurriedly buried it back in the wardrobe, telling me not to read it. So I read the book secretly. It was about Nazi atrocities. It had a blue cover. That is all I can remember of it. I don't think I understood it at all, beyond recognising that it was filled with horror. I grew up frightened of such things. How many times did I argue with Harold about violent movies? I didn't talk to him for several days after he had taken me to see *Psycho*. I can't understand how watching violence of a most horrifying kind can constitute enjoyment. More recently I read Djamila Boupacha's account of the torture meted out by the French troops in the course of the Algerian war, and I knew that the South Africans had sought out and learned from the French troops.

As they storm out of the office, Swanepoel says, 'I'm going to fucking well kill those fucking bastards. I'm going to get them. I'm going to fucking kill them.'

Although I am no activist, I have always sympathised with the battle to confront and end apartheid, and felt proud of the stance that Harold has taken. I always knew that my life would be inextricably linked to Harold's early on, when we first started dating in my second year at university. And although I had fancied all sorts of men who nearly approached the ideal man – someone who would order wine with aplomb, open car doors with a flourish, be assertive and determine the course of my life and have money without exploiting anyone – I stuck to Harold, who was interesting and gentle and kind. We married seven years after first going out with each other. I knew when we did marry that I would have to come to terms with his politics, even though I shared neither his enthusiasm, nor his ability to be a disciplined part of a movement.

For the last few years it has not been easy to resist the government, and each successive year makes the opposition that much more dangerous. For some time I had been convinved that the white people, in particular, who are few in number and known to the secret police, are like sitting ducks, waiting to be picked off one by one, Harold included. I had little doubt that I would land up with sole responsibility for my children. Now events have overtaken us all. At this moment I feel extreme anger with Harold. He has landed me in the shit; I am being interrogated, a situation I could never have foretold; and I resent him for the part he has played in getting me into this mess. What have I done to deserve this treatment?

A man whose name I think is Van Zyl comes in after they leave. He is the exact opposite of Swanepoel and his colleague. He is debonair, articulate and highly intelligent. I know him from various raids, and he has been particularly friendly towards both Joe and Ruth. He would joke with Joe and say, 'Man, if I had been born different, I would have been on your side. Anyway, man, at least I know where I stand with you. It's better than those liberals who say one thing and mean something else.'

There is instant relief. He does not harangue me, or say very much. I start to weep, but stop almost as soon as I have begun. 'Why do you have to have people like that in the police force?' I ask, stupidly. 'Well, the police force is like marriage,' he explains. 'You get all types. It's like life – some are good, some are bad; you get the rough with the smooth all mixed up together.'

'If you let those men near me again, I'll jump out of the window,' I warn him. We are on the sixth floor, and momentarily I mean what I say. I would prefer death to the physical and hideous abuse which I think they can inflict on me. As soon as I say this I realise that there is no way I could do it. Who would look after the children? Even if I land up in jail for a few years, I can at least come out and look after them after that. Who knows what will happen to Harold? I do not believe that the escape will be successful. They are all such amateurs fighting against a force of what seems like evil, almost wantonly violent men. The responsibility of looking after the children is mine, and mine alone. I have to make sure that I am in one piece to do it.

Van Zyl must think I mean what I say. He keeps an eye on the window, and from then on someone sits near the window all the time.

'Listen, I must phone home and find out how my baby is,' I say to Van Zyl. He agrees. I cannot believe it. I dial home with trembling fingers. Marlene answers the phone. 'Listen, Marlene,' I say, 'for Christ's sake make sure that Jimmy checks with the police tomorrow to see if I am still alive. I'm frightened they may do something terrible to me. You must get Jimmy to check. He will be able to get access to Colonel Klindt, head of Security.' I know Jimmy and Barbara are at Hartebeestepoort Dam for the weekend. Marlene reassures me that Nicholas is all right, and that the girls will be home only later that night. I don't know whether Van Zyl has been listening. He says nothing.

I realise that the Special Branch are getting desperate to know what they think I know. Time might be running out for me. Perhaps the best thing is to give them some scraps of information so that they will leave me alone. I desperately try to recall everything that has happened, and what Greef would have known. My resentment against Harold resurfaces. 'You know,' I say to Van Zyl, 'I am really very angry with Harold for landing me in this mess. All I want to do is to look after my chidlren, and now here I am being threatened by such horrible people. Of course I had to help him, but there was only a little bit I could do. What do you think? There must be a massive organisation behind this escape. You don't really think that somebody like me could have done all this. I've got my hands full with my children. And you know perfectly well that I've been through hell with my baby's illness.' I tell him that I received a message by phone, and that I had smuggled in some blades for them to saw their way out. More than that I don't know.

Oh what a clever ploy that is, I think, talking about an organisation and diverting attention away from myself. Yes, I admit to knowing that Harold was planning to escape – after all, I am his wife, and duty bound to help him. Wouldn't they expect that of their wives? Van Zyl looks interested. He perks up and makes some sympathetic clucking noises. 'Yes, how terrible to take advantage of you like that,' he responds. He can well sympathise with me. That is all I need. I wax quite eloquent about Harold's ungentlemanly behaviour in landing me in such dire trouble when I have never before been involved in anything. It just isn't fair.

Van Zyl is followed by another two men who continue to

probe. Be careful, I think, because you can trip yourself up if you contradict yourself. You must remember exactly what you have said before. Then suddenly I am summoned to Colonel Klindt's office. It must be late afternoon by now. The low-angled rays of the late sun illuminate the Venetian blinds, and the gold cigarette lighter glows. The temperature is beginning to drop. Klindt asks me just one question: 'Well, can you tell me where Harold and Arthur are?' 'No.' 'Take her away,' he commands, and I return to the little office, passing a phalanx of angry-looking men.

The group outside must have spent a long time pondering what to do with me. Six of them storm into the office, looking at me very slowly and deliberately. Luckily, Swanepoel is not amongst them. Maybe he isn't capable of talking over anything. One man stands out. He is the one who mocks me every time I go to the toilet. He has the most remarkable eyes I have ever seen. They are a luminous green. He looks as though he is in his late twenties, good-looking and well built. When he looks at me, it is as though he can see right inside me. We make eye contact. Without turning his head and looking directly at me he says, very slowly and deliberately, 'Sy lieg. Sy weet alles', and just in case I didn't understand he says, in the staccato tones of an educated Afrikaner familiar with English, 'She's a bloody good actress. She knows absolutely everything. Don't believe a word she says.' My heart sinks, but I avoid looking down. I keep looking straight into his eyes. He is the most dangerous person here, I think. I must be on my guard with him. He is not easily fooled. I dread the possibility of being subjected to any interrogation by him. I will not be able to fool this man.

They appear to be ready to do something. I have not given them any information they can act on. Perhaps now the bulk of them do believe they are up against a bigger organisation than they had reckoned with.

My body is beginning to stiffen and ache. I have sat still too long and too tensely. Darkness is replacing the dusk. There is a flurry of activity. Men come in and out of the office. The filing cabinet is pulled open. There are no files in it at all, only guns. They are coming to arm themselves and I realise that I have never thought of the Security Police being armed. I cannot help expressing my surprise at this. My original captor says, 'Those guys are going out to hunt down and shoot those two bastards. We're sorry for you, Mrs Wolpe, because you're going to be a widow by tomorrow morning. It doesn't matter where they are, we'll get them. And if not today, tomorrow. They'll never get away from us. They can go to Timbuktu, but we'll get them.' Their anger has not abated. Now it is being directed away from me towards the two escapees. No mention of Abdullah and Mosie – just Harold and Arthur.

My interrogation has ceased. Time moves on slowly. The building is quieter. Two men, one of whom escorted Harold at the funeral, enter and say, 'Come on, you're coming with us. We're going to take you to jail, and you can rot there. No use going on talking to you. You won't help yourself, so you can rot in jail.'

It is now about nine o'clock. Off we go to Marshall Square. Fourteen hours since my arrest, and still no sign of Harold. Good news, I suppose.

The lights are quite dim, accentuating the institutional grey, and I am led to the charge office to be stripped of my bag, with its precious cigarettes and matches. My belt is removed and the shift dress, the fabric of which matches the dull grey atmosphere, drops shapelessly, accentuating the gape where the button is missing. I feel humiliated. As I am escorted to what I presume is a cell, I see the tall black warder walking towards me. He does a turnabout. Neither of us acknowledges the other's existence.

A cell door is opened, and I'm left on my own. It is really strange, and reminds me of a shelter I had once been taken to when I was hitching to Italy and I did not have the correct travel documents. I was short of money, and needed a cheap place to stay overnight. It turned out to be a home for 'fallen' women. No women could have fallen recently, because I was the sole occupant of a large dormitory, bleak and eerily empty. This cell is similar. It has about six or eight beds. Again I am the sole occupant. It is dark, dimly lit, with a toilet in one corner and a stone sink in another. The woman who escorts me says not a word. She thrusts some blankets into my hands and refuses to tell me what the time is. I now no longer have a watch.

Sleep does not come easily. I am cold, the room is cold and bleak, and I am exhausted and frightened. I must have fallen asleep, because I begin to dream. I am surrounded by tall faceless grey men, looming over me, threatening me. I keep wanting to talk, but no sound comes out of my mouth. I suddenly see myself in a mirror – no eye make-up, no lipstick, pale and drawn, with my mouth gaping open like a grey Francis Bacon painting. It's the big gaping silent mouth that strikes me. My night terror is halted by the bang of a cell door and the clatter of a tin tray. The same silent wardress thrusts the tin tray into my hands. 'What is the time?' I ask. It is as though I am addressing a deaf-mute. No answer. 'I haven't any clothes or toothbrush.' Again no response. 'When can I get something?' I realise that I will get no help from this source.

The tray holds a tin plate with a hard-boiled egg, and a tin mug with coffee and a slice of dry bread. The coffee is undrinkable. It has the dry, acrid taste of acorns. I struggle to eat the egg. It sticks in my throat. Nor does the dry bread go down any easier. It is still very dark, and it strikes me as a ridiculous time to be eating anyway. It must be close to daybreak, because I can hear the sounds of movement in the street outside. I crawl back under the blankets after rinsing out the awful taste of the egg and stale cigarette smoke from my mouth. I am beginning to want a cigarette, but the bastards have stripped me of everything. I feel dirty, unwashed, grotty and cold.

It is not long before the same wardress returns and instructs me to follow her. I can get no sense of where I am as we walk down bleak corridors into a small bare cell with nothing except an iron cot bed, a thin mattress covered with blankets, and a hard pillow. There are no washing or toilet facilities – just the hard bed standing on a highly polished red-tiled floor.

Now I am awake. I feel overwhelmed by self-pity. I lie on the bed and let the tears run down my cheeks. Only once during the previous day did I allow myself the luxury of some tears, and that was late in the afternoon. Now I do not have to pretend and show a strong face to the world. I cry quite silently.

Without any warning the cell door bursts open and the room is filled with black women in prison dress. Down on their hands and knees, rubbing my highly polished floor with old rags. Not a word is spoken. 'I want to see the Matron,' I say to the white wardress. 'I have nothing with me, and I am menstruating. I need some Tampax and I want some clean clothes and a toothbrush. Please make sure that I see her.' From what Jimmy said I have learned that there are matrons in jails. Still the wardress does not answer.

As suddenly as the women had appeared, they disappear. It is bizarre. Even in jail the white women are serviced by the black women. If I was not feeling so miserable, I might well laugh out loud. Suddenly I hear my name being called. It is Ruth Slovo's voice. I am astounded. It is only a few days since she was arrested under the Ninety Day law. I have been too engrossed in my own problems. She begins to talk in what I can only describe as a stage whisper and comments, laughingly, on my imperious request to the wardress. She says how good it is to hear my voice, and how pleased she is that I am her neighbour. I certainly don't share her delight. 'I hear that four of them escaped last night. That's fantastic news,' says Ruth.

I do not feel at all communicative, and I do not trust myself not to burst into loud sobbing.

Again the cell door opens. This time I am told that I am to see the visiting magistrate. I'm in no state to do so. I haven't washed since yesterday morning, I haven't changed my clothes, brushed my hair or put on my eyeliner. And I am craving a cigarette.

The magistrate is a small man behind a giant-sized desk. I plead with him to give me a cigarette. My head spins slightly from the nicotine deprivation. He refuses. 'Please give me a cigarette,' I plead. He ignores my request and then, as an afterthought, says, 'It's against the regulations.' I think he is a miserable bastard. He does not explain why he is seeing me. 'I want you to tell me what has happened to you.' I don't need much prompting. Much to my own surprise, I begin to sob –

great big sobs rack my body. In between asking him repeatedly for a cigarette, I describe the police's behaviour, especially that of Swanepoel, and his partner. He steadfastly refuses my request, but digs a tissue out of the desk drawer and hands it over to me. I proclaim my innocence and say they have no right to keep me. I am guilty of nothing more than obeying my husband. He had asked me to do certain things and I did them. Any wife would do the same. While I sob part of me hopes that the sobbing will have some effect, though exactly what I cannot begin to know. Everything seems so hopeless. I am now faced with imprisonment for ninety days. I suppose there is some comfort in knowing that somebody in authority knows what happened at the Gray's Building, despite his obvious lack of sympathy.

I am moved to another cell, which I am told was Hazel Goldreich's. I can hear Hazel arguing and saying she will not move unless she can have her mattress: 'I'm used to it and I won't go.' I am still too traumatised and intimidated to shout out anything to her.

My new cell is really small with a high window in the one corner, a thick door with a peephole, a cot bed and mattress, cream-coloured walls and a bare bulb hanging a few inches from the ceiling. I stand on the bed and try to look out of the window. It is much too high. At least I can hear street noises. There is the a sound of traffic, and I think that this will give me some idea of time. There are the sounds of black voices and laughter; only the thickness of this wall separates me from life outside.

What does one do in a cell? I wonder. Many a time since Harold's arrest and the subterfuge, organisation, rushing from one place to another, visiting Marshall Square nightly, I have thought how peaceful it might be to sit in a jail. There would be nothing to do. There would be no trauma. There would be no tension. Well, that is what I thought. The reality is very different.

I get up from the bed, and pace the cell. It is four by three big steps. Maybe I can do some ballet exercises. I stand up in first position, heels touching, feet outstretched, and try to do a plié. My legs are stiff, and it strikes me as ludicrous to pretend that I can do any ballet exercises. It is twenty years and one severed Achilles tendon since I last tried doing anything like this. I stop. I try to recall the book by Stefan Zweig in which he had described the imaginary chess game played on the board formed from the light through the bars of the window. Was it his own imprisonment? I cannot recall. Whatever the circumstances, I recognise that chess is not a game I really enjoy playing.

It must be mid-afternoon; the cell door is opened and a small suitcase is flung in at me. I open it up eagerly. It is a major disappointment. There are minimal toilet requirements, a change of underwear, a nightshirt and nothing else, not even a change of clothes. I am still in the shapeless grey shift that I so dislike. Marlene must have got this together. Such a pity that she has no imagination. I bang on the door, calling to be let out to the toilet. That would prove a distraction. The response is slow, and I am told to hurry. The toilet is one of two in a little courtyard outside the cell, so the distraction is limited. I am escorted back to the cell and huddle under the blankets for warmth. The prospect is bleak.

It seems to be dusk. I can see that the outside has got darker, so it must be about six o'clock. The cell door opens unexpectedly. The two policemen who brought me here last night are standing there. 'What do you want?' I ask querulously. They don't answer me. My immediate thought is that they are going to take me to another jail, out of town. At least in Marshall Square I know that Hazel and Ruth are here. It is small comfort, but comfort nevertheless.

I repeat the question. 'Just wait and see. Maybe you're going to be moved,' is the reply. 'But where?' I plead. No answer. I follow them to the charge office. 'Here are your things. You can go home now.'

I don't believe it. 'Are you sure? You're not going to arrest me again?' I say. I am answered with a truly hollow laugh, and the policemen walk away. 'I have to use a phone,' I say to the desk sergeant. 'I will phone my brother James Kantor to fetch me.' I assume that his name is well known, and that they will respond appropriately. It is, and they do. The phone is moved so that I can dial.

I call Jimmy and tell him to fetch me from Marshall Square. 'Please hurry,' I plead with him. I am desperate to leave the premises, and want to get out before they change their minds.

It does not seem too long before Jimmy appears at the charge desk. He is quite jocular with me: 'About time you went home.' And he makes some feeble joke about my neglecting my children. I say nothing. I wait until I am safe in the car, then I break into uncontrollable sobbing.

'Oh James, they were unbearable. They were unbearable. I thought they were going to kill me yesterday. They frightened me terribly. They were so horrible.' I am surprised at the intensity of my sobbing. I don't recall ever having sobbed like this before.

Jimmy is clearly shocked. I know he has a temper, and a quick one at that. This triggers it off. He swings the car violently around and says, 'They will pay for this. I won't have them behaving like that to my sister.'

'For Christ's sake, what the hell are you going to do? I want to go home.'

'I'm going to the Gray's. I am going to lay a charge against the bastards who threatened you. They can't behave like that.' This really frightens me. I entreat him: 'Please don't go near the place. You don't know what they're like. I don't want to go near the building ever again. Please, Jimmy.'

It seems that the more I sob and beg of him to desist, the more he is inflamed. 'Nobody, but nobody, is going to treat my sister like that.' 'You really don't know what they're like,' I plead. 'They torture. They're demoniacal. You just don't have a clue.'

It's no good: he refuses to be deterred. We get to the Gray's building, and Jimmy disappears inside. I sit in the car outside, literally shaking. Thank heavens, he returns quickly. 'There's no one around,' he says, 'but I have arranged for you to attend an identity parade tomorrow morning to pick out the thugs who have assaulted you.' I have told Jimmy that the magistrate said that technically I had been assaulted. The police are not supposed to threaten or shake the prisoner in a chair the way they did to me. If that is technical assault, I think, then God help those who are actually assaulted.

We return to Jimmy's house. There is no one there. 'Baba is staying at the dam with the boys,' says Jimmy. 'We both thought it would be better for everyone if she was out of town at the time. I called the press,' he adds, 'just before I left to pick you up. They'll be here any minute.'

I feel absolutely dreadful and totally demoralised. I am still wearing the horrid grey shift dress I put on yesterday morning. It feels as though I have been living in the garment. Well, I suppose I have. I slept in it last night, and haven't yet had an opportunity to wash or change my underwear. I haven't brushed my teeth since Sunday morning. And I have no make-up on at all.

I do not feel in a fit state to meet anyone, let alone the press. Jimmy is insistent. 'They want a picture of you. You see, there was a report in this morning's paper that you had been assaulted. Marlene was interviewed and said that when you phoned you said that you had been hit across the face. They want to hear from you what happened.'

I protest: 'I'm so tired. No one hit me I just want to go home to my children. I don't want to see anyone except my kids' – to no avail. He is adamant.

I am chain-smoking by now. Suddenly there is a flurry of activity. The room seems to be filled with reporters and photographers. I go through the story much as I told it to Jimmy, and the ordeal is soon over.

'The Fischers also want to see you,' Jimmy says. Not long after the *Rand Daily Mail* reporter and photographer leave, the doorbell rings, and it is Bram and Molly. They come in beaming. They are nothing short of jubilant. 'We've beaten them for the first time in ages. The townships have gone wild. People are absolutely thrilled about the escape. It's come at a time when everything looked so bleak for the forces of resistance.'

They don't seem to hear me saying that it was horrible. What happened to me is unimportant in comparison with the effect of the escape, and anyway, I'm out of jail. Although they stay only a short while, it seems interminable. Eventually I am on my way home.

Marlene is out. Angelina is babysitting. As I walk into the house and I see her I burst into tears again. Angelina puts her arms round me, guides me to the small settee in the sitting-room and sits down with me, holding me in her arms.

'Sho sho,' she tries to soothe me. 'They mustn't see you like this. The little girls mustn't see you like this.' And she is right, of course. 'They don't know what happened. We told them when they came home on Sunday night that you were away for a few days. So they don't know anything.'

'Oh, Nina, I was so frightened,' I tell her. 'And I thought I wouldn't see the kids for years and years. I thought they would just hold me for ninety days and then another ninety days and then just make sure that I didn't get out of jail for years and years.'

This is the first time the two of us have behaved in such a way that there are no more barriers between us. The deep chasm created by race and mistress–servant relations has disappeared. In the midst of my misery I recognise the amazing effect that this situation has created. I have no need to explain anything to her and she is able to comfort me like a mother or sister.

For the past five years that this woman has worked for me she has looked after my children and loved them as her own. She has never had children of her own, and it is clear to me that she would have made a superb mother. She once told me that she could not afford to have them. She has always maintained a distance between the two of us, irrespective of what I have said. I recognise that she has every reason to be suspicious of me. After all, I am the white madam and she is the black servant.

Somehow, tonight, that barrier has been broken down completely. We are women on an equal footing, and in her quiet yet strong way she is giving me strength to carry on. I go to bed, feeling calmer than I could have imagined, to await the next day's events.

Days of Freedom

DAY ONE

HAROLD WOKE instantly after what seemed like only a catnap, although he had in fact slept for three hours. The smell of percolating coffee seeped into his consciousness. For the first time in what now seemed like an eternity he felt truly hungry; he drank the welcome coffee and ate a slice of hot toast with lashings of butter which soaked into the bread. He ate as though he were at a magnificent banquet. No food ever tasted sweeter or more tempting than this simple breakfast on the first morning of freedom.

Barney turned on the radio. Not only was their escape the main news, but every fifteen minutes the regular programmes were interrupted by a shrill bleep, followed by an announcement that four political detainees had escaped from Marshall Square. Their names were broadcast, and an appeal was made to the public to give every assistance possible that could lead to their apprehension. Reward for information was offered. Already information was coming in, it was predicted that their arrest could be expected shortly. They also heard how Greef had been arrested. There was not much news on this.

The news bulletins continued throughout the day. They had made history. It seemed that never before had a news item dominated the radio so much as their escape did. The security forces were using every possible device to recapture them, and the media were among their instruments. Harold heard with horror of my arrest. The news was short and sharp: two of the wives of the escaped prisoners had been taken in for questioning, but I the only one being held.

The urgency of the bleeped messages contributed to the

tension of the day. Barney had to go to his parents' house for Sunday lunch; anyway he had been advised by Mannie to keep clear of the flat until both fugitives were moved elsewhere in case anything went wrong. He needed an alibi, however slender. All day long Arthur and Harold took turns in keeping an unobtrusive watch at the window. Apart from a police van which parked nearby for half an hour, there was no other indication of any problem. So far so good.

By eight that night both men felt exhausted. Neither had had much sleep over the past forty-eight hours, and the nervous tension was taking its toll. They both fell into a heavy sleep, only to be suddenly awakened by the awareness of someone's presence. Arthur sprang out of bed, ready to fight. 'Relax, man, it's only me,' laughed Mannie. 'You two have got to move. We're not sure how long you will be safe here. I'm going to drive you to an empty house we know about in Norwood. We know that some time tomorrow an estate agent is supposed to be coming to have a look around. You'll have to keep yourself out of sight. Probably get into the attic or stay in the servants' quarters. The agent just wants to see what the place is like. Let's hope you'll not be seen. We'll move you again to a safer venue.' He paused and added, 'Hopefully.'

Harold and Arthur exchanged worried glances. 'That sounds really crazy,' ventured Arthur. 'Moving us twice doesn't seem the most sensible thing to do. Haven't you heard the radio today? They're pulling out every stop to get their hands on us, and boy, I don't fancy landing up in their hands again. They'll give us a real going over, to say the least.' Harold nodded in assent. He knew what the security forces were capable of. Mosie's eardrums had been pierced and both he and Abdullah had given them graphic descriptions of the torture they had been subjected to. Mannie became serious for a moment. 'It isn't easy finding safe accommodation. We've tried Cyril Jones's place. We've used it quite often. It's helluva bad luck, something's happened to a member of his wife's family and she's going down to Cape Town, so that place is out. People are really scared since Rivonia, and you two are hot stuff at the moment.

Babette drew up a list of people's names to try, and we haven't been very successful.'

There was no alternative: they had to travel three miles to their destination in Norwood. It was eleven at night. Arthur crouched down on the front seat, and Harold squeezed himself on to the floor space at the back. Without incident they arrived at their destination, a dark empty house. Hazel's cousin was there to meet them. Mannie repeated the warning about the estate agent's visit the next day, and they were exhorted to be extra careful to avoid detection. 'By tomorrow night our committee will have come up with something better,' Mannie assured the two fugitives. 'I bloody well hope so,' retorted Harold, who had worked on just such a committee at the time when they had been trying to get Nelson Mandela out of jail the previous year.

The temperature had plummeted fourteen degrees, and it was bitingly cold inside the empty house. There was nothing except a carpet on the floor of what must have been the sitting-room. Both men curled up on the floor. Each felt vulnerable and scared, and finally drifted off into a troubled sleep.

DAY TWO

Harold woke at daybreak with a migraine attack, to which he was prone, and which could leave him unable to move. 'Maybe it's just cold and hunger,' he consoled himself.

Together they cautiously peered outside. The front of the house was some way back from the street. There was a low fence; a once-neat lawn was now overgrown. The place looked neglected and uncared for. The house seemed to have been unoccupied for some time. There were some unremarkable shrubs and a few trees in the front. The back yard was blocked off from the front garden by a wall. From the kitchen window they could see a high brick boundary wall with a door, probably leading into another road. High hedges took over where the brick wall ended. There were the usual servants' quarters, two small rooms in a bad state of repair, a shower screened off from a toilet which had long since lost its seat, and a bowl that was stained black. The kitchen had a stack of old newspapers, and one of the servants' rooms had the remnants of a torn and aged curtain whose floral print was barely visible.

'This is it,' Arthur said assertively. 'We'll hide in one of these rooms. Let's cover the window with the rags and newspapers so nobody can see in, and lock ourselves inside until the agent has been. What do you think?' Harold agreed. Arthur had been able to lock one of the servants' rooms with a key from a bunch lying on the kitchen sink. It was better than trying to get into the attic and hiding there in darkness all day. And they both felt they would be secure locked into one of the rooms. It was highly unlikely that a potential buyer would be all that much concerned about the state of the servants' quarters. It was the number of rooms available, rather than their condition, which would be of interest.

The two men settled down for their long wait in their secure little prison. The sun removed the early cold of the day, and directed its warming rays against the door. Neither could resist the temptation to squat outside the kitchen door and allow the heat to radiate through their cold bodies. They seemed to be safe from prying eyes. Arthur was getting more and more fidgety, and wanted to explore his surroundings. 'Don't be a fool, man,' Harold admonished, as he moved back into the one room. Arthur could not contain himself, and kept walking up and down in the back yard.

Thump thump. The sound of heavy, urgent, insistent knocking on the locked garden door broke the quietness of the wintry suburban day. Arthur hurried towards the servants' quarters, a look of fear on his face. 'My God, I think whoever it is jumped up to look over the wall,' he said, rather tremulously. Harold realised there was no point in upbraiding Arthur for his folly. 'What do you think will happen?' Arthur asked urgently. If he had been seen, and the person knew that the house was supposed to be empty, he might go and report the matter to the police. 'If the guy is black – and it's unlikely that a white would come banging on the back gate – then it'll take him some time to get to a police station. It'll take about an hour for something to happen,' Arthur worked out. For the next sixty minutes they kept an anxious lookout at both front and rear entrances. Time tiptoed silently by. The sixty minutes passed, and they were able to breathe more freely once again.

Harold tapped on his front shirt pocket, checking that the newspaper cutting showing Nicholas's homecoming was in place. He found himself feeling that as long as he had the cutting with him, all would go well.

Arthur and Harold did not chat much. Each wondered about the plight of his wife. It was too painful to discuss. Hazel was stuck in Marshall Square, and Harold knew that I had been arrested. He worried inwardly. They kept a silent watch, each one thinking about the possibilities of the success of their venture.

Their vigil was broken by the arrival of a relative of Hazel's with some food. It was now five o'clock, and unlikely that any estate agent would arrive. They began to relax and wolfed down the cold beef, pickled cucumbers, and bread and butter. She couldn't tell them what arrangements had been made; she said they would have to wait for Mannie, who would come and move them to a safer place.

With the setting sun the cold began to descend, and they found themselves shivering. They felt it was safe to move back into the house. At least the room inside was carpeted, and they were bound to be warmer than on the concrete floor of the servant's room. Arthur had brought a loose brick he had found in the back garden as a weapon – hardly effective, but at least something. It was close on eleven o'clock when they heard the front door open and light footsteps coming towards the room in which they were crouching. Harold felt his blood chilling, and the hackles on the back of his neck rising. In the softest of voices he asked Arthur, 'It's too quiet for the cops, don't you think?' In the darkness he could make out Arthur's shrug of his shoulders. They crept towards the kitchen, hearts beating rapidly.

'Where the hell are you guys?' Mannie's voice sounded like a cannonball. The two men burst out laughing. It was the first time either of them had laughed in many a day. Relief flooded Harold's body, and he felt like jumping up and down in sheer delight. He tapped his shirt pocket.

They were to be moved. First they were to be given a meal

and a chance to wash, almost like condemned men. They crisscrossed the northern suburbs, resuming the same positions they had held in last night's car to the home of friends of Arthur. Children and servants all safely out of sight, the two fugitives were given a stiff whisky each. They both asked to see the day's paper. Photographs of all four men appeared, the picture of Nicholas's homecoming, with me holding him, and one of Mosie's wife. Harold's heart sank as he read about my detention. He said nothing. The atmosphere was tense, but the whisky and the food had a tranquillising effect. They started with a piping-hot barley soup, followed by a fried fillet steak and chips, and then a fruit salad. Both men ate with gusto, and by the end of the meal Harold felt filled to bursting point. Arthur suddenly came to life and kept up a lively chatter, alternately amusing and gripping his audience with a brief description of their flight.

At the end of the meal each man went off to have a hot bath, and Harold found himself drowsy while the hot water lapped round his shoulders. He got out of the bath in a leisurely manner, wrapped the big bath towel round his body, and massaged himself dry. He washed his underpants, and was wringing them out when he heard the shrill ringing of what must have been the front-door bell. This set the two ridgeback dogs barking furiously. Harold's immediate thought was that they had finally been traced. Nobody except the cops would ring a doorbell at that time of night, he thought. He dressed hurriedly, waiting in the bathroom.

There was no thundering noise of a police entry. Instead, a timid knock on the door brought him out. Standing there was Mannie. 'I've come to take you fellows away,' he said. 'We're sure you'll be OK there. We'd better get moving quickly.'

DAY THREE

It was well after midnight when they set out once again. This time they had to drive for some distance along Louis Botha Avenue, the main road that passed Alexandra Township and led to Pretoria and the North – a road which they thought would be heavily patrolled by the police.

Luck was still with them: no police controls.

They were taken to a cottage in Mountain View which stood in the large grounds of a house belonging to the Kreels. The cottage had been used by the underground movement. 'We're not happy about putting you here,' Mannie said. Kathy – referring to Kathrada – 'was the last person to use the place, and we have a vague feeling that the police may have got wind of it. We've been unable to come up with anything better than this. Everyone's running shy. We've tried every possible contact, but nobody wants to know.'

The fugitives arrived without incident at 1.30 in the morning. Quickly and stealthily they were led to their new home, a one-roomed cottage. The story was that the Kreels rented the cottage to a businessman who was away from time to time, although he did have friends coming to stay. At the moment he was known to be away. 'You two will have to be invisible. You won't be able to put on lights or cook or do anything that could indicate that the cottage is occupied. It has to look empty.' Mannie emphasised this. He went on, 'Leon and Maureen are both out at work all day. They have a five-year-old daughter, who is at nursery school in the morning. She is likely to play out in the garden in the afternoon. There are two servants – a man and a woman, who both sleep on the premises. So you two have got to be' – and he paused to emphasise his words – '*deadly quiet*. I mean quiet. We haven't been able to find you any other place to be, and we're not a hundred per cent sure about this place. So day and night you've got to make like you're not here.' Mannie was talking softly, but the men looked at each other and felt like muffling him. His voice seemed to ring out in the large room.

Mannie made sure the curtains were drawn, and then he switched on a small lamp so that they could get their bearings. The walls were painted white, and there was a poster advertising an exhibition. They found some black material lying about and Arthur tried to fix it around the windows. There were two single beds at right angles to each other, with brightly coloured blankets. A round wooden table with water marks and some wooden chairs stood in the middle of the room. One corner had a makeshift kitchen – just a shelf with a single hotplate, a few chipped white plates, three mugs, and a sugar bowl. In the other corner stood an old-fashioned wardrobe and a whitewood chest of drawers. A small bathroom led off the other corner of the room.

Mannie produced a bottle of whisky and poured them each a tot. He obviously felt relieved to have them safely ensconced in the house, and began to regale them with an account of the effect of their escape: 'Man, the papers have had the biggest headlines I've ever seen: GOLDREICH AND WOLPE, 36 HOURS AND STILL NO TRACE OF THEM. The hours of your freedom are being counted; it sounds like countdown to your capture.' He gave a shallow laugh. 'Everyone's being told to keep a lookout for you two. The government is in a mess! The Minister of Justice has been made to look like a complete asshole. He had been bleating out everywhere that they have completely smashed the Communists and all the subversives, and now you two have ruined it all. Those buggers have got to capture you to prove that they are on top of all the subversives. They're just not bothered with Mosie and Abdullah. Shows you what racists the buggers are. Because they're Indians they don't count!' Both men were eager to hear what had happened to Mosie and Abdullah. 'You'll never believe it,' Mannie said. 'They were walking down Commissioner Street when a car drew up next to them. It was Dasso Joseph, who had just finished his shift at a restaurant and was on his way home. He recognised them, and has taken them to a place of safety. The cops just aren't bothered with them, it would seem. So they're lying low for the present.' He went on, 'The townships went absolutely wild with delight when the news broke about your escape. Everyone there has been talking about it. They're over the moon. It's the biggest defeat these bastards have had, and there's no way we're going to let them get hold of you.' Harold and Arthur exchanged wry smiles. They felt the same way.

Later in the morning they woke, stretched, and Harold yawned noisily. 'Watch it, Harold,' cautioned Arthur. 'We don't know who's around and how the sound carries.' Arthur was right. They would have to be extremely wary during the day. The curtains could not be opened, nor the windows. Even the rasp of the match on the flint sounded like an explosion, and they were worried that the gardener would hear and wonder.

They breakfasted on uncooked bacon, some dry water biscuits and a cup of water . The kitchen wasn't exactly well stocked. The food was passable. So continued their third day of freedom. Mannie had thoughtfully dropped some old newspapers the night before, and they settled down to read. Sipping what passed for morning coffee – yet another cup of water they poured carefully from the jug they had filled the night before – they read avidly, both fascinated with the accounts of their escape.

'I haven't got a clean pair of underpants,' said Harold. 'I left my only pair in the bathroom when I was washing them last night. Bugger it.' He started to look round the room. He found a pair of underpants neatly folded in the drawers. 'Good God, Kathy's been here.' His name had been written on the inside waistband. 'I'm sure he won't mind me wearing his pants.' It was a visible reminder to them of how closely they were linked to those arrested at Rivonia; Kathrada was one of them.

They found a chessboard in the wardrobe, and spent the morning playing. The last time Harold had played was during the 1960 Emergency, when he was locked up with all the others; chess had been one of the detainees' most popular games. Their new prison was pleasant by comparison. By lunchtime the air was heavy with smoke from the cigarettes they puffed at. There would be no visitors during the day. Contact could be made only late at night, when the chances of detection were minimal.

Harold realised how much more acute his hearing had become since his imprisonment. He noticed sounds that previously would have passed him by. So it was not surprising that he heard the five-year-old come out to play. She took up a position on the veranda of the cottage and kept up a constant chatter. It sounded as though she had an imaginary friend. He found her presence reassuring. She represented a real world that existed outside.

The day went by slowly. They could not flush the toilet. It would make too much noise. They could not run a tap. The water going into the drain would be a giveaway. They could wash only at night, when there was less chance of being heard. By mid-afternoon they both felt restless. They did not even dare whisper in case the little girl heard them.

It was 11.30 that night when Bram and Ivan Schermbrucker knocked gently on the door and whispered their names. They had come laden with food.

The two men eagerly unpacked: juicy navel oranges, apples and a pawpaw, some polony, bread, powdered milk, Nescafé, a bottle of brandy, a loaf of bread, and a bottle of apricot jam. Harold grimaced at the sight of the jam. 'My mother gave me apricot jam sandwiches every day of my life for school,' he said. 'I can't stand the taste of it now. How about bringing me a slab of Cadbury's dark chocolate?'

This was the beginning of the nightly visits from members of the escape committee that had been formed. Usually it was Mannie who came, but on the third night Hilda Bernstein arrived. Both Hilda and her husband Rusty had been activists for years, and were close friends of ours. One or the other was always being arrested, and Rusty was one of those picked up by the police at Rivonia. Hilda was unrecognisable. She was wearing an old raincoat that looked as though it had come from a school jumble sale, a scarf over her hair, dark glasses, and gym shoes. She had taken her car into Berea, then got on to a bus going in one direction, off a few stops later, and changed direction. She made sure nobody followed her. The three of them sat sipping brandy and talking over the various possibilities. There weren't many options.

Getting across the border at Bechuanaland was the obvious choice. How to get to the border was the obvious problem. 'We think there are massive border posts,' Hilda said. 'We've been going through the maps carefully. The snag is how to disguise you in a motorcar. There are probably blocks on all the main roads out of Johannesburg, so that is really the major danger point.'

In the early evening, when their room grew dark and there

was no way they could read or play chess, even though they could now whisper without fear of being heard, their conversation was desultory and finally petered out, each man withdrawing into the silence of his own thoughts. Harold was not one for recriminations. He did not regret his involvement at all. He had come to politics through the rigours of intellectual debate and thought. His was not an emotional reaction. He hated apartheid and the misery it caused. He rejected racism and its consequences. He believed that a racially free society was possible. He could not allow the doubts that entered his mind to dominate. It was difficult enough doing what he had been doing without this. Yet he was fully aware of the traumas he had caused his family, and worried about them.

He had read with great care the report that had appeared on the front page of the *Mail*, with a picture of me looking away from the camera, talking to someone and smoking. My face looked strained, and he had shuddered at the thought of what was happening to me.

Harold and Arthur were becoming accustomed to what soon became a routine way of living. They postponed getting up in the morning and would lie in bed until well after eight o'clock, taking it in turn to bring one another a cup of coffee in bed.

Today it was Arthur's turn. Harold was lying in bed, lazily blowing smoke rings into the air. *Bang, bang, bang.* His blood froze. Thunderous knocking on the door. Each man looked at the other, but said nothing. Again an insistent knocking on the door. Then, as suddenly as it had come, the knocking ceased, and they heard heavy footsteps walking away. Neither got up to see who the intruder was. It happened again the next morning. This time the banging was at the kitchen door of the Kreels' house, and they heard a rough voice, with a heavy Afrikaans accent, saying, 'Where's the missis?' Each man thought: This is it. They've finally caught up with us. They couldn't hear the answer. The man must have gone into the kitchen. It was just moments before they heard him walking away.

They had been in hiding for ten long days. On some nights

the monotony would be broken by a visit from one or other member of the escape committee. It was Thursday night. Mannie arrived at eleven o'clock. It didn't seem to matter what the problem was, Mannie always maintained an easy-going, joking style, as though he took nothing seriously.

'Well, we can't stand you fellows around any more.' He laughed, gulping a swig of brandy. 'It's too much bother bringing you razors and food and papers. You're on your way out.' He paused to see what effect his words were having.

They both put their glasses down, as though on cue. 'Well?' Mannie enjoyed the moment of tension, and delayed his response. 'I bought a car today for cash. It's a big Ford. You two are going to be disguised as women, and you will be driven by someone. Neither of you know him. He is absolutely trustworthy. He'll drive you to Swaziland. We've had various people driving all over the place, and it seems that the roads to Swaziland are virtually clear. There're road blocks everywhere else, particularly the roads to Bechuanaland.'

He stopped. Both men let out a laugh of sheer delight. The prospect of being on the move again was wonderful.

'Look what I've brought for you.' Mannie had two parcels of women's clothing, and some concoction for removing their body hair.

For the next hour Mannie and Harold could barely contain their laughter as Arthur went through a series of mimes in the different garments Mannie had brought. He was a sophisticated woman in a tight black skirt and a white blouse, puffing seductively at a cigarette. He was a dumpy depressed woman from Fordsburg with a scarf hiding her curlers. He was a young, eager, bright kugel. He put on lipstick, he fluttered his eyes, he minced along the carpet swinging his hips from side to side. Tears fell down Harold's cheeks, and eventually he rolled on the floor.

'It's no good, Mannie,' he said finally. 'If Arthur looks like somone in drag, can you imagine what I'll look like?'

Mannie wiped his eyes dry. 'I've got to agree. You chaps just don't look like women. It won't work. The first cop that sees you will know immediately it's you two pretending to be women.' The three of them contemplated the possibilities. 'There's only one way to do it,' Mannie said. 'The two of you will have to travel in the boot.' At least the boot of the car was likely to be roomy.

At eleven o'clock the following night, Mannie arrived once more at the cottage. 'We've got some tarpaulins in the boot to cover you two with. We've taken out the loudspeaker from the radio on the back window. This should let sufficient air into the boot, and the back window will be left open. You two won't suffocate,' he said encouragingly. Neither of them had thought about this. They had only contemplated what would happen if they met a road block.

The house was on a quiet road. Even during the day, it seemed empty. Mannie had checked this out. And at this time of night there was practically no chance of being seen in the road – or so Mannie had told them. He went first, with Arthur and Harold hard on his heels, to the waiting car, with its open boot.

No sign of anyone except the driver. 'This is Crawford, who's going to drive you to Swaziland.' Besides registering that Crawford was a young man who looked no older than his early twenties, Harold did not notice anything more. The three men shook hands speedily, and then Arthur and Harold climbed awkwardly into the boot. It wasn't easy stretching out and fitting themselves into position. Their heads were towards the back seat, their backs to the opening. 'Here's something to keep you going.' And Mannie threw in a small bag of oranges. It must have been he who covered them first with the blanket and then with the tarpaulins. 'Nobody would know there're two bodies here.' Somehow they didn't believe Mannie. The boot was banged closed, there was a thump on the metal, and they heard the car rev up.

So began the long journey to Swaziland. They had to cover about 230 miles to the border, and the driver estimated it would take him about six hours' driving. Although it was really cold, both Harold and Arthur quickly warmed up under the blankets and tarpaulin.

'Hey, you two.' They heard Crawford's voice. 'We've just

passed Benoni. The roads are pretty empty, and not a sign of a cop.' This was the first of Crawford's commentaries. 'We're going to go on tarred roads from Johannesburg to Ermelo. These are main roads and not too bad. We'll be passing through Leslie, Bethal and Ermelo.' Bethal was notorious. The white farmers of that area were known for their use of black convict labour, and it was Ruth who had exposed their foul practices. 'You'd better be comfortable because you two have a long spell in the boot.' He laughed encouragingly, then started singing Frank Sinatra's 'My Way'. Arthur joined in.

They must have been going at least two hours, and the two men found their limbs getting stiffer and stiffer. There was nothing they could do. They couldn't stretch their legs. All they could do was flex their muscles and wiggle their toes. At least my gout's better, Harold thought to himself. 'I'm going to stop for petrol at Leslie,' Crawford said, 'so don't be worried. Obviously I'll check that there're no cops around.'

He gave them time checks. He described the places they drove through. He spoke of the stars in the night. 'It's a wonderfully clear night, and if I look away from the lights of the road into the sky I can see the Milky Way,' he said cheerfully. The trip came alive for the two men trapped in the back.

'We've passed Ermelo. We're now moving on to a dirt road. We're more than halfway now, about ninety miles from the border.' He laughed. 'Ermelo's a really one-horse town. Would you believe it – I nearly missed the turning to Breyten. I'm going to take smaller roads now, and they're likely to be a bit bumpy. Sorry, there's nothing I can do.'

When he reached a tiny village called Lothair he was able to report: 'We're now about thirty-seven miles from the border.' The two men in the boot felt reassured. 'We're meeting up with someone who is going to guide us across the border. He knows all the roads inside out, and will know the best way for us to go. We've arranged a rendezvous at a small junction with a road that should take us across the border.'

It was now almost five o'clock, still pitch dark, and no sign of the rising sun. The car came to a halt. 'I'll let you two out for a stretch,' said Crawford. 'I can see for miles around, so no one can take us by surprise.' The boot was opened, and the two men felt a gush of cold air coming in as the tarpaulin was lifted off them. Neither could get out at first. Each was fixed into a foetal position, and could not move his legs. 'My bloody legs are filled with pins and needles,' Harold complained. 'I can't get them to move.' As the blood coursed through their stiffened limbs, they extricated themselves from their sanctuary. Arthur was the first to clamber out, and Harold followed clumsily. They stretched their arms up, they rubbed their limbs, and both lit up cigarettes. 'Christ, I can't face getting back in,' said Harold. They jumped up and down and swung their arms. 'You've had enough of a break,' said Crawford. 'The other car is due to arrive, and I want you both inside before he comes. We still need to be cautious.' He was remarkably cool and self-possessed for so young a man.

The two men resumed their positions, and Crawford covered them with the tarpaulin. 'Here he comes,' and they could hear another car braking, a door being slammed, and then muffled voices. It was Crawford talking to someone else. The Ford took off again, with the stranger leading the way.

They drove for ten minutes. The car stopped yet again. This time Crawford did not have time to tell them what was happening. The two men heard a car door slam, and then a loud banging on the boot: 'Get out, this is the South African police.' Both Arthur and Harold froze. They had got so far and so close to the border. The tension was broken by a loud, raucous laugh. 'You can get out now. We're across the border.' It was their border guide, who would now take them to Mbabane. He had, as Harold was later to say, a macabre sense of humour. For him it was 'fun and games'.

Getting out of the boot was not so bad this time. They had not yet had time to stiffen up so completely. They both embraced Crawford, who shyly turned tail and took off into the morning light, back to Johannesburg. There was no time for thank-yous. 'How do you say thank you to someone like that?' Harold said as they sat with their guide from Swaziland. Their destination was a Mission.

The realisation that they were free soon dawned on both men. 'Yeah,' screamed Arthur. Harold responded with a yelp. They laughed out loud, they shouted and screamed. It was the first time in almost two weeks that they had spoken above a whisper. They were like two little schoolboys, unable to contain their excitement. 'Free at last, free at last . . .' that refrain again. They were in a British Protectorate, safe from the avenging wrath of the South African Special Branch. Free. Free. Free. They laughed raucously; they said over and over again: 'We're free'.

REPORT FROM THE STAR: 12 SEPTEMBER 1964

Leon and Maureen Kreel were acquitted and discharged this week at the end of their year-long trial in Johannesburg. The 28-year-old pharmacist and his wife had been charged under the Suppression of Communism Act, and with harbouring Arthur Goldreich and Harold Wolpe after their escape from Marshall Square on August 10 last year.

The State alleged that the Kreels allowed the fugitives to hide in a cottage in the grounds of their home in Terrace Road Mountain View.

They pleaded not guilty before Mr. W.G. Vos. This morning the magistrate alluded to the Rivonia raid and the subsequent raid on the Kreels' home and cottage which, a listed Communist (arrested at Rivonia) had pointed out to the police. On this raid, the fingerprints of Goldreich and Wolpe were discovered on various articles and charred scraps of paper, later proved to be portions of Communist literature, were found lying on a compost heap. There was evidence about an attempt to cover the windows with black cloth and shade the lights.

. . . Two men, who gave their names as Donald Williams and Pedro Perreira, later turned out to have been Ahmed Kathrada and Dennis Goldberg (Rivonia trialists).

Mr. Vos said the State had failed to prove that either Kathrada and Goldberg, or Goldreich and Wolpe, had stayed at the cottage with the knowledge and consent of the Kreels.

Evidence was that these 'cunning and ruthless men,

Goldreich and Wolpe, had taken the greatest precaution to conceal their presence, and identity from everyone.'

There was no evidence to show that Maureen Kreel had deliberately tried to clear the cottage of incriminating evidence. If this was so, Mr. Vos said, she would not have left so many incriminating articles including a jacket of Goldreich's with a Nelson Mandela badge, for the police to find.

My New Image

I AM FREE and Harold is free. I don't have any strong feelings about his freedom. I am so completely drained by yesterday's events that I don't really care, one way or the other. I have done my bit for him. Now I am on my own. Or so it feels.

Jimmy's wife, Barbara, comes round to the house. 'You look terrible,' she says. 'I'm going to do something about it. I'll take you to my hairdresser for a cut and trim. You need to do something to buck yourself up.'

I feel I am unable to make any decision for myself, so I let myself be persuaded by her. Normally I go to hairdressers only for a cut. I never have my hair set.

We enter the salon, which is in Rosebank. The sickly smell of hair spray permeates the air. There is a bustle of activity catering for the needs of all these fashionable women. Opposite me a woman is sitting under the hair dryer, with one hand resting in a small bowl of soapy water, while the other hand is caressed by a woman who holds the limp hand on a small towel and massages the cuticles. The two are having a loud conversation about the dinner party the customer will be holding tonight. The place is abuzz. Barbara has a word with her man; and a gown is put round me, and my hair is washed. Instead of cutting or drying it, a woman puts a foul-smelling lotion on my hair. I don't realise until too late that it is being coloured, and I sit for an hour before the hairdresser examines me. He looks at me in the mirror, picks up strands of my hair, fluffs it out and *tsks*. 'I'll cut very little,' he says. 'What I'm going to do is straighten it. It's far too curly, and quite shapeless.' I nod. Who am I to question this man, who is reputed to be one of the best stylists in Johannesburg?

While I sit there I cannot ignore the absurdity of the situation. Here I am, the wife of one of the most wanted men in the country – 'the biggest fish', as Vorster would have everyone believe – sitting in this up-market hairdresser's salon being dolled up. I can't help wondering if anyone knows who I am. Maybe they wouldn't be so solicitous if they did, although Barbara has probably had a word with her man.

There is something to be said for making some effort with one's appearance. I remember Rica's description of how she had worked on all the women with whom she had been locked up during the 1960 emergency. Rica Hodgson has always been glamorous. In the 1950s she wore her hair in a Rita Hayworth style. She has well-manicured nails, and wears tight-fitting skirts with thin high heels. She smokes endlessly, sporting a long cigarette holder which, she claims, is for filtering the cigarettes. I think it's more for effect. Rica, like her husband Jack, has long been involved in politics. The two of them are Communists. Jack escaped arrest at the time of the Emergency, but Rica was picked up. She made sure that the women she was with in jail had their hair done every week, she taught some of them how to use make-up, and she manicured their nails. Rica had originally trained as a hairdresser. 'They all felt much better for it, you know,' she said, referring specifically to those women who looked as though they never spent any time on themselves. 'They really blossomed,' she insisted. She kept up her standards no matter where. When she was moved on her own to an open jail in the countryside, she would sit in the evening sipping a potent cocktail she had concocted from fermented fruit peel. She could enjoy the beauty of the Transvaal sunset, listening to the ever-enveloping quietness of the evening as the crickets stopped their frantic clicking and the sounds of the day diminished, drinking her cocktail and smoking.

I emerge with wonderful glowing chestnut hair, all traces of grey obliterated, softly curling under. All signs of the obstinate curls have disappeared. I am pleased with the result and relish entering this world of make-believe, even if only for a short time.

Home is a haven of peace. Nicholas is outside in his pram

next to the glass-fronted sitting-room, kicking his legs, free from any covering in the warm winter sun. It is amazing how normal the child is looking. His large dark eyes, which used to follow the movement of everyone in his hospital room, are now sparkling. He is just wonderful, and I cannot quite believe the miracle of his being alive. He gives me more comfort than anything else, and when I'm with him I can forget the problems of everything that surrounds me.

There are not many people who do come to see me, and certainly nobody from the movement. I have a sense that people are avoiding me. I don't have expectations, and certainly don't anticipate that they will come – if I'm honest, I probably don't want them to either.

Rumours are flying about, and the newspapers are dominated by speculation on the fugitives. The *Daily Despatch* has big headlines: SEVERAL HELD AS HUNT FOR MEN CONTINUES, and, in smaller print, POLICE BELIEVE ESCAPE WAS CAREFULLY PLANNED. The paper claims that people have been held for questioning. Senior officers refuse to say whether any arrests have been made. The search is on – it is said to be the 'biggest manhunt'.

Maggie Smith, a *Sunday Times* journalist, tends to drop in quite regularly to keep in contact with me and tell me anything she has heard. When we talk we go into the bathroom and run the tap. I have no idea whether these precautions are necessary, but I assume they must be. 'There are stories circulating that you're going to be arrested again,' she warns me. My heart sinks. I can't face that thought. I simply do not know what to do about it. She suggests that I should think of leaving the country. This is drastic, but it's something I have to face up to. Better to be out of the country and struggling than languishing in jail. I am being consumed by fear.

The next time I see Michael I tell him about this, and he says he will talk to a contact of his in the Dutch Embassy to see if there is any way they can help me. The problem is: how the hell can I leave the country, and what do I do about the children? I become obsessed with this idea. Michael arrives one day with a man from the Dutch Embassy. We walk in the garden. He is perfectly charming. Unfortunately, he says, there is nothing he or the Embassy can do to help me.

It is a week since I got out of jail. My sister Betty telephones me from Umhlanga Rocks. 'A very close friend of ours has been killed in a plane crash,' she says. 'Tommy and I are coming to Johannesburg for the funeral. It's on Wednesday. We're leaving tomorrow and will stay with Jimmy and Barbara. Tommy is in an awful state because Dave was a really close friend of his.' She was brief. Trunk calls are so expensive.

That is something to look forward to. I welcome her arrival. Betty is always like a breath of fresh air. She is curt, matter-of-fact, indomitable, and her very presence will be comforting. She is also not judgemental and that in itself is important. I really do need as much support as possible, and preferably from my family. My mother has fled to Durban. She tends to run away from problems, and my problems are just too great for her to handle. Anyway, she has to come to terms with her recent widowhood and how to plan out her life.

Betty and Tommy come round on the Tuesday night after supper. I tell them about the phone calls I have started getting. The first one was a sugary-sweet voice that said, 'Hello, Mrs Wolpe. I am a nurse at the Nightingale Hospital, and I wanted to find out how your little boy is.' I reacted with spontaneous warmth at this friendly request, so I told her how well Nicholas is doing, and what a miracle it is that he is alive. She listened and then said, 'It's a pity he has such vicious parents. For my part, I think he would have been better dead. You are a fucking bitch, your husband is a traitor and he will be caught and then we will kill him.' She continued in this vein with a string of invective. I pretended I hadn't heard what she was saying. Ruth once told me that the way she dealt with hate calls was to say to the caller, 'I'm sorry, I can't hear what you are saying. Would you mind repeating what you have said? Talk a bit louder,' and keep on saying this. I tried this out, but didn't think I had been very convincing. The caller ignored what I had to say, and didn't stop to listen. She just continued, so I banged the phone down. And I still have that voice ringing in my ears, wishing my baby dead.

They both listen to me. The phone goes again while we are talking. Tommy picks it up and then, in a rage, pulls the plug out of the wall. He won't say who it was or what the person said. I'm more than horrified. Now I don't have contact with the outside world, and I prefer having a phone that works, in spite of the hate calls.

The next day I arrange for the telephone department to repair the phone.

Betty and Tommy return that evening at about seven o'clock. It is the 21st of August. Betty looks grim-faced. 'I've got bad news for you,' she says. 'It's not about Harold,' she adds comfortingly. 'Jimmy has been arrested.' This news is really shattering.

'I arranged to meet a friend of mine this morning. He's a CIA agent. He told me that Jimmy was going to be arrested today. So I went to Jimmy's office, and got him to come out with me. I warned him that this was going to happen. He just laughed at me and said that it was impossible. He told me not to worry. Anyway, I met Barbara for lunch and then we went back to their house. I tried phoning Jimmy later in the afternoon. I got a strange man's voice. In my usual manner I told him to fuck off, I wanted to speak to Mr Kantor and he was to put me on to him. The phone call was transferred, and Jimmy picked up the phone. In answer to my question of what the hell was going on I heard him say to someone, "Can I tell her?" The answer must have been no and I said, "Tommy and I wanted you to do something about our will. We've had it drawn up but I wanted you to see it." All he would say is that he would see me at home later that afternoon. I guessed something must have happened. I told Barbara about the conversation when she returned later with the boys. She tried phoning. She also got no information from Jimmy, except that things were wrong. We both realised he must have been arrested. He was brought to the house later on with a horde of bloody cops. They went through all his personal letters. Barbara and I were allowed to sit in the room with him. He looks absolutely awful. His face is ashen and he really has aged instantly.' I cannot believe what I am hearing. Betty adds, laughing somewhat hollowly, 'Jimmy looked at the will, and one of the bastards witnessed it for us.'

Jimmy is innocent. Jimmy is inviolable and inculpable. He is the top criminal lawyer in the country. His cases always hit the headlines. He is known to the police, he is Colonel Klindt's lawyer. He is blameless. Why arrest him? They must know that he has done nothing.

This news is perhaps even more shattering than all that has preceded it. If the police can arrest Jimmy, then they are capable of doing anything and everything. My last semblance of security evaporates with the news of Jimmy's arrest. Now I feel even more vulnerable than before.

Tommy is not very solicitous. He has made it clear that he disapproves of Harold and all his colleagues. I probably fit into that category as well, by virtue of my association. I am guilty by my affiliation, if marriage could be called that.

Marlene is out on one of her many dates. She has been less in evidence lately, particularly now that I am home a good deal more than before, particularly since my nightly visits to the jail have ceased.

I go to bed as soon as Betty and Tommy leave. Sleep eludes me. I can't bear the thought of Jimmy in jail. I don't even know where he is, and I feel so guilty. Nor do I have the strength to offer Barbara any comfort. Betty tells me she is fine, and not at all shattered by what has happened. Nothing seems to upset that glamorous exterior of hers, and I have no way of knowing what she is truly feeling.

I seek advice the next morning from a lawyer I have known really well. I make an appointment with him. He is distinctly cool when I come into his office. There is no welcoming smile, no banter. I tell him just how shattered I am by the news of Jimmy's arrest. 'I know that he is absolutely innocent,' I say. 'Believe me, I know it. I'm terrified,' I go on. 'Now that Jimmy has been arrested, there is no one who can look after me. What can I do to protect myself and my children? I'm at a loss.' His tone is cold: 'There's absolutely nothing I can do to help you, I'm afraid. I would rather you did not call to see me again.'

I leave and return home. The GP is coming this afternoon

for a routine check on Nicholas. When he is there I say, 'I think I'm on the verge of cracking up. I haven't slept properly. I need something.' He gives me a really strong tranquilliser. I take it that night, and nothing happens. Eventually, the following morning, I sleep. The signs are clear. I am in a state of anxiety. I find eating difficult. I find sleeping difficult. And I am petrified that I will be arrested again, and this time incarcerated for months on end.

The *Sunday Times* journalist's warning has to be taken seriously. I tell Betty about my fears, and say that I think I should try to leave the country. She sets up a meeting between me and her friend, the CIA agent. I have not had the time for the full import of this to sink in. Now Betty tells me that she was approached before she moved to Natal to act as an informer for the Americans. She had been working for African Artists, a group committed to breaking the colour bar in theatrical enterprises. They had been responsible for putting on Athol Fugard's first play, *The Blood Knot*, at the Bantu Men's Social Centre with a black and a white actor. This was unique in the country. The CIA wanted anything she could tell them about this group. Even though she refused, she has not lost touch with the man who approached her. Betty never ceases to amaze me.

The meeting is like so much of my life now. I'm beginning to think that maybe B-movies are not concoctions by hackneyed scriptwriters. The meeting is in the cocktail lounge of the Carlton Hotel, the only place where middle-class women can go for a rendezvous in the afternoon without any eyebrows being raised. A red rose is pinned to the lapel of my home-sewn beige jacket. A tall man in a loose-fitting suit, with short crew-cut hair, comes up to me. We shake hands solemnly and sit down. I order a whisky sour. It's the only drink with an exotic name that I know.

He is concerned. 'We would like to help you very much,' he says, sounding very sincere. 'We all have tremendous respect for you and would like to help you get out of the country. But can you imagine the scandal if it ever came out that the American Embassy had assisted someone like you in getting out of the country? We think the government is on a collision course. Of course we don't approve of the tactics employed by the Communists. At the same time, we recognise that there has to be a change in policy towards the blacks. People like your husband, at least, are working together with the blacks, and the Americans would like to see an end to apartheid.' It is the Kennedy era, and segregation in the deep South has finally been confronted. He talks about false travel documents, but the whole thing is a futile exercise. I am no further than I was before.

The feeling of isolation is increasing. The only bright event is a delegation from King David School. Two men in suits arrive at the house one afternoon. Clearly they aren't police. I have never seen them before. The usual polite exchanges take place. One says to me, 'Mrs Wolpe, I want you to know that the Jewish community views your husband's activities and those of Mr Goldreich with horror. We do not approve at all. Such things can only bring down the wrath of the government on our heads.' I feel stunned. Surely the Jews, of all people, should recognise oppression and fight it wherever it occurs. How ridiculously naive I am. 'We are very sorry for you, Mrs Wolpe.' I am seen as an innocent bystander. In spite of his admonishments, the man has come to tell me that the board is prepared to waive the girls' nursery-school fees until such time as I feel I am able to pay. Well, that's some comfort.

Betty is due to return to Umhlanga Rocks. Before she goes she calls round at the house. 'I'm prepared to smuggle Arthur and Harold to Durban if you want me to,' she says. 'There's an Israeli ship in Durban at the moment, and I'm sure they could get on to that boat.' I tell her I have absolutely no idea where they are, and at this stage I really don't want to know. 'Anyway, I would never dream of letting you do anything like that. You're crazy. You could go to jail. And in any event, Tommy wouldn't agree to do anything like that.' She says: 'To hell with Tommy.' The whole idea is crazy, and she certainly wouldn't get very far with two fugitives like that.

The papers continue to talk about the big escape. Then one day, the news breaks. My friend Moira arrives at the house in the afternoon. I have only recently become friendly with her, and she is such a gorgeous, bright person that I welcome her presence. She is flushed and breathless. 'They've done it,' she says. 'They've got away. Oh, isn't it wonderful.' And she flings down the newspaper with its banner headlines. It seems that the two men have arrived in Bechuanaland, having flown there from Swaziland dressed as priests. Momentarily I feel a sense of relief: it hasn't all been in vain. I am keen to phone Barbara. 'They must let Jimmy out of jail now,' I say to her when I've told her the news. 'It must be obvious to them that he had nothing whatsoever to do with the escape, or the flight from the country.' I know absolutely no details of what has happened beyond what I read. 'Let's try and do something about it.' She replies that she has already heard the news, and has been in touch with the Special Branch, who just laughed at her. 'Let's try the press,' I suggest. The two of us meet at the offices of the *Rand Daily Mail*, and go to see one of their leading journalists, who is on the phone when we arrive at his desk. He is talking urgently with someone, and the talk is about Harold and Arthur. He puts the phone down and says, 'I'd better make up something for tomorrow's copy. They say they don't know very much and I'll have to give our readers something more than that. Can you tell me anything?' he asks me. I am incredulous. I am learning all the time, and my ideals are being shattered one after the other.

Barbara and I talk earnestly. 'It's obvious,' she says, 'that my husband has had absolutely nothing to do with these two men's escape. I want you to put something to that effect into the paper.' The journalist laughs. 'That's not news,' he says, and adds that nobody will believe it anyway. 'You can see,' I say shrilly, 'he couldn't have had anything to do with their getting out of the country. He's been locked up himself. You must understand that Jimmy is quite innocent.' It is useless. I see that what makes news is its capacity to entertain. It does not have to correspond with truth or reality. It just has to be a good story and Jimmy's lack of involvement in the great escape is not a good story. It's quite simple. We leave the office. I am amazed at how well Barbara seems to be taking Jimmy's incarceration.

I am obviously happy for Harold and Arthur, but I can't help feeling angry at them for the mess they have left behind. Hazel is still in jail. I could be picked up any day. Jimmy is in jail. All three of us are the innocent players in this great game. The only relief is that if they pick me up I don't have to worry about divulging any information about their whereabouts. At least I am spared that dilemma. Now it seems as though I can be charged only with helping them to escape, but the penalty for that must be at least three years, if not more. Even though the fear of torture recedes into the background, my horror of imprisonment does not diminish.

Mafuta Berger is another person who arrives out of the blue to see me. Mafuta is a nickname. It means big, but in fact he is quite short and rotund. Maybe the name is derived from his position rather than his stature. He is a highly successful businessman, a key figure in a hosiery factory. He is of German origin and his wife, Vera, is from Yugoslavia. They have both known what it is to struggle. Vera is very conscious of the difficulties she experienced during her first years in South Africa. She, together with her father, worked in a fish-and-chip shop which, she said, was sweated labour. Now she enjoys the luxurious life that Mafuta provides for her. They live in a sumptuous Killarney flat. They have no children, but a favourite little dog. Mafuta is extraordinarily generous, and throws lavish dinner parties. I have no recollection how or where he met the Slovos, but clearly he will help Ruth in whatever way he can now she is on her own. He has the guts to see me, and I am grateful for that.

'Mafuta, I can't go on much longer. I think they're going to arrest me, and I just haven't the strength to cope with that. I want to get out of the country. With Jimmy's arrest anything can happen, and I'm terrified for my life.' I know it sounds melodramatic, but that is how I feel.

We're sitting in the garden on the little wall of the terrace that Harold built. It has a paddling pool in the centre for the girls. The sun is hot and the air is dry. The warmth of the sun burns through the sweater I was wearing, and gives me a feeling of comfort. A Willie wagtail eagerly hops along the dry lawn, hoping for some delectable insect to come into its line of vision. Mafuta's round face looks serious. 'You know all my business associates have been smuggling money out of the country for years now. They're all terrified of the nationalist government's collision course, and they want to protect their assets. I've got contact with Customs officials. There's a Customs official in Durban who has been very helpful, and for a sum of money he'll help you get out of the country.' This sounds rather extreme to me. 'How the hell can he do that?' I ask, somewhat taken aback. My mother has laughingly spoken about some wealthy woman who was reputed to pad her French knot hairdo with pound notes when she flew out on an overseas trip to pay for her extravagances. Systematic smuggling is something I know nothing about, and being smuggled out of the country is quite a different ball game again. 'I'll give you his name. You go down to Durban, arrange to meet him, and he'll be able to get you on board a boat leaving the country.' Strangely enough it is the thought of bribing someone that I find so unpalatable. 'It's so embarrassing to bribe somebody. How do I do it? Mafuta laughs at my innocence. 'You go along with a hundred-pound note. You start a discussion with him and tell him there's a hundred in it for him if he can get you on a boat. There are boats going via the east coast to Europe. You pay your passage once you're on the boat.'

I haven't got a hundred pounds. 'Borrow some money from one of your wealthy friends,' Mafuta counsels me. Michael Gluckman is the only person I can approach. I hate the thought of bumming money like this. There is no alternative. It sounds a harebrained scheme, but at this stage I am willing to try anything.

I get the hundred pounds and book a flight to Durban. I take with me a small suitcase with a pair of warm trousers, and some summer clothes. Durban is likely to be quite hot even at this time of year. It has a tropical climate, and the temperature seldom drops as it does in Johannesburg. The sea is warm, the days are hot, and the pawpaws and avocado pears are flooding the market.

Betty fetches me from the airport and takes me to her

home. Tommy looks so much better than he did in February. His cancer seems cured, and he is back at work in the advertising business. His hospitality does not match his improved health. He makes it quite clear that I am not welcome at their home. It's not because there's no space since my mother is there as well. He is damned if he is going to be tainted by association with so notorious person as myself. It is bad enough having me as a sister-in-law. Poor Betty is distraught, but there is nothing she can do about it.

My mother comes to the rescue. She approaches a woman whose husband has been convicted and jailed in connection with some financial scandal, a woman who is familiar with innuendos and smears. She knows nothing about politics, but in an act of solidarity with another woman caught up in her husband's activities she offers me accommodation and takes me in.

I tell no one of my intention to flee the country, not even my mother. I simply say that I need a break away from Johannesburg. I have the telephone number of the Customs official and in the course of a morning's shopping I go off to meet him at the appointed place. It is so simple. Handing over the hundred pounds is no problem at all. He is clearly an old hand at this sort of transaction, and tells me that there will be no difficulty. He will find a suitable ship for me, and I must dress in a sari and cover my head. The only problem is that there is no suitable ship and I shall have to wait. It is just a question of time. He pockets the money without counting it, takes my phone number and says he will be in touch with me shortly.

Every morning I set out for the beach and my hostess goes off to the golf course. Her flat is on the sea front. More often than not my mother joins me. I sit on the beach, with a brightly coloured hat pulled down over my face, completely masked by sunglasses. Nobody could recognise me, not even the police, I comfort myself. Young Indian boys – they could be not more than eight or nine – struggle up and down carrying a load of daily newspapers, shouting out the latest headline. The escape countines to dominate the front page. Sometimes I buy a copy.

SABOTAGE SUSPECTED IN GUTTED PLANE

The paper tells me the two men are in Bechuanaland, hanging out in the local jail to avoid being kidnapped. The plane that is due to fly them out is burnt out. The next one crashes. There they are in Francistown, playing draughts or chess or some game or other, waiting to get out of the country. I seem to have reached a point where I no longer care about what happens to Harold. I have done what I can for him. Now I feel I have to look after myself and so, eventually, my children. It is unpleasant to acknowledge that I have become fear-ridden, a victim of gross anxiety. I feel incapable of making clear-cut decisions and unable to relate to other people or situations. I have become the centre of my universe. I have no more tears inside me. And I think: Well, he's fine, he's safe, and even the stories of the blowing up of the aircraft do not perturb me.

I watch the public response as the young boys cry out the latest headline. The slim, tanned, bikini-clad bodies of women, matched by the muscular tanned bodies of the men, react to the cries and eagerly pursue the latest event in the drama. It is the only thing that disturbs their sun worship. I idly wonder what those complacent holidaymakers would do if they had any inkling of who I was. Perhaps they would freeze in their comfortable oil-baked positions. My mother remains detached from the news. The only way she can cope with problems is to act as though they are not there. While the sun shines, and I smile and talk naturally, everything is all right. The minute she comes face to face with reality, she is likely to crumble. But even she cannot ignore Jimmy's imprisonment. She is getting herself geared up towards returning to Johannesburg because she wants to be near him.

A message is left for me to meet my contact again. At last, I think, it is time to move on. I meet him downtown. He tells me there is a major snag: the boat that he can get me on is scheduled to stop at Beira. 'If you're worried about the South African police, I can tell you the Portuguese are far worse,' he tells me solemnly. Their reputation for violence and physical torture is legendary. But my crooked Customs official can come up with no other suggestion. The hundred pounds has disappeared.

There is no alternative but to return to Johannesburg. When I tell my mother I am returning, she says she will come back with me. At least I will have company on the plane.

The Long Wait

T HEY WERE free, free from the thousands and thousands of police and army reserve that had been called up following their escape, traffic police and keen citizens aching to help the government apprehend them. Now they were on their own with no escape committee to oversee the plans.

Their destination was the Mission run by the Reverend Charles Hooper, a priest who had worked among the people in the Zeerust District, a man known for his indomitable opposition to apartheid and his willingness to assist South African refugees. He knew all about them, and would help them. At the same time he would have to protect his Mission.

Hooper hurried them into the house. 'It's small, and not easy to keep you out of sight,' he said. 'We will have to be extremely careful to keep your presence here absolutely secret. After all, we're in a landlocked oasis. If those bastards get a whiff of your presence, it will be almost impossible to get you out of the country.' They found it strange yet reassuring to hear a priest swear.

They sat in a dark, simply furnished sitting-room. There was a 1930s lounge suite with wooden arms and worn upholstery, some prints on the wall – clearly a home where there wasn't much extra money to spend on any luxuries. Hooper's wife brought in a tray of tea, which she put down on the round brass six-legged table. She left the room discreetly.

Hooper didn't pry. He asked no details of their escape. 'The main problem is getting you out of this country,' he said. 'There is a small charter aeroplane company here. I know the director well, and I am sure he is absolutely reliable. He has a pilot's licence, and I can book a flight to Bechuanaland for the two of you.'

Arthur and Harold exchanged glances. They could think of no other solution. 'How do we protect you – and ourselves, for that matter?' Arthur asked. Hooper had a simple solution: 'You'll have to become priests for the occasion,' and all three men laughed. Harold said, 'But what about my Jewish nose?' 'Put on an English accent, and you'll resemble a good upper-crust Englishman,' Hooper reassured him. 'I'll find you some suitable clothing, and you had better start wearing it now, just in case.'

He left the room, soon returning with two alpaca jackets, black trousers, and two dog collars. 'That depletes my wardrobe,' said Hooper. 'Luckily we're all more or less the same size.'

Harold and Arthur went to their room to don their clothes. Arthur started to play his new role of Reverend Mitchell, and Harold rolled on the bed with laughter. 'You really have missed your vocation in life,' he spluttered in response to Arthur's portrayal of an English priest with a hot-potato-in-his-mouth-type accent.

The meal that night was simple good home cooking, washed down with Lion lager. Both men ate ravenously. 'Berrangé has organised the flight for the two of you,' Hooper said. It was some time since Harold had been in contact with Vernon Berrangé, a senior barrister at the Johannesburg Bar, known for his brilliance at cross-examination. Berrangé could reduce even the most hardened police witness almost to a jibbering idiot using tactics which involved somewhat theatrical gestures like wiping the lenses of his glasses and then holding one up towards his eye, which effectively magnified it. The poor witness would be unnerved by a glaring enlarged eye, while he was bombarded with questions. 'The flight has been booked,' Hooper told them. 'Berrangé has arranged for the director of the charter company to act as pilot. All you have to do is to wait a few more days. You'll leave Tuesday morning.'

This was no hardship. Hooper had a good supply of green-backed Penguin thrillers, and both men settled down to read

Ellery Queen's *French Powder Mystery* and *The Dutch Shoe Mystery*, and Raymond Chandler's *Trouble is My Business*. Chandler is one of Harold's favourite writers.

Tuesday 27 August: a clear, bright morning. Harold and Arthur paid special attention to their appearance. Arthur had shaved his beard, which gave him a very different look to the pictures that had been appearing in the press. They had all agreed that they needed to be aged slightly. 'I always knew that amateur dramatics would come into their own one day,' Hooper's wife laughed, as she combed the silvery powder carefully into their hair. They were each given a small haversack; and inside Mrs Hooper had put some sandwiches, a toothbrush, soap, and the books neither men had quite finished. 'You can always post them back to me one day,' she said.

Hooper drove them to the small airfield in the car in which they had arrived at his Mission station. The arrangement was that Hooper could sell the car and put the money towards the funds he needed for aiding refugees.

Harold looked around him, marvelling at the sight of trees and grass and blue skies. He realised with a shock how quickly he had become accustomed to living what was tantamount to a twilight existence.

Hooper dropped them at the airfield, where they were met not by the director but by one of his pilots, a man called Truter. Hooper introduced them. 'Here is the Reverend Shippon,' he said, pointing to Harold, 'and this is the Reverend Mitchell,' he said, presenting Arthur. 'These men are visiting from one of our Missions in a place called Mirfield in Yorkshire.' Everyone shook hands, and the pilot went towards the cockpit. Hooper said quietly, 'Let's hope the guy has no idea who you are. We don't trust him. He's known for being sympathetic towards the South Africans. Well, there's nothing we can do about it now. The die is cast.' He left hurriedly. He did not want to be too closely associated with these two men.

The two 'priests' said goodbye to the Reverend Hooper quite formally, climbed into the two back seats of the small single-engined Cessna plane, and waited for take off. There had been no formalities at all, and they were beginning to relax when two white British Security men strolled towards them. They had no travel documents. It was an anxious moment, and they both felt a wave of fear well up. 'Good morning, gentlemen,' said one of the men courteously. 'We're from the Security Police,' and then he asked them what they were doing there. Arthur replied in a firm, clipped English accent: 'We've been visiting the Reverend Hooper here, and now we're *en route* to Bechuanaland, where we are due to spend a few days. We've been on a routine visit on behalf of our order.' He went on to detail some of the aims of the visit, then extolled the virtue of Hooper's Mission and the wonderment of Swaziland. 'We shall be returning here after a few days,' Arthur added. My God, thought Harold, let's hope the cop doesn't ask for any details. Arthur must have sounded convincing. No documents were asked for. The policeman saluted them and wished them a safe journey. Harold lightly tapped his chest, confirming that the newspaper cutting on Nicholas's homecoming was still in place. It reminded him of his family, and momentarily he wondered how things were. He realised how caught up he had been with the escape, so that worries about the family had been pushed aside.

The roar of the engine was loud and it was difficult for them to talk to each other, but it didn't matter, since they had to be careful about what they said. The plane flew due west. They flew low – no more than six or seven thousand feet up, so they could see much of the countryside below them. Harold realised, with a sinking feeling, that he was flying over the route he had taken with Mike that fateful day a few weeks ago.

Truter, the pilot, shouted to them that the trip shouldn't take more than three hours. The wind was helping them along. They flew over the small towns of Ermelo and Bethal, and then over the Magaliesberg range. Harold couldn't reminisce with Arthur about the wonderful weekend parties he had attended there while he was still a student.

They both knew they were coming close to Pretoria, and if Truter had any suspicions about them, this would be the critical moment. There was Swartzkop military air base, and all he would have to do was radio signal to them. Turning them in would net him a handsome reward. The offer was £5,000 on each of their heads.

Both men tensed themselves. They had pocket knives, with short sharp blades. They weren't exactly deadly weapons, but they could inflict some damage if necessary, and they made them feel a little more secure. Arthur nudged Harold and held out his knife. Harold nodded complicitly. They could see Pretoria looming up. They waited anxiously. The plane dipped, and their stomachs churned over with the movement. It was Truter's way of demonstrating the famous landmark of the administrative seat of government, the Union Buildings designed by Sir Herbert Baker. They flew in, and over Pretoria. Truter clearly did not suspect them. Like schoolboys they linked little fingers as evidence of their delight when they realised they were over that hurdle.

As they flew towards Bechuanaland, the terrain changed quite dramatically. Everything looked parched and dry. The redness of the scorched soil over the vast plains was crisscrossed every now and again by a farmstead with a few trees and then, some distance from that, a small cluster of farm workers' huts.

The flight was quick. They had reached the Bechuanaland border. Truter was to fly them to Lobatsi, a small town said to be crawling with South African agents. Dr Abrahams, a man from Cape Town, and three associates, who had fled South Africa, had recently been kidnapped by farmers who were clearly sympathisers with the South African government. Although this had happened in a relatively deserted spot some distance from Lobatsi, both men felt uneasy about the town. They wanted to conceal their point of entry into this British Protectorate.

'Could you let us off at the far end of the runway?' Arthur yelled at Truter above the roar of the engines. 'We don't want to go through any routine checks. We've left all our documents in Swaziland, and we don't want the inconvenience of bureaucratic inspections.' Truter didn't seem to find this at all strange. Maybe it was the type of request he was used to. He taxied to the end of the runway. The two men jumped from the plane and hurried off towards a nearby hill, clutching their haversacks.

As they half-walked, half-ran, they discussed what they should do. 'Jack and Rica are now in Lobatsi, you know,' Harold said. The Hodgsons, who had been involved in the struggle for years, had had to make a quick getaway from South Africa, and they had been more fortunate than Harold. They had now been there for more than a month. 'They are the people we should contact. They'll be able to get us in contact with our people in East Africa. We need to keep as far away as possible from any officials.' Their plan – somewhat foolhardy – was to remain on the hill until dark, then make their way into Lobatsi. They squatted in what they thought was a vantage point, then decided that perhaps they would be better making contact by phone. They set off towards a little cluster of houses, hoping that they would be able to find a phone there.

They were close to what turned out to be a school, where there was obvious activity when a Land Rover screeched to a halt. Apparently their arrival had not gone unnoticed. It was the same Land Rover that had been cruising up and down the runway, and it had now met up with them. 'Are you looking for us?' a policeman asked.

Their reaction was identical. Both men beamed, and Harold said, 'I've never been so happy to see a policeman before. We had been thinking of staying on that hill over there,' he continued, pointing to where they had come from, 'before making our way to Lobatsi. We thought we should find a phone to contact our friends.' 'Reverend, this is your lucky day, sir,' the one man replied. 'A small boy was savaged by a leopard there only last week.' Although this sounded far-fetched, it was later corroborated.

The two men smiled at each other. Their luck was continuing. They were beginning to chalk up their lucky breaks. They had further exchanges with the police. They nodded when they were told, 'We'll take you to the District Commissioner's office.' They realised that they would have to make their presence known to the Commissioner. It could not be avoided.

The District Commissioner's office was unremarkable, with

a roll-topped desk, a wooden filing cabinet and a picture of the Queen prominently displayed on the wall. He was an Englishman with a florid complexion and a mass of tiny blue veins on his face. Either high blood pressure or too much whisky or both, Harold thought. It was clear that the time had come for them to reveal their true names. The man looked as though he would explode. 'This is a travesty. This is outrageous. This is blasphemy. How can you have dressed in the cloth of the Lord? And why didn't you come direct to me?' He was more than affronted, he was almost apoplectic. When they explained their fear of being kidnapped like Dr Abrahams, he ridiculed the notion. 'What a lot of tosh,' he said. 'You couldn't possibly be kidnapped here, in this built-up area. Abrahams was taken in a remote spot near Ghansi.'

The two men apologised, and tried to appease the Commissioner by pointing out that they had been on the run for two weeks and had not wanted to jeopardise their chances through a chance meeting with a South African agent. They said they wanted to be given political asylum.

'I will give you asylum,' said the Commissioner grudgingly, 'but I want you out of the country as soon as possible. You will have to make some arrangements yourselves, and do so immediately. Nor are you to leave Lobatsi without my permission. You should be all right in the local hotel. Before I get one of my men to drive you back to the hotel, you need to answer some questions.'

They were escorted to another office, where a British Security officer started questioning them. 'What organisation are you members of,' was just one of the many questions. 'Are you Communists? How are you politically involved?' Harold's legal knowledge stood them in good stead. Quietly and firmly, he replied that they would rather not discuss any of these questions. The officer was not aggressive at all. It was almost as though he had anticipated that kind of response. After a few minutes he called out to a sergeant to drive the two men to the Cumberland Hotel.

The buildings in the main street were like all buildings in rural areas: single-storey, flat-roofed, with paint peeling from the walls. The streets were not crowded; small pockets of people sat on the pavement, inevitably waiting for something to happen. 'Look there,' Arthur pulled at Harold's sleeve. 'There's Jack.' The driver stopped the car, and the two men jumped out. Jack's jaw dropped in amazement, then he laughed his husky smoker's-cough laugh. The men embraced, and off they went to the Hodgsons' flat nearby.

Rica was as delighted as Jack with her visitors, and immediately asked for details of what had happened. They felt starved of real news. The men filled in as much as they thought they could. The news of their arrival spread, and soon the flat was packed with other South African refugees.

Luckily, a number of the refugees were leaving that night for Francistown in the north where they were due to fly out in a few days to Tanzania in an East African Airways Dakota. It was a three-hundred-mile journey, and after feasting and drinking they took off at midnight. Someone was sent to the District Commissioner's Office to tell him of the departure of his unwelcome visitors.

It was a long trip. The road was straight, and the driver had no difficulties. Every now and again the headlights would pick up the luminous eyes of some wild creature, transfixed by the brilliance of the headlights. The men dozed off after a while, and woke to see a wonderful African sunrise magnified by the wide space around them.

Francistown was bigger than Lobatsi. Its main road was tarred and wide, and it sported more shops than the smaller town. Not a lot seemed to be happening there. They were driven directly to the home of the District Commissioner, Mr Steenkamp, who was known for being sympathetic to refugees from South Africa. They were not going to repeat the mistake they had made at Lobatsi.

Mr Steenkamp turned out to be a delightful man. He was tall, with dulling blond hair that kept falling into his eyes – eyes that smiled a lot – and straight white teeth, which contrasted with his deeply tanned face. His long slender fingers played with the match he had used to light their cigarettes. He talked easily, and immediately made it clear that he would help them to leave the country as best he could, and give them whatever assistance they required while they were in Francistown. 'The place was crawling with journalists yesterday. There had been a rumour that the two of you had arrived in Francistown. The pack got fed up when there was no sign of you, and they have all left. I think you will be fine at the local hotel. Nobody is around, and it might be better politically for you not to be staying with me. It might cause the British government some embarrassment.' He could not spend long with them, and after a welcoming cup of tea and some toast he sent them on their way to the hotel.

It seemed typical of small-town hotels. The long bar, an essential item in any hotel, was to the left of the entrance lounge. Electric fans suspended from the ceiling, which was darkened by smoke from the countless cigarettes, indicated the heat of the country, although at that time of the morning it was still relatively cool. They went to the desk to register. They did not notice a man slouched in a chair nearby. He turned out to be a lone journalist from an Afrikaans newspaper – a man who, they learned subsequently, was thought to have close connections with the Security Police. The journalist had heard that a refugee plane was due to leave Francistown the following day, and had come on the off chance that the two men would somehow have found their way there. His hunch paid off. He recognised them immediately, and the telephone wires started buzzing.

The journalist's story must have hit Johannesburg within an hour. It proved the clarion call to all the hungry journalists eager to get the story at first hand. The small airfield at Francistown suddenly had to cope with several charter planes from all over Southern Africa. Local and foreign journalists poured in. This was a story that the world was interested in. One after another they banged on the room Arthur and Harold had moved into. One after the other they pleaded and insisted on a story. Both men felt harassed by the journalists' insistence. They could divulge no information. Too many people had risked too much to get them out of the country. 'We're not prepared to give you any statement,' was what they took it in turn to say. It had already become known that they had arrived at Lobatsi dressed as priests. In spite of their lack of co-operation, the reporters did not give up. Their adventures were now a *cause célèbre*.

Finally, the BBC television reporter persuaded them to be interviewed in his room.

Off they went to his bedroom, where the bright lights for the cameras had been set up. The two men sat upright next to each other on the bed, with its faded striped cover, beside a small bedside table with a rickety table lamp. Microphones hung round their necks. Neither had ever been interviewed for television before, and both stared directly at the cameras, feeling foolish. 'You two men have just completed an amazing escape from a Johannesburg jail. There has been a price on your heads, and every policeman in the country has been on the lookout for you. And now you suddenly emerge in Francistown, in Bechuanaland, hundreds of miles from Johannesburg. The world is waiting to hear about how you achieved this.' With that he turned to Arthur, and asked him to give some com-ments. Arthur made the standard response: 'I have nothing to say.' The interviewer then turned to Harold, posed the same question and got the same response. Both men felt somewhat ridiculous, but the interviewer was undaunted and went on to describe how the two men had arrived at Lobatsi dressed as priests, and were then driven to Francistown with a number of black refugees. He put their arrest into the context of the struggle against apartheid. It was his way of coping with the lack of information.

That day the reports started appearing in the South African press. The *Star* carried a photograph of the two men walking together with Ismail Bhana, a refugee, who had driven with them from Lobatsi. 'Goldreich and Wolpe Escape to Francis-town' was the front-page news item that evening. The next day the *Rand Daily Mail* headline said: 'I Was Duped – Priest', with an account by Hooper who 'angrily claimed that he had been the "unwitting dupe" of Goldreich and Wolpe'. He was quoted as saying that he had never met them before, and that they had appeared at his door, posing as Congregational clergymen, saying 'that a prominent English clergyman had suggested that I might be able to accommodate them for a few days'. Prime Minister Vorster was quoted in the *Chronicle*: 'The escape was a great loss in the campaign against subversion. You don't lose a war by losing a skirmish now and again. There can be no doubt that two of the big fishes have got away – but some very important ones still remain in our net.'

After the interview with the BBC their refugee friend Bhana arrived at the hotel and advised the two men to stay put and lock themselves into their room. A town with three thousand white people, most of whom were sympathetic to the South African government, was not a particularly welcoming place in which to seek refuge. Bhana was beginning to feel nervous at the attention they had already drawn to themselves. He said he would share their bedroom, and arranged for some young men from the nearby refugee camp to act as guards and to monitor the press demands. They talked well into the night, not stirring from their room.

Finally they slept, secure in the knowledge that two of the young men were keeping guard over them. At four in the morning there was a frantic banging on the window. A tousled-looking man said, in an agitated voice, 'Your plane is burning up on the airport. It is hopeless. You'll never be able to fly away.' Nobody believed him, nor could they understand why he should be there at that hour of the morning. They went back to sleep. When they woke a while later, the destruction of the plane and the closure of the airstrip were confirmed. The Witwatersrand Native Labour Association, which had built the airstrip, would no doubt have it repaired soon because it was vital for transporting the black migratory workers to the gold mines of South Africa. That wouldn't help them. 'The bloody Security Police certainly mean to make life as difficult for us as possible,' said Harold over breakfast.

The news soon spread. The *Rand Daily Mail* ran a special edition that morning with banner headlines: 'Refugee plane is Gutted'. The plane was a complete write-off; burned for two hours before the fire could be controlled. Only the tailplane and one wing remained intact. Later the refugees learned that a man had phoned the offices of the *Star* that morning and said, in what sounded a disguised voice, 'Unfortunately, we failed the first time, but we will get Mr Goldreich and Mr Wolpe. They will no longer be on the face of the earth after thirty-six hours.'

The Chief of Police was frankly worried: 'We have no doubt that this was an act of sabotage instigated by the South African police. We have a good idea of who is behind this, but we have no proof. Clearly they are going to do all they can to prevent you from leaving. But more than this: they will do their level best to get you back to South Africa. It is my considered opinion that you would be safer taking refuge in our local jail.' He paused to see what effect he had on the two men, who had been brought to his office later that day.

Neither Harold nor Arthur needed much convincing. Their bedroom on the ground floor of the hotel could easily be broken into through either the window or the door, which looked decidedly flimsy. Maintaining any form of security was almost impossible. Nor were the white guests' reaction to their presence in the hotel favourable. After one photo session with Arthur, a hostile atmosphere developed and a scuffle almost broke out. The white people made it clear that they found it an affront to have the two fugitives there. And both men had received threatening phone calls. They both concurred that there was nothing to beat a friendly prison, so they packed their bags and left for the jail under escort. Some wry comments followed them out of the hotel.

Bhana confirmed that afternoon that East African Airways would send a relief Dakota the next day to pick up all the refugees, including the two now famous ones. This time the plane would fly in and take off the same day; no stopover was planned. Clearly the company felt uneasy.

They settled into their spacious new quarters. There was a courtyard leading to an ablutions block with separate lavatories and showers. Ismail Bhana moved with the two of them into a 'suite' of cells. The governor of the prison, Mr Delville Knight, a dapper Englishman, was hospitable. He arrived at six that evening with a plate of sandwiches, beer and a bottle of gin. He obviously liked his evening drink, and poured himself a stiff gin and tonic. Harold joined him; Arthur and Ismail took the beer instead. In a strong northern English accent the governor made his feelings clear. 'I want you gentlemen to know that there is no way that I condone or agree with any of your actions. I do not support your views, sir, but by gad I will defend to the death your right to express them. And I will have you know,' he said, emphasising each word with a jabbing of his finger, 'that your safety while in my prison will in no way be endangered.'

As the evening wore on, they all felt the better for the liquor, and a feeling of warmth and relaxation welled up in Harold. He realised just how uneasy he had felt in the hotel. A cool breeze wafted into their cell, and that night all three men took their bedding into the courtyard and slept under the bright star-studded sky. Lazily Harold watched for a shooting star, and remembered how superstitious I am and how I would shut my eyes tight as I wished for the impossible. He found himself drifting off into an easy sleep, thinking of pleasanter days – of holidays and the children playing on the beach. He avoided thinking of the troubled times the children and I would be having. And tomorrow at that time, or maybe the following night, he anticipated being in Dar es Salaam.

This was not to be. They heard that the plane had taken off, but been diverted. East African Airways took fright – or rather, their insurers took fright. They were taking seriously the threats that had been made by people who reaffirmed their resolution to prevent the men from reaching Dar es Salaam. Insurance on any plane that would carry Harold and Arthur seemed unlikely. The spotlight was on the two men, and nothing could be done secretly.

The journalists vied with each other to get photographs and interviews. Together with Bhana, Harold and Arthur monitored carefully those whom they allowed in to see them. Other reporters were seen at the prison gate, or ignored entirely. They also received guests in their cell – like Dr Abrahams, recently released by his kidnappers.

It seemed they could well be Mr Knight's guests for some time. Friday passed. Saturday passed. Sunday came and went.

And still no progress. Indeed the South African *Sunday Times* carried a highly threatening report:

'We will get Goldreich and Wolpe,' Mr. P.S.R. Willers, leader of the South African Nazi Party, said in Pretoria yesterday. He said that the two Francistown refugees would not reach Dar es Salaam alive.

I spoke to Mr. Willers after an anonymous telephone call to the SUNDAY TIMES which suggested that Mr. Willers and members of his party were behind the explosion that wrecked the aircraft which was to take the refugees from Francistown this week.

When I put this allegation to Mr. Willers he replied: 'No comment'.

Offered an opportunity to refute rumours which could be damaging and dangerous to him, he said: 'It is not damaging to suggest that I had anything to do with attempting to annihilate the scum; nor is it more dangerous to think they will die than it is to believe that my throat, and the throats of all Whites in South Africa, will be cut, by leaving them alive, so that they can go overseas and plan.'

Mr. Willers said that if he brought Goldreich and Wolpe – dead or alive – to the South African authorities he would claim the reward offered for their capture.

Mr. Willers founded the South African Nazi Party two years ago. He refuses to disclose the number of members of the party.

The long wait had begun. The days were hot and, by contrast, the evenings were wonderfully pleasant. The two men, with the constant companionship of Ismail Bhana, talked with other refugees, and drank with Mr Knight at the end of the day. Mr Knight kept reiterating his firm belief in the law, and in freedom of speech. Yet all these pleasantries could not disperse the feeling of tension at the constant surveillance and the threats that were pouring in.

The New Prison

W HILE THEY were in Lobatsi, on the Hodgsons' advice, Harold and Arthur had approached Mr Bartoni, who owned a charter air company, to fly them to Dar es Salaam. Mr Bartoni was not keen. He vacillated, and then refused. Not long after they had arrived in Francistown, a Mr Nash appeared. He was a pilot employed by Mr Bartoni. 'Mr Bartoni has changed his mind,' Nash told Harold and Arthur. 'He now says that if he doesn't fly you out, somebody else will. And you know what businessmen are like. He would rather make the money than let it go to one of his competitors. The only snag is that I have to return to Lobatsi and can only take you tomorrow. We can't fly at night, you know, because there are no facilities at the airports or airstrips for landing.'

The men were delighted, and wanted to communicate their good fortune immediately to Chief of Police Steenkamp, who gave it his blessing. The next morning they prepared for their departure, but Nash didn't turn up. 'I guess we'd better phone Bartoni to check if there is any reason for the delay,' Harold suggested. After the usual problems of making a connection, they finally got through to Bartoni. He was abrasive. 'I don't know anything about this arrangement,' he told Harold, and hung up. Steenkamp arrived. 'I've had word from our intelligence that Nash has just flown in from Jan Smuts Airport in Johannesburg. Not only has he been offered a reward of £10,000 for flying you two back into South Africa, but he has also been told that he will be given the right to operate a charter air company in South Africa. The man is clearly in the pay of the South Africa government.' Steenkamp sounded breathless. They were back to square one.

Their confidence in the sanctuary of the jail was marred by rumours of impending attacks on the prison itself in an attempt to kill both fugitives. The South African papers were promoting an image of two desperate men anxiously waiting to flee from Bechuanaland, to flee from the long arm of the South African regime which was determined at all costs to get them back into the country. The question of extradition was being mooted. The extradition treaty between South Africa and Bechuanaland following the initiative of Prime Minister Vorster was not yet in place. The British government had already been involved in a diplomatic row over the kidnap of Dr Abrahams, and clearly wanted to avoid a similar situation with their embarassing 'guests'.

Getting out of jail in Francistown was beginning to look even more complicated than leaving Marshall Square. They settled into a routine of reading, playing some cricket in the prison yard, and entertaining acceptable visiting journalists. George Clay was one of them. Clay was a South African by birth; he worked for NBC, the American network, out of Dar es Salaam. (He was killed some years later in an ambush, covering the civil war in Zaïre.) It was George Clay who came to the rescue. He said that NBC would pay the cost of an aircraft to fly them out if they gave him an exclusive interview, assuring them at the same time that they would not be expected to divulge anything that could imperil anybody.

Clay arranged for a small Tanzanian Charter Air Company, owned and operated virtually single-handed by a man called Tim Bally, to fly into Francistown. He had used this company on a number of occasions, and not only knew Bally but had learned to trust him implicitly. Bally sent a small six-seater aircraft to fetch the two men. It set off on the first leg of its journey and got as far as Mbeya, in Southern Tanzania. It crashed early in the morning.

Harold and Arthur heard of the crash just an hour later, when they were called to the office of the warder on duty. 'We've been told by the *Rand Daily Mail* of the crash of a plane said to be coming here to fly the two of you out,' he said, a wry smile on his face. 'You two are obviously bad news,' he added.

Arthur and Harold both immediately assumed that the plane had been sabotaged. As the *Mail* reported on 7 September 1963: 'One of the aircraft's twin engines failed. In the crash landing the propeller was smashed and the aircraft severely damaged. The pilot was unhurt.' This time no one could be blamed, although the *Mail*'s report ended with a statement from the civil aviation authorities in Nairobi, which said that 'they had received a threatening cable on Wednesday night from Parkview, Johannesburg, warning that any aircraft ferrying from Francistown would be "shot down or burnt on the ground". The cable, signed Bwana Ndge [literally Big Bird] said: Please endeavour to stop East African Airways interfering with our Communist criminals'.

All the threats and the latest crash had an impact no one had anticipated. It seemed that no commercial aviation company would touch the two men now. Apart from anything else, the underwriters would not extend cover to a company that tried to fly the fugitives out.

It was George Clay, on his return to Dar es Salaam, who came to the rescue once more. He conceived of a plan together with Dick Hall, who worked on the Northern Rhodesia *Financial Mail* in Lusaka. He would hire two planes from Bally's company – one to take him to Bulawayo in Rhodesia, and the second to bring his cameraman and equipment to Bulawayo. The first plane would take Clay and his cameraman to Francistown; Bally would remain in Bulawayo awaiting confirmation from Clay about flying in to pick up two passengers. Clay did not spell out in so many words who Bally's passengers would be, hoping to overcome the problem of insurance. The finer details would have to be discussed and confirmed with the British government representatives in Francistown. As Oliver Carruthers, another actor in the drama, was to say years later: 'The British government, embarrassed by the affair, could not be seen to be helping, but their connivance was needed. The plane had to be allowed into Francistown, Harold and Arthur had to be persuaded it was OK . . .'

Once back in Francistown, Clay first met Harold and Arthur. Neither needed much persuasion on the viability of his plan. This seemed to be their last chance to fly out of the country. They all recognised the need to take Mr Steenkamp and Mr Knight into their confidence. Nothing could be done without their co-operation and assistance. When all of them were gathered together in the cells later, Clay gave them some of the details: 'Once I had told Bally that the passengers could not land in any of the countries making up the Central African Federation because of the problems with the police there, he worked out a route. He said that he could not fly over Northern Rhodesia without coming down to refuel, and we all know that if the Rhodesian police got their hands on the two of you, you would be sent back to South Africa *tout de suite*. The distance is too great. He suggested that the best way would be to fly to a small town just inside the Bechuanaland border, where he could refuel. It's a place called Kasane.' Steenkamp interrupted Clay: 'We've got a forest ranger there, a thoroughly reliable man whom I could contact and make sure that he is around when the plane lands. But I will need to have some idea of the timing.' Clay acknowledged this suggestion, and went on: 'Bally would fly to Elisabethville in the Congo, refuel, and then go on to Mbeya, refuel again, and finally go on to Dar es Salaam.' The name Mbeya elicited wry smiles from everyone. The problem was how to get Harold and Arthur to the plane secretly. Doing anything secretly in Francistown was no easy task. The place was too small to escape the eagle eyes of the waiting journalists, let alone the agents of the South African government.

Steenkamp had been listening intently. 'I don't think it is a good idea for Bally to land in Francistown. It will be impossible to keep things quiet. It would make much more sense if he could land at Palapye. It's roughly a hundred miles south, and has a small airstrip. I'm convinced that none of the journalists would anticipate such a move. We could just spirit you away there,' he said, smilingly to Harold and Arthur.

Clay beamed at the idea. 'Brilliant. I can easily arrange this with Bally, and I have a colleague who writes for the *Daily Telegraph* in London. He's a Rhodesian, here with his own car. He's told me that he is quite willing to help out, and hopes he can get some of the story printed after I have filed mine. He could drive the two of you to the plane. I can let you all know at what time the plane could get there. If they left Palapye round about half-past six in the morning, they should get to Kasane within a couple of hours.'

Steenkamp registered that, and added, 'We've got to move fast and secretly. We obviously need two cars, one to act as a decoy and the other to convey our guests to their plane,' he said, smiling towards Harold and Arthur. 'The one car with the decoys will leave first and travel northwards, so that any prying eyes will assume that our two guests are in the first car.'

'I'm prepared to act as one of the decoys,' volunteered Mr Knight. Both Harold and Arthur recognised that this was a courageous offer, knowing full well that if the South Africans got wind of any of this they were likely to blast the car if they could not get to the men inside it. 'We'll need one other man,' Mr Knight added, 'someone we can trust.' Ismael Bhana fitted the bill. He was probably the only one they could involve without knowledge of the impending flight getting out and about. There were too many talkers and too many listeners in Francistown. Bhana simply smiled and said of course he would do that. 'That's settled,' said Mr Steenkamp. 'I'll drive the car.' The generosity of spirit of all these men, particularly the governor of the prison and Mr Steenkamp, was overwhelming.

The discussion had taken on the tone of a war game. 'We'll need to keep guard in the area surrounding the prison all night,' said Mr Steenkamp. 'I'll arrange for the army to mount guard in the hills surrounding the prison. We'll get the men in position when dusk falls. We don't want to make anything too obvious.'

It sounded so simple and straightforward. This time the impending departure held none of the tensions that had preceded the night they left Marshall Square. The three men had their usual evening drink with Mr Knight, admist an air of festivity. Mr Knight produced some snacks, which looked ridiculously dainty and out of keeping with the harsh, stark prison environment. George Clay arrived with his cameraman when they were drinking their second gin and tonic, and joined in the celebration. 'Look, I've got a letter from the Chief Immigration Officer in Tanzania, permitting the two of you to enter the country. I haven't been able to get you something to allow you to enter the Congo. You're going to need some official-looking document for that country,' warned Clay. 'At some stage you'll come across a bureaucrat who'll demand some document from you. So prepare something.' There was no way that the British officials could provide them with an official document. They had to improvise.

Harold borrowed the prison typewriter. It was an old machine whose letter 'h' did not type in line. On an ordinary letterhead he typed: 'To whom it may concern: This is to certify that the person named in the letter and whose photograph is attached is one and the same person. The photograph is signed and dated.' Luckily, George Clay had arranged for them to have some passport-size photographs available. Mr Knight gave Harold the use of the prison stamp, signed the letter and witnessed the two photographs. By the time he had finished it looked like an official document.

The visitors left, and the three occupants of the cell block settled down for their last night together. A feeling of warmth and camaraderie pervaded them all. The night air was clement and comforting and, as usual, the sky was glittering.

All three men were washed, dressed and ready by 3.30 the next morning. Bhana made some strong coffee; they drank it quite silently, and were then escorted to the governor's office. At four o'clock exactly Mr Steenkamp drove up to the prison in an official-looking black car, and Bhana and Mr Knight rushed into it. The approaching dawn would have enabled any observer to make out two figures hurrying into a waiting car which revved its engine and took off speedily in a northerly direction towards the Rhodesian border.

Fifteen minutes later another car drew up at the prison. It too was an English car with a Rhodesian numberplate. Harold and Arthur clambered into the car, which immediately went in the opposite direction. They were followed by a police car, which had been waiting in a side street next to the prison.

They arrived at Palapye at 6.30 in the morning. The drive was uneventful. The accompanying police car had kept a reasonable distance behind them, and the two cars maintained a steady 60 miles per hour. The colour of the rising sun filled the sky with a glorious salmon-pink colour, and the morning light was pure. Harold felt his spirits surge with the rising sun. They were on the move again. The adrenalin was flowing, and the unreality of their sojourn in the Francistown jail began to dissolve into the morning light. Their first destination was the police station at Palapye, where they went through Customs and emigration formalities. Harold smiled at what seemed a somewhat eccentric exercise. Neither he nor Arthur had any document except the flimsy bit of paper that the Reverend Hooper had given them. They had no possessions beyond the clothes they were wearing and the haversacks the Hoopers had given them. Yet they had to be cleared for leaving the country. Each man was given a document which they would give their pilot. Then they drove westwards towards the airstrip.

It was a small airstrip, marked out in the midst of the countryside. Their car parked at the side, with the police car close by. The wait for the arrival of the small aircraft began. 'Tim Bally has been given strict instructions,' George Clay had told them the night before. 'He has been told to make sure that your car is parallel to the airstrip. If it is, then he should land, but if it is at right angles to the airstrip, then he must fly off. That will be an indication that all is not well, and there is some danger involved.' George had added that Bally did not know the identity of the passengers he was scheduled to fly out.

The wait began. Seven o'clock, the time Bally was due to touch down had come and gone. Neither man could avoid looking at the hands of his watch as the minutes moved on slowly. Seven-twenty. Harold was convinced that Bally would not appear. They had no contingency plans. Another ten minutes, and another. It was coming up to eight o'clock when a faint hum of an engine could be heard followed moments later by a tiny aircraft which landed smoothly on the ground close to the car.

Both men scampered out of the car, shouting their thanks to the driver and waving to the police in the waiting car, and rushed towards the plane, not looking back. Bally opened up the door and set out a couple of steps. As the door opened, a sheaf of papers blew out on to the runway. Arthur clambered into the aircraft, followed by Harold. 'Do you need those papers?' Harold stopped to ask. Bally's answer was a simple 'Yes.' With that, Harold turned round and chased after the elusive papers that were blowing in a wind created by the propellers of the small plane. So much for the high precision surrounding their departure, thought Harold as he got back into the plane, clutching the errant papers in one hand. 'Strap yourselves in,' Bally told them, as he got ready for the takeoff. Harold sat in the passenger seat next to Bally, with Arthur behind them. The takeoff was smooth: they soared upwards and steadied off in a north-westerly direction towards Kasane, just on the border between Bechuanaland and Northern Rhodesia, on the Zambezi River west of the Victoria Falls.

Tim Bally was an unlikely sort of man to be running an airline company – not that the company was large. This was a far remove from the historian he had set out to be, having read history at Trinity College, Dublin. He was short, his face was quite genial, made rugged and freckled by the sun of Africa. He appeared vague on first meeting, and this impression was reinforced as the day proceeded. Every now and again his right hand would flail about next to him, and Harold would ask, 'Are you looking for something?' Bally would reply, 'Yes, I'm looking for my map.' Harold did not know which map and would ferret around the fifteen or twenty maps that were scattered all over the floor until he came across the one Bally required. For all that, he appeared to be a highly competent and confident pilot. He wasn't all that talkative – in fact he said very little. Suddenly he said, turning to Harold and smiling, 'I wonder if there's a jet aircraft chasing us? Yesterday the papers carried a story that any aircraft which attempted to fly you guys out of Bechuanaland would be blasted out of the sky.' Harold didn't know how to respond beyond giving a wan smile. Bally asked no questions, and let the matter rest there. He made no more mention of this, and Harold did not know whether he was vague, disinterested or antagonistic. He opted for the first.

Bally flew north until he hit the unmistakable wide-banked lush Zambezi River. They seemed to be flying straight towards the Caprivi Strip, a long, narrow band of land, under South African control, which bordered on Bechuanaland, Angola, Northern Rhodesia and South-West Africa. It was reputed to be a heavily armoured area, given its strategic position. Harold worried that they would fly over the territory. Bally turned right, though, and landed at Kasane to refill before making for Elisabethville.

They landed, and were met by the forest ranger whom Steenkamp had contacted. He was there with his jeep and said, 'We can all go to my office, where you can go have a wash and a drink, once Bally has refuelled.'

Bally soon returned, expressing his irritability with the facilities. 'Could you believe it,' he said, 'they simply do not have the correct octane fuel I need. This is quite ridiculous. There is no other alternative except to fly to Livingstone, which does stock the right stuff. You fellows can wait with him, if he doesn't mind,' he said, pointing to the forest ranger. 'I shouldn't be gone for more than an hour or so.'

It was midday when they set off for Elisabethville. Bally had returned with a full tank of petrol and some sandwiches, apples and oranges. Once again they were in the air. They had a vast distance to cover before reaching Elisabethville. They had to fly over Northern Rhodesia. Bally was right. There was nothing to stop the authorities from sending up a plane to try and force them to land; radio contact could be made only when they were within reach of a landing area, and that was far from frequent. The radio was pleasantly silent. Bally was occasionally asked to report his whereabouts to air traffic control. Luckily, no awkward questions were asked. Bally estimated six hours' flying time before they reached their destination.

The unfurling of the scenic beauty of untamed Africa captivated both men, who marvelled at the sight, every now and again, of flights of birds, graceful buck, giraffes and zebras running as hard as they could away from the sound of the intruding plane. There wasn't much sign of human settlement.

After five and a half hours a town came into sight. Bally smiled broadly. 'We've made good time. There's Elisabethville.' His voice tailed off when he and the others saw a green cricket pitch and the white-clad figures playing beneath them. 'Oh hell, that's certainly not Elisabethville. You wouldn't find a cricket pitch there.' It was Chingola in the copper belt of Northern Rhodesia, not all that far from the Congo and more or less due south from their destination.

Not long afterwards Bally made contact with air traffic control at Elisabethville. After tuning in, he turned to Harold and said, somewhat irritably, 'The blighters have given me a conflicting series of positions. Anyway, we should be in Elisabethville inside of half an hour.'

Half an hour went by, and no sign of Elisabethville. Bally made contact with air traffic control again. They acknowledged that he appeared to be lost, and told him they would relay the news to other aircraft in the vicinity, and instruct them to keep a lookout for the small plane. From then on he turned off his radio speaker and kept his earphones on so that his two passengers would not hear any more disturbing news.

Bally got more and more angry with the controllers. Eventually he said, 'Well, that's that. I'm turning off the bloody radio. Those assholes have been giving me incorrect information.' He deliberately turned off his radio, made some calculations and did a U-turn.

The situation was tense. The needle on the fuel tank was edging towards empty, and Bally said somewhat forlornly, 'Not more than twenty minutes' flying time left, chaps. And even if I did have more fuel, this plane isn't equipped for night-time flying.' Harold looked over his shoulder at Arthur, and they both simultaneously took out their packets of cigarettes. 'Oh well, we may as well have our last drag,' they both thought.

There was nothing except dense jungle beneath them, stretching endlessly. A forced landing would be disastrous. 'Look,' Harold called out jubilantly after ten minutes. 'A road – we can land on it.'

Bally thought the suggestion ridiculous. 'There's no way I'm going to try and land this plane there,' he said. He dismissed their pleas. Then a railway line loomed up. Immediately Bally connected once more with air traffic control. 'Listen, you guys, it looks to me as though there's a mine on my left and a railway straight ahead of me.' The good news came back, telling him to follow the railway line – they were close to Elisabethville, and the railway line would lead them there.

Ten minutes later they landed, with little fuel and in fast fading light. Harold and Arthur beamed. Later that night, at a hotel, they discovered that each had said to himself: 'Well, I've tried my best, there's nothing more I can do, and it has been a fine adventure while it lasted.' Strangely, neither was fearful at that stage.

They were armed with their official-looking letters and attached photographs, and these they flourished in front of an official-looking man, who took the letters, looked at them carefully, obviously not understanding a word of English yet satisifed with the official-looking nature of the documents he was handling. He too added his rubber stamp to the papers. Their entry into the Congo was official. In addition, George Clay had been in constant contact with Oliver Carruthers, editor of the Northern Rhodesia *Financial Mail* and in charge of the Copperbelt office of the *African Mail* in Ndola. As Carruthers was later to write, in a private communication:

My role was to ensure that everything went all right in Elisabethville. Elisabethville was then in the hands of the UN, but only just, with the route from Northern Rhodesia (about ninety miles) being perilous and subject to constant banditry. Neither Clay nor Hall wanted to go to Elisabethville – Clay, as a South African, did not want to be overtly connected with the plan; while Hall was about to go on holiday in South Africa with his five sons. In any case, my French was better than either of theirs.

I needed a UN escort to make the trip. (This was done on a regular basis, but my trip was in a sense an emergency, so needed special arrangements.) Nobody in Elisabethville knew they were coming, except the UNIP [Kaunda's United National Independence party] rep, who had difficulty in persuading the government officials of the significance of the event.

The journey to Elisabethville (by car) was uneventful,

but I had a full day persuading the political officials, and then
the airport officials, that they had some VIPs on their way.
The airport officials, a stage removed from the mainstream,
were the more difficult, particularly as I said that Harold and
Arthur would be arriving at about 4.30 without making radio
contact until they were within fifty miles (having left Northern Rhodesian air space). At 5.30 there was still no radio
contact, and dusk approached. Rather too late for comfort,
they arrived.

Carruthers had also managed – with great difficulty – to
negotiate with Kaunda, Future President of Zambia, to assist
the men with safe passage while they were in the Congo.
Carruthers was waiting at the airport with his future wife,
Jocelyn, and triumphantly he waved a letter approved by
Kaunda. 'I've managed to get you this document,' he said, after
introductions had been completed. 'You'll be given protection
by the Congolese government while you're both here. And I've
arranged for your hotel accommodation.'

The two men's relief was reinforced by Carruthers's warm
greeting. They had no inkling of the difficulties and, indeed,
the traumas that he had undergone to make all the arrangements. His communication continues:

The arrival formalities, if they could so be described, were
easier than I thought they would be. I told Goldreich and
Wolpe to keep quiet for their own good, but they were too
excited, partly because of the escape and partly because they
were in black Africa. The problems of black Africa soon
became apparent in that Bally discovered that Elisabethville
airport, for all its apparent bustle, did not have the correct
octane fuel: he and I would have to fly to Ndola the next day
to fill up. A day would be lost. On the other hand the joys of
black Africa, vibrancy and *joie de vivre*, kept our heroes busy
for the night.

The three men were whisked off to the centre of town, where
they were booked into a hotel by Carruthers. After a bath and a

shave, they were introduced to some leading government officials who had come to welcome them.

It was a jovial meal that night. They drank some French wine, and Arthur was in top form, amusing the company with his many stories. They all set out for some sightseeing and landed up at a nightclub called Black and White. The band was playing loud music which successfully combined French and African jazz. Gyrating bodies given up to drink and the pulsating music filled the men with sheer delight. They drank greedily, relishing being among people, both black and white, who were drinking, smoking, laughing and dancing. They were alive and they were free. By the time they returned to their hotel at two in the morning all of them were quite drunk. It had been a long, wonderful day. Carruthers wrote:

Bally and I set off early the next day, leaving Goldreich and Wolpe in my wife's Jocelyn's hands. They would have to avoid the press, but I had no way of telling the ANC in Dar what had happened, any more than I could tell Dick Hall. Equally, everybody knew Goldreich and Wolpe had left Francistown, and as they were in hiding somewhere, then where were they? You did not have to be that clever to work out that Elisabethville was a possible destination. Would the Security Forces react?

By the time Bally and I got back, the team were jumpy. The AFP stringer had discovered them. A much more difficult evening was spent in skulking around seedy bars. (I had been able to phone Dick Hall from Ndola, so at least the conspirators knew what had happened, and Dick sent off various pieces around the world, blaming me for the whole affair.) Early the next day it was back to the airport. Jocelyn and I drove back in the regular convoy.

On the second morning they left, and a few hours later they landed at Mbeya, a small town nestling in the mountains of Western Tanzania. George Clay met them, together with the local District Commissioner of the Tanzanian government, who provided a little welcoming ceremony for the two men. They were taken to see the remains of the plane that had been due to fly them out. It was here that George Clay got his exclusive story.

Within an hour they took off for Dar es Salaam, arriving late in the afternoon. The further they were from South Africa, the warmer the greetings became. The crowds were at the airport in full force to greet the men, who were accorded the status of heroes. The crowds sang and danced, and people came up to hug them. It was an emotional occasion, captured by the Western world's press and TV cameras.

The Long Farewell

D URBAN HAS been another segment of the perpetual nightmare that I feel is my life. Waiting for something to happen that does not happen. Now, as I sit on the plane heading once more for Johannesburg, my mind skips from one thing to another in no coherent way and no logical sequence. I realise that I feel deep resentment towards Harold. It is there. I felt particularly angry when I read an account of their arrival in Elisabethville, and the presence of some mysterious woman with them. It sounded as if things were working out really well for the two of them – they were welcomed in Dar es Salaam like heroes, and meantime Hazel and I are stuck – Hazel much more so than myself.

I cannot eradicate the fear that seems to have become a part of me. I am quite simply terrified of being incarcerated. My experience of that for just one day was enough to show me that I am no stalwart heroine. I wonder about my capacity to do things for myself. I seem more than able to fix up other people's lives, but when it comes to myself I seem hopeless.

I am finding it more and more difficult to eat properly. I simply have no appetite or desire to eat. Not even sweet things can tempt my palate.

What will I do when I return to Johannesburg? What will happen to me? Will they come and arrest me at home again? I cannot tolerate the suspense of not knowing. If they are going to arrest me, then let them come and do so now.

Polly is sitting quietly beside me. Every now and again she tries to engage me in conversation. I am not very communicative. She probably recognises the hopelessness of her task. She is thoroughly miserable about Jimmy's arrest.

The house is looking lovely. Angelina has kept everything ticking over during my ten-day absence in Durban. Marlene is there, holding Nicholas in her arms. I snatch him from her greedily and hold him tight. Nanette tries jumping up at me in delight at my return. On the face of it, everything is normal.

I phone Joel Joffe, who has taken over the winding down of Jimmy's practice. Joel was due to emigrate to Australia with his wife Vanetta, and he has been persuaded to stay on for a while to take care of Jimmy's outstanding matters and organise the office. Joel, who was a partner of Jimmy's until he went to the Bar, is a brilliant lawyer. Where Jimmy is flamboyant, Joel is quiet and self-effacing. Where Jimmy is a strategist in the legal game, Joel is an interpreter of the law. Joel is cerebral. He is a tall, thin, myopic man, with a prominent Adam's apple and a gentle appearance. When he is serious he hangs his head down and looks over the rim of his glasses in an effort to make contact. He smiles a great deal. He does not appear to be highly confident, yet his reputation for brilliance has long been established.

I don't care who is listening in to my conversation. 'Joel, I've just returned from Durban, where I spent some time having a bit of a break. I simply can't go on any longer, not knowing whether the rumours I have heard are true or not.' I explain everything to him. 'I'm beginning to crack up. All I want to do is leave the country. I've got a valid passport and I want to get the hell out. I'm sick to death of Harold and all the shit he has landed me in. I don't care any more where he is. He can go to Timbuktu for all I care.'

Joel is softly spoken. At times you really have to strain yourself to hear what he is saying. 'I think you had better get yourself off to a psychiatrist and have yourself assessed,' he suggests. 'Tomorrow morning I will make sure that I discuss the matter with Klindt, and ask that you be allowed to leave the country. It would help if you had a report to the effect that you are in a state of anxiety.'

That wasn't difficult to establish. My GP gave me the name of someone to see, and off I went.

It is good to be home again, and with the children. I feel so guilty about Peta and Tessa. I realise with horror that three months have gone by since Nicholas was first taken ill – three months of unmitigated misery. During my pregnancy, when I said glibly that I would be fleeing when Nicholas was six months old, I did not anticipate anything like this.

Joel phones me to tell me that he has arranged to see the police, and will let me know their decision as soon as he hears it.

I am restless all the while, and talk earnestly with Marlene about what will happen if I am allowed to leave the country. I decide the best thing is to give her power of attorney to manage my affairs, because clearly my mother has no heart for this and there is no one else I can turn to at this stage. Diane is out of the country, and I don't seem to have any close friends. Angelina, whom I trust implicitly, is unfortunately not literate and has no education. It would be impossible for her.

It is afternoon, and I decide to take Peta and Tessa to Polly's for afternoon tea. At least it will provide some diversion, although Polly is not all that keen on little children. It is four o'clock. The phone rings. 'It's Joel for you,' Polly calls out.

I grab the phone from her hand. I can barely say hello. Joel senses my urgency, and wastes no time in pleasantries. 'The police have been in conference all day, deciding what to do about my request to them to allow you to leave the country. They have finally reached a decision. You can go. But go now, go tonight.'

I can't believe what I hear, and ask him to repeat it just to make sure I have made no mistake. I cup the receiver with my hand and say to Polly, 'I can leave the country. Joel says I must go immediately.' Her face hides any emotion she may be feeling.

Joel continues: 'The police told me that they knew you were down in Durban and wondered what you were doing there. They knew you had returned to Johannesburg and were clearly surprised at my request. I think they are so accustomed to people doing things in a secretive and underhand way that they did not quite know what to do. I suppose that is why it took them so long to reach a decision. I must insist that you leave immediately, that you go tonight.'

Somewhat breathlessly, I reply, 'I have no money, I need to pack some clothes, I have to make arrangements for the kids and sort out some finances. I need a day to get myself together.' Joel's reponse is that I must leave by the next evening at the latest.

There is no time for Polly and me to discuss the matter. We haven't really talked at all about the implications of the last month's events. She has not openly blamed me or Harold for Jimmy's crisis, but I know that she feels it, as do other members of the family. There is not much sympathy around for Harold – or for me, for that matter.

I rush home with the girls. There is so much to do. Perhaps it is as well that I have so little time to prepare my departure from the country. I phone Ellen Hellmann, who is the Chair of the Isaacson Foundation Bursary Fund, which I have run for the past four or five years. My maternity leave is not yet over. Ellen was very supportive during the 1960 Emergency, and counselled me about my fears for the children and what Harold's absence could do. At that time she told me how she felt her own daughter had been manipulative when her husband had died, and could reduce Ellen to tears by asking for her dead father. Ellen told me then to be firm with Peta – Tessa was too young to understand – and I listened to her. I tell her that now I am planning to leave the country, and she offers to come round and see me.

We walk outside under the big oak tree, and talk. I plead with her to try and do something about Jimmy. I don't know what she can do, but she' is well connected. Her response is: 'Where there's smoke there's fire.' I argue fruitlessly, but continue saying that I know – and I emphasise this – that Jimmy is quite innocent. She thrusts a hundred-pound note into my hand and says, 'That should help you.' It certainly will, because I have no idea of my financial state. There is no money coming in. I still owe the hospital a fortune, I have no idea if Gerson Katz has ever been paid for saving Nicholas's life, although no amount of money could ever pay for that. There are all sorts of expenses, and I must be operating in overdraft. Both Hessie Sachs and Michael Gluckman have offered me help, and I accepted it willingly. Hessie says she will pay my mortgage until I sell the house.

Somehow the financial mess seems the least of my problems. Ellen leaves after a short time, and wishes me good luck in a stilted fashion. I get the feeling that she is not too happy about having come round to the house, but I respect the fact that she has done so. Then I start sorting out clothes. I scrabble through my winter clothes and realise that they all need a thorough cleaning. Well, that can be done first thing in the morning. There is an excellent same-day cleaner on the main road. There is an airline ticket to be purchased. I call Angelina, Isaac and Peter, Angelina's partner, into the house, and sit them down. I explain to them that I am allowed to leave the country, and why I think it is the only solution for me. Otherwise there is no guarantee that I won't land up in jail, and that won't help the children at all. At least I shall be able to start my life over again, together with the children when I am able to make adequate arrangements for them. Angelina is very wise. She agrees, and wishes me every luck, as does Peter. Peter tells me not to worry, and that he will help look after the house and the children.

I haven't thought through what will happen to the children. For the time being I will have to keep on the house and let them remain there with Angelina and Marlene. Marlene will be there as long as Nicholas needs her care, but everyone is of the opinion that his progress is such that the vigilance and special care can soon cease. There simply is not the time to work out all the details, nor am I in a fit state to do so. Somehow I trust to luck and assume that Marlene will keep things ticking over, even though I recognise that this is a tall order.

I start the day early.

I don't want to think of the departure. There is not sufficient time to get everything done. It is four o'clock. I change my clothes and get ready for the ride to the airport. Polly has said that she will take me, and my cousin Pauline will provide a second car so that the girls and Angelina can come along as well.

We arrive, and I am nervous. I clutch my passport tightly

in my hands, and go through passport control. The place seems to be swarming with sinister-looking men whom I take to be Special Branch policemen. The one man who examines my passport carefully is frankly hostile. I am anxious in case the decision to allow me to leave the country is reversed. The passport is stamped, and I can resume talking to everyone. Partings are bad at the best of times. This one is horrendous. The girls are playing around, not fully aware of the consequences of the events but clearly upset. Angelina cannot sit anywhere. How ridiculous this apartheid system is. She is black, good enough to love and care for my children, but not good enough in the eyes of the law to sit comfortably on a bench or a seat. Oh how tragic it all is!

The call comes to board the plane. I hug everybody, and hold the girls specially close and tight to me, and hurry away through the barrier and walk to the plane. I do not dare look back, because I feel as though my heart will break.

I board the plane, strap myself in at the window seat and find I can't see very much through tears. I have abandoned my children. I have left my country. I am bound for England.

Epilogue

July 1993

Postscript

Just before this book went to press my attention was drawn to a newspaper report of March 1994 in which Greef, who had been traced (contrary to what I wrote in this Epilogue), referred to the fact that he had never been paid the money promised to him. That money was used by the movement for legal defence and support of families of political prisoners. Steps have been initiated to compensate Greef.

I T IS thirty years to the day since my old world collapsed. I
am sitting in a friend's garden in St Roman de Malegarde,
Provence. It is hot, but the sun is masked by a film of
cloud. The incessant clackety sound of the cicadas gyrating
their scale-like stomachs breaks the silence. The fig tree is laden
with its aubergine-coloured fruit. It is impossible to pick the
delicious fruit because the hornets are in control. Four olive
trees have been transplanted to the lawn surrounding the pool.
An old blue cart nestles under one of the trees. I feel at home in
Provence. Even though my French is appalling, I manage to
communicate, and I wallow in the ease and untrammelled
freedom of life here.

Harold and I have come from South Africa for our annual
holiday, and Tessa, now thirty-five, has joined us. Harold has
to return to Cape Town before me – too much work and too
many pressures. Tessa and I will remain for the whole month. I
need the break, as I have had a dreadful year with dislocations
of the one hip and another massive operation on it. My mobility
is still restricted. We all want to be with Peta, who at thirty-six
has had a second child – a daughter, called Alicia Gaëlle, born
on the 29th of June. Peta is delighted we are here, and says she
already went into a state of decline before we arrived in
anticipation of our departure.

Both she and Tessa feel acutely the distance that separates
us all. At least if we were in London we would be able to see
her and her children far more often. *Tant pis*! Tessa lives in
London, and says she cannot envisage living anywhere else, but
she still feels that we have abandoned her – an expression used
by so many children of exiles, irrespective of their ages. The

film world is so insecure, and she is looking for work once again. Nicholas, who is thirty, could not get leave, and regrets he is unable to be with all of us. He decided on the spur of the moment to settle in South Africa, and after an initial period in Cape Town, he took a job with a large non-governmental organisation – Operation Hunger – which, through its own fund-raising activities, provides two million meals a day for near-starving people. He prefers living in Johannesburg to any other city in which he has lived, and ignores the violence that rocks that city daily. He doesn't even lock his car door inside when he drives through certain areas, unlike everyone else. It is not that he is unaware of potential danger, but simply choses to ignore it; he will not give way to it.

A whole lifetime of events has elapsed since those dark days in South Africa in 1963. Within days of my arrival in London, Harold and Arthur followed. Only through the intervention of the British Labour Party, and Barbara Castle in particular, were they granted asylum.

We had to obtain state permission for Peta and Tessa to fly to join us in London. A month after I arrived the two of them, aged six and five, flew out, clutching their dolls and a bag of sweets each. Nicholas was still not well enough to be moved, and it was not until the following February that a friend of ours, returning from South Africa, was able to bring him to us. I had not seen him for five long months, and could not recognise the large, blond, delightful baby that arrived. That crucial period of the first months of his life was lost for ever. Years later a woman was to say incredulously, 'How on earth could you have abandoned your children? I could never have done such a thing.' How could I possibly have explained to her what it is like living under the constant threat and fear of arrest and lengthy detention? My only salvation lay in leaving the country before the police changed their mind. And that meant 'abandoning' my children. Even now there are certain aspects of those days which I cannot discuss with any degree of equanimity.

I no longer remember how I dealt with my anger at Harold. I was caught up in the excitement of his arrival and the attention he and Arthur received, which no doubt dissipated some of it. Harold though, says he recalls my resentment and frailty. The subsequent months were filled for him in work on behalf of the anti-apartheid movement – he probably had little time to deal with me. And no one else was interested in the plight of Harold's wife and family. I had to learn to adjust on my own.

And so began the long journey towards creating a normal family life in England, where we spent all but four years in London. All this was to be broken, yet again, by events in South Africa.

Hazel was held for quite some time following the escape. When she was released she, too, came to London with her two sons, but she and Arthur separated. He moved to Israel, where he married an Israeli woman. We have seen him only intermittently since 1963. Perhaps he and Harold had had enough of each other's company to last them a lifetime.

Greef, of course, was charged, and sentenced to six years in jail. He did not serve his full sentence and was given the usual remission. Sadly, he never did receive the money he had been promised. The police extracted a confession from him in the early hours of the morning, when the escape was discovered, and he must have told them, among other things, exactly where he was due to pick up the money. The police took him to the appointed address somewhere in Fordsburg, Johannesburg, but someone recognised the police cars and avoided the trap. The money was subsequently swallowed up by the movement. No one knows where Greef is, or what became of him.

In those early days in London I avidly read the newspapers to see what was happening in South Africa. What became known as the Rivonia Trial dominated the news about the country. My interest in the case was fuelled by my concern for my brother Jimmy, who was charged with treason together with all the others. He was acquitted. His practice had been sold off for virtually nothing, and he was penniless. His professional life in South Africa was in shreds. His personal life deteriorated following a sordid divorce from Barbara. He was granted custody of all four children – two of their own, and two of

Barbara's sons whom he had adopted. He died in 1974, ten years after he had come to London, at the age of forty-seven, following a massive heart attack. I was appointed executor of his estate, and this proved a difficult task, as relations between Barbara and myself deteriorated irrevocably and created what seems an insurmountable barrier between us and Jimmy's children.

The full force of Jimmy's feelings of betrayal by Harold and myself was contained in a letter he sent, while still in prison, to David Susman, one of the few friends who stood by him through the distressing days of the trial. David gave me a copy on my return here. Although Harold did have a long talk with Jimmy shortly after his arrival in London, it was not adequate. I have always regretted our inability to discuss this period in any depth with him, but he was loath to speak of such matters.

My mother followed Jimmy to London and lived on and off with us, returning periodically to stay with my sister Betty in the Cape. She was in South Africa when Jimmy died, and clearly never became reconciled to his untimely death. She fell ill, and lost all her faculties. Betty was desperate for me to come out and help her, but I was not given safe passage and never saw her again, nor did I attend her funeral.

The explosion in higher education opened up a way for me to become an academic. It was not easy. I started off, unbelievably enough, in a unit for Yugoslav studies. Quite bizarre. I even learned Serbo-Croat out of a book while trying to run a house, look after three children, and generate a research project. Harold returned to sociology, using a Nuffield fellowship to enable him to read and study. He has always been concerned with analyses of South Africa, and much of his written work has been highly influential there, read clandestinely in the 1970s.

In due course we both contributed in our own way to our disciplines: I in feminist analyses and Harold generally in the field of development. For me, the cost was high. Doing what I did and at a relatively late age – I was already in my late thirties when I started in academic work – without any support system took its toll. In the early years there never seemed to be enough money, and I could afford only minimal domestic help, if any. For many years it was a hard slog, and I was often exhausted. Now, looking back, in spite of all the difficulties, it was interesting and well worth all the drudgery. And we did have fun, and we laughed and enjoyed ourselves.

We began holidaying in Europe in 1971. Camping was the only way we could afford to do so. Those holidays were wonderful, restorative and often highly amusing. In contrast with the excessively organised German and French campers, our efforts often attracted a ring of amused bystanders. We were not efficient; our tent could blow away. Unlike the French, who sat down at a table with a plastic cloth and plastic flowers in a vase, our eating arrangements were makeshift. Finally we bought a ruin of a house in Provence and have been there every summer since, working on restoring the place to a habitable state.

It is only now that I have full realisation of just how deleteriously our early life experiences affected our children. Peta and Tessa gave interviews to Hilda Bernstein when she was gathering data for her book on exiles, and Nicholas wrote an account for her. Both Harold and I find these accounts spine-chilling and very sad. Peta said that she never divulged to anyone that she came from South Africa, for two reasons. The first was that she felt she had to be careful because of some imminent danger; the second was that she did not want to be associated with South Africa in case she was judged a racist. She felt alien. Everything about her was wrong – her curly hair, her name, her background. Tessa, like Peta, felt different at school, unlike the other children. All sorts of things contributed to this: her surname, being Jewish, and having parents like us. She craved 'normality' – which in her terms meant being ordinary and unremarkable, and merging into the crowd. She became a dropout at school, largely through her anger at what had happened.

Nicholas suffered too, and even though he was only an infant when he arrived in England, he has never felt fully integrated. He describes his childhood as a constant fight against us because of his anger – particularly at Harold – for the disruption in his life. As the youngest, and as a result of his illness, I always tended to protect him. He saw this as a denial and lack of recognition of his right to know about everything, and to be recognised as growing up and responsible. Nicholas wrote that 'secrecy and protection' were ever-present. 'Death and assassination was a real fear, but it was a fear I never discussed.'

The threat of disaster has always been there. When we were away in America, Peta recalls how we instructed her on how to check the mail for any letter bombs. Tessa has had constant nightmares.

All three feel that had they grown up in South Africa they would not have had to cope with a range of problems their peer group never had. Peta said, 'I feel we've been deprived of something by not having been brought up there. That should have been our home. I think a lot of the sort of difficulties that I have arise from not really belonging here [in England].' All three expressed their concern about people who are politically involved having children. 'They should have thought about us as children. You make a decision about what you're going to do; you have children, and you are aware that you're bringing other people into the world, so therefore you have to think of them first,' Tessa said.

Nicholas wrote: 'I never really spoke to AnnMarie or Harold about how I felt, how I wanted to reach out to them and commend them for what they had done, but at the same time show how hurt I was inside. All they saw, and all I was willing to show, was this person who blamed them for what had happened to me.'

Harold and I now live in Cape Town. Since our return we have heard, for the first time, the versions of the 1963 events from some of the people who were intimately involved in the escape, and how their lives were affected in one way or another. Other stories abound, many apocryphal. I have not been able to verify some accounts, like the one which claims that all the locks in all the prisons were changed immediately after the escape. They – so I was told – became known as Greef locks, a double form of lock with two different people responsible for each key.

Integration, socially, politically and workwise, has proved quite complex and, at times, difficult to understand. We both work at the University of Western Cape. Harold's work is extremely demanding. As Director of an Educational Planning Unit he is concerned not only with building up a viable research unit and training researchers, but also with conducting research related to all aspects of secondary education. This will feed into policy formulation for a new South Africa. He and the Unit will no doubt make a significant contribution, and he feels tremendous satisfaction in this. He has no time to pursue academic interests, and longs for the day when he can read, contemplate and write.

My work at the Centre for Adult and Continuing Education involves research. Like everything else here, it has not been straightforward. I have learned a great deal, and I eventually settled into the Centre. I was regarded initially with a fair amount of reserve, caused not least by my 'Western' brand of feminism, which is suspect here because it is white and obviously middle-class. My political pedigree was acceptable, but not much else. It is much easier now. It is sad that my knowledge of Women's Studies and my wide experience as a teacher in this area have not been drawn upon. The reasons for this are, as far as I can understand, largely political, and relate to my being white and a returnee. I could have made quite a significant contribution in this area had I been given a chance.

Political integration has also been trying. Attempts to join the Welfare Committee of the ANC foundered, for inexplicable reasons. Both Harold and I are on an education subcommittee, but even here I do not feel fully involved. There is no doubt that my physical incapacity has contributed to this, but that is by no means the full story. There is a sense – and Harold shares this view with me – of a resistance to utilise to the full the abilities and capacities of returning exiles – except, of course, for those who fitted full-time into existing ANC structures.

We had been warned about the insularity of Capetonians. They do not take easily to strangers. But we have made new friends, all of whom have been incredibly supportive and warm-hearted. We enjoy seeing those members of my family who live in and around the Cape, especially Betty, and have even discovered new relatives. In spite of this the loneliness has been hard to bear at times, particularly during the long period of recovery following my last operation, when I missed Peta and Tessa sorely. They were such pillars of strength after my first hip operations.

Contary to the way the media portrays it, the majority of the violence is driven by gangsterism – fuelled, no doubt, by the alarming level of deprivation that overwhelms the black ghettos or townships. We are constantly fed gory details of dramatic violence characteristic of present-day South African society. There is no hesitation about showing dead bodies and their spilled blood. This spurs private individuals to arm themselves.

Our lifestyle is completely different from London. Apart from anything else, we have a wonderful home with spectacular views of Table Mountain. In the mornings, while we breakfast, Harold looks up at the cable car making its way to the top of the mountain, and I can just see the sea from where I sit. Our two black half-breed chow-chows provide me with ample protection when I am on my own at night. Harold travels a great deal.

I realise that in spite of all the difficulties, I am beginning to enjoy life in Cape Town. Interesting it certainly is – one of the most beautiful small cities in the world, entirely negotiable without the snarl-up of traffic; excellent wine, and a few but sufficient new friends to take the place of those left behind in London, and a great deal of work still to be done. It has all the ingredients for a paradise on earth.

Yet – are we really home?